GW00602129

Where the Brave will Live Forever

A Portadown Journey of Remembrance

Ronnie Harkness

Published by:
Breagh Lodge Books

<u>Cover Picture:</u>

Delville Wood Cemetery, Longueval, Somme

Last resting place of **Sgt. W. H. Lewis 13885, 7th Royal Irish Fusiliers, 9th September 1915, XV E 9, Jervis Street, Portadown.**

This book is dedicated to my mother.
Alice Elizabeth Harkness,

Died: Friday 13th April 2012

Acknowledgements

The culmination of several years of work to complete this publication cannot be attributed to the sole work of the author. Therefore I wish to pay tribute to a number of people without whose help, this Portadown Journey of Remembrance could not have been undertaken.

Many thanks to my wife, Lesley for her patience and valuable assistance in driving thousands of kilometres during our innumerable visits to the battlefields of World War One; for the taking of photographs; for the timeless hours spent on the computer recording my thoughts and experiences and for her constant encouragement in supporting me to complete this guide book.

Barrie Crawford, a colleague and friend who has given so freely of his time and expertise and who basically has been responsible in that all my reminiscences in written and photographic form have been channelled into this publication.

Dr Ian Adamson and his colleagues in The Somme Association whose companionship I have enjoyed on many occasions and who have imparted their knowledge both freely and generously.

Ian and Jeannie Alexander and their associates in Battlefield Tours whose knowledge of the Western Front was second to none.

Ross Hussey MLA, who brightened up many a visit with his wit and musical expertise.

Keith Adams, IT section of Craigavon Borough Council who was instrumental in ensuring that a lot of my data was retained following a nasty computer virus which threatened to destroy many years of work.

The World War One Committee on Craigavon Borough Council for their grant contribution.

Finally to those wonderful and inquisitive Primary Six and Primary Seven pupils from Bocombra Primary School, Portadown, who on a school visit to Belgium over twenty five years ago, awakened my interest in Ulster's and Ireland's involvement in the Great War.

Contents

Route 2 - The Somme 97

Route 6 - Bailleul to Ieper 217

Route 7 - Ieper (Ypres) and the West 243

Introduction

Foreword

It is nigh on a quarter of a century ago that I first encountered a World War One cemetery – Tyne Cot at Passchendaele in Belgium. I had been taking a large group of primary school children on a cross community trip to a theme park at nearby Bellawaerde and were on our return journey when we stopped to have a look at the last resting place of so many young men. The pupils bombarded me with questions – I couldn't answer them!

I had never in my grammar school days heard of Tyne Cot or for that matter the Somme. I made a promise to my young inquisitive pupils that day – if ever we returned to this hallowed place, I would answer all their questions.

So started my regular visits to the Western Front, to the silent cities of the First World War battlefields. I became engrossed, if not somewhat bewildered as to why this period of Ulster's and Ireland's heritage had been kept from my peers and myself.

I was appalled at the huge loss of life, the fact that two generations had been cruelly taken from us. Every town and village in Ulster was affected and like others Portadown particularly so.

A few years later, I was again on a school visit, once more to Flanders when the pupils actually followed the life of Pte William John McGaffin, 9th Royal Irish Fusiliers, 36th (Ulster) Division. He had lived in Bleary, a short distance from our school in Portadown. The pupils held a Service of Thanksgiving at his grave in Tyne Cot Cemetery, Passchendaele. Our trip was covered extensively by BBC Radio Ulster and several local newspapers. Some of the pupils involved, during their next stage of education, continued their studies of the Great War.

I have lost count of the number of visits I have made to the Western Front, albeit each one memorable as I always learned something new and kept written and photographic evidence.

In more recent years, I have had the privilege of being an elected representative on Craigavon Borough Council and I have been honoured and indeed humbled, on behalf of the citizens of the Borough, to lay wreaths at the Ulster Tower, Guillemont, Wytchaete, Messines and in far off Gallipoli.

In August 2010 I participated in The Last Post Ceremony at the Menin Gate in Ieper (previously Ypres), representing Portadown Masonic Brethren.

I began to realise that whilst there has been a plethora of books on Ulster's and Ireland's involvement in the Great War,and now many more publications during 2014, relating to the centenary of World War One, these have been mainly geared towards the avid war enthusiasts and battlefield "gurus".

What I believed was required was a simple guide for the casual tourist, perhaps the visiting school groups or indeed those who enjoy a leisurely read in the comfort of their own home – one that would not narrate statistics, dates, regimental details and so on – but one which would be easily enjoyed and informative, pointing out relevant places of interest which would appeal to young and old alike.

I appreciate this opportunity to highlight the sacrifices made by those men of my adopted home of Portadown and the surrounding area. I have also included a wide range of talented individuals - professional footballers, rugby players, athletes etc who lie in the cemeteries or who are named on the memorials in Northern France and Belgium alongside Victoria Cross recipients, Brigadier Generals and the ordinary private soldier who lie alongside the Portadown fallen.

Each and everyone played a significant part in the battles of the Great War. They have all one thing in common – they did not return. Mothers, wives and sweethearts were left bereft of their menfolk and children denied the opportunity of enjoying a life in the company of their fathers. May we never forget those who made the supreme sacrifice, those who returned maimed in mind and body and those at home who gazed forlornly at so many empty chairs.

Ronnie Harkness - 19th May 2015

1

The First World War

In 1914 following the outbreak of World War One, the German army opened up the Western Front by first invading Luxembourg and Belgium. It then turned its attention to the industrial regions in France.

The advance was halted by the Battle of the Marne.

Following the race to the sea both sides dug in with a line of fortified trenches stretching from the North Sea to the Swiss frontier with France. Essentially this line remained the same for most of the war. Along this front there were several major offensives. The Battle of Verdun left a combined 700,000 dead.

The Battle of the Somme had more than a million casualties whereas Passchendaele totalled a further 600,000.

The German Spring Offensive of 1918 saw them advance 97 km to the west and they nearly succeeded in forcing a breakthrough. However during the second half of that year the Allies advance was so great that the German government was forced to sign the Armistice.

The terms of peace were agreed upon with the Treaty of Versailles in 1919.

Casualties from the major Western Front battles:

BATTLE	YEAR	ALLIES	GERMAN
1st Marne	1914	263,000	
First Ypres	1914	126921-161,921	134,315
Verdun	1916	400,000 - 542,000	355,000 - 434,000
Somme	1916	623,907	465,000 - 595,294
2nd Aisne	1917	118,000	40,000
3rd Ypres	1917	200,000 - 448,000	260,000 - 400,000
Spring Offensive	1918	851,374	688,341
100 Days Offensive	1918	1,069,636	1,172,075
TOTAL	1914-1918	3,619,838 - 4,077,838	3,370,731 - 3,684,025

Notable Events of the First World War along the Western Front

1914

Mons	August
Aisne	August
Le Cateau	August
Nery	September
Aisne	September
1st Ypres	October

1915

Givenchy	February
Neuve Chapelle	March
Ypres Salient	April
2nd Ypres	April
Aubers Ridge	May
Festubert	May
Artois Offensive	May
Loos	September

1916

Somme	July 1st
	July 2nd - 17th
	July 18th - September 9th
	September 10th - October 3rd
	October 4th - November 18th

1917

Arras		April
Messines		June
3rd Ypres	Pilkem Ridge	July
	Langemarck	August
	Menin Road	September
	Polygon Wood	September
	Broodsiende	October
	Poelkapelle	October
	2nd Passchendale	October
Cambrai		November

1918

Somme	March
Lys	April
3rd Aisne	May
Marne	July
Amiens	August
Somme-Arras	August
Havrincourt	September
Cambrai / Hindenberg Line	September
2nd Le Cateau	October
Selle	October
Sambre	November

The Irish on the Western Front

On 28th September 1912, almost half a million Ulstermen and women signed a "Solemn League and Covenant", pledging their willingness to fight to remain part of the United Kingdom. In January 1913, the Ulster Volunteer Force was formed.

This date, now referred to as Ulster Day, saw 237,368 men put their names to the Covenant and 234,046 women signed the accompanying declaration.

At Seagoe in Portadown, following a church service 569 men and women signed their names.

In August 1913, the Irish National Volunteers came into being. Following the shooting of Irish Nationalists in Dublin on 2nd July 1914 after guns for the Irish Volunteers were landed at Howth, there was a distinct possibility of war in Ireland.

Only the outbreak of war in Europe saved the situation and Unionists and Nationalists believed that loyalty to England would be rewarded when the war was over.

Sir Edward Carson on behalf of the Unionists stated, "*I say to our Volunteers, go and help serve our country*".

In response John Redmond urged the Nationalists, "*It is these soldiers of ours whose keeping the Cause of Ireland has passed today.*"

From each corner of the island, northerners, southerners, protestants and catholics enlisted in their thousands.

In various parts of Ulster the Ulster Volunteer Force and Irish National Volunteers marched side by side.

Thus, from this point on, the 36th (Ulster) Division and the 16th (Irish) Division became a part of folklore in Irish history.

The two Divisions were to later fight side by side at Wytschaete but each was involved in many conflicts during the Great War.

For those in Ulster the 1st July 1916, the first day of the Battle of the Somme, will be a date that never will be forgotten. The glorious feats of the 36th (Ulster) Division meant that they were one of a small number of British Divisions who reached their objective, only to find that reinforcements from other Divisions failed to negotiate No Man's Land leaving the Ulstermen, isolated and surrounded. They had no option for the remnants of their men, but to retreat.

At the end of the day the 36th (Ulster) Division had suffered 5,766 casualties of which 2,069 had been killed.

In early September the same year the 16th (Irish) Division took the villages of Guillemont and Ginchy, showing the same bravery and courage as their counterparts in the 36th (Ulster) Division had shown in July.

Within 10 days the 16th (Irish) Division, which had been 11,000 strong had lost half of its strength, killed or injured.

It was to be November before the Battles of the Somme - there were three of them - came to an end. The total casualties from the Somme amounted to 419,654 British, 204,253 French and 500,000 German.

In June 1917, both Divisions were to fight side by side in Belgium, in the Battle of Messines, their objective being reached in taking the village of Wytschaete. The Ulster Division lost 61 officers and 1,058 other ranks whereas the Irish Division sustained almost 1,000 of all ranks, killed or injured.

From July to September, the Third Battle of Ypres, better known as Passchendaele – a name synonymous with death - involved the brave soldiers of Ireland yet again.

The British sustained 244,897 casualties and there were roughly 337,000 German casualties.

The two Divisions were involved in the Battle of Cambrai in November 1917 when 380 tanks were used in the assault.

During the German Spring Offensive in 1918, The Royal Irish Regiment, part of the 16th (Irish) Division lost heavily at Lempire whilst the 12th and 15th Royal Irish

Rifles of the 36th were eventually overwhelmed in this stage of the campaign at Fontaine-les-Clercs.

Brigadier A E C Bredin commented, *"The 16th and 36th Divisions suffered the heaviest losses of any formation during the great German Offensive of March 1918".*

When the Allied armies launched their successful counter-attacks, the Germans eventually succumbed.

In other memorable quotes:

"I am not an Ulsterman, but yesterday, 1st July 1916, as I followed their amazing attack, I felt I would rather be an Ulsterman than anything else in the world". **Captain W B Spender.**

"Our greatest success (on 3rd September 1916), was the capture of Guillemont by the Irish troops. They advanced on Guillemont with an impetuosity which carried all before it: charged through the German positions with the wild music of their pipes playing them on". **Frank A Mumby, "The Great World War - A History".**

"The record of the Thirty-sixth Division will always be the pride of Ulster. At Thiepval in the great battle of the Somme on July 1st 1916, at Wytschaete on June 17th 1917, in the storming of Messines Ridge, on the Canal du Nord, in the attack of the Hindenburg Line of November 20th in the same year, on March 21st 1918, near Fontaine-les-Clercs, defending their positions long after they were isolated and surrounded by the enemy, and later in the month at Andechy in the days of "backs to the wall", they acquired a reputation for conduct and devotion deathless in the military history of the United Kingdom, and repeatedly signalised in the despatches of the Commander-in-Chief" - **Sir Winston Churchill.**

"It is these soldiers of ours, with their astonishing courage and their beautiful faith, with their natural military genius, with their tenderness as well as strength; carrying with them their green flags and their Irish war-pipes; advancing to the charge, their fearless officers at their head and followed by their beloved chaplains, as great hearted as themselves; bringing with them a quality all their own to the sordid modern battlefield; exhibiting the character of the Irishman at its noblest and greatest". - **John Redmond MP**

"I recall the deeds of the 36th (Ulster) Division, which have more than fulfilled the high opinion formed by me on inspecting that force on the eve of its departure for the front.

Throughout the long years of struggle, which have so gloriously ended, the men of Ulster have proved how nobly they fight and die". - **King George V.**

36th (Ulster) Division

107th Brigade – 8th (East Belfast); 9th (West Belfast); 10th (South Belfast); 15th (North Belfast) Royal Irish Rifles

108th Brigade – 11th (South Antrim); 12th (Central Antrim); 13th (1st Co. Down) Royal Irish Rifles; 9th Royal Irish Fusiliers (Armagh, Monaghan, Cavan).

109th Brigade – 9th (Tyrone); 10th (Londonderry); 11th (Donegal, Fermanagh); Royal Inniskilling Fusiliers; 14th Royal Irish Rifles (Young Citizen Volunteers, Belfast).

Pioneer Battalion – 16th Royal Irish Rifles (2nd Co. Down).

1st Service Squadron, 6th (Inniskilling) Dragoons

153rd, 154th, 172nd, 173rd Royal Field Artillery

121st, 122nd, 150th, Field Company Corps of Royal Engineers

108th, 109th, 110th Field Ambulance, Royal Army Medical Corps

36th Divisional Signal Company Corps of Royal Engineers

36th Divisional Cyclist Company

36th Divisional Train Army Service Corps

76th Sanitary Section Royal Army Medical Corps

48th Mobile Veterinary Section Army Veterinary Corps

16th (Irish) Division

47th Brigade – 6th Royal Irish Regiment; 6th Connaught Rangers; 7th Leinster Regiment; 7th Royal Irish Rifles

48th Brigade – 8th; 9th Royal Munster Fusiliers; 8th; 9th Royal Dublin Fusiliers

49th Brigade – 7th; 8th; Royal Inniskilling Fusiliers; 7th; 8th Royal Irish Fusiliers

"Pals" Battalions

In England ready made friendship groups began in Liverpool in the prelude to war which became the forerunner of the "Pals" Battalions.

The most notable were the Accrington Pals, Barnsley Pals and Grimsby Chums. These men came from close knit communities. Some may simply have been at school together others worked in the same professions or in local factories.

The authorities welcomed such groupings probably believing that such groups would create a sense of comradeship.

What was not realised at the time was that if such a battalion would suffer major casualties then the effect on the local community would be catastrophic.

In Ulster and around Ireland it was little different. The 36th (Ulster) Division was divided into brigades and consisted of men who had enlisted in particular areas. The 107th Brigade which included the 8th, 9th, 10th and 15th Royal Irish Rifles were men basically from various areas of Belfast.

Men from Tyrone, Londonderry, Donegal, Fermanagh and the Young Citizens Volunteers comprised the 109th Brigade which included the 9th, 10th and 11th Royal Inniskilling Fusiliers and the 14th Royal Irish Rifles.

The 11th, 12th and 13th Royal Irish Rifles hailed mainly from South Antrim, Central Antrim and County Down and formed part of the 108th Brigade. This Brigade was completed by the 9th Royal Irish Fusiliers by men enlisting from Armagh, Monaghan and Cavan.

Therefore with regard to servicemen from Portadown and surrounding district, the majority joined the 9th Royal Irish Fusiliers, where scores of them made the supreme sacrifice on the killing fields of France and Belgium.

Their selfless contribution , to their local equivalent of the English "Pals" battalions would leave a devastating effect on the Portadown area in general and throughout Ulster as a whole. Their huge loss was to prove a crippling blow as two generations of servicemen would never return home.

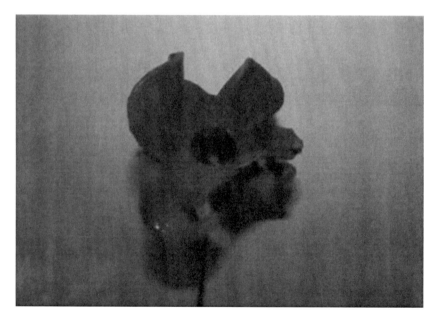

One of the ceramic poppies which had been on display at the Tower of London in 2014

Commonwealth War Graves Commission and its architects

The Commonwealth War Graves Commission, formerly the Imperial War Graves Commission is responsible for the upkeep and maintenance of war memorials and cemeteries throughout many parts of the world.

Those memorials and cemeteries within France and Belgium are meticulously maintained by horticulturists and gardeners employed by the CWGC.

Make a point of praising their endeavours should you meet them as you travel along, they will appreciate your comments.

The former Imperial War Graves Commission deserves the utmost credit by first of all appointing three principal architects to undertake the construction of hundreds of memorials or cemeteries commemorating the fallen of World War One.

These three, **Sir Edward Lutyens**, **Sir Reginald Blomfield** and **Sir Herbert Baker** set the tone for others to follow. A fourth principal architect **Charles Holden** was later appointed and he refused a knighthood on two occasions.

Other notable architects such as **R Truelove, H Chalton Bradshaw** and **W H Cowlishaw** also contributed much following the Armistice.

These talented individuals were responsible for many fine buildings in many parts of the world but space permits me to mention just a fraction of their endeavours throughout the Western Front.

Sir Edward Lutyens

The Stone of Remembrance

Thiepval Memorial to the Missing

St Georges Memorial Church

Arras Memorial and Cemetery

Etaples Military Cemetery

Dartmoor Cemetery

Sir Reginald Blomfield

The Cross of Sacrifice

Menin Gate

Artillery Wood Cemetery

Ancre British Cemetery

Essex Farm Cemetery

Brandhoek Military Cemetery

Sir Herbert Baker

Tyne Cot Cemetery

Delville Wood Cemetery and South African Memorial

London Cemetery and Extension

New Zealand Memorial in Caterpillar Valley Cemetery

VC Corner Fromelles

Bailleul Communal Cemetery and Extension '

Terlincthun British Cemetery

Charles Holden

Louvencourt Military Cemetery

Forceville British Cemetery

New Zealand Memorial in Messines Ridge Cemetery

Pavilions in Wimereux Communal Cemetery Extension

Baupaume Post Cemetery

Poelkapelle British Cemetery

R E Grave

H Chalton Bradshaw

Ploegsteert Memorial to the Missing and adjoining cemeteries

Cambrai Memorial

J R Truelove

He served as an officer with the London Regiment.

Vis-en-Artois Memorial

Le Touret Memorial

Lone Tree Cemetery

Spanbroekmolen British Cemetery

W H Cowlishaw

Pozieres Memorial to the Missing and Pozieres Military Cemetery

Prowse Point Cemetery

Devonshire Cemetery

We are very much indebted to the sterling work contributed by the above individuals who have allowed many war pilgrims and enthusiasts throughout these past ninety years to pay their respects to the fallen buried on the Western Front or to those with no known graves whose names are etched on various memorials in order that they will never be forgotten.

Commonwealth War Graves Commission

Formerly named the Imperial War Graves Commission, the CWGC had by 1937 built over 1000 architecturally constructed cemeteries consisting of fifty miles of brick and stone walling, almost 1000 Crosses of Sacrifice and 560 Stones of Remembrance. In addition were eighteen large memorials to the missing and in excess of 600,000 headstones.

Certain memorials are special to particular Commonwealth countries. Vimy to the Canadians, Villers-Bretonneux to the Australians, Delville Wood for the South Africans, Neuve Chapelle for the Indians, Thiepval for the British and Menin Gate for all with the exception of New Zealand who did not want their war dead names inscribed on it.

Headstones

The standard headstone is 81 cm (or 2 feet, 8 inches) high. On each is allowed details of the fallen. At the top is the emblem badge of the regiment or service for the British and Indian.

The maple leaf represents Canada, the badge of the Australian Imperial Force for the Australians, a fern leaf for the New Zealanders, the springbok for the South Africans and the caribou for the Newfoundlanders.

There are over 1500 different national, regimental and departmental corps badges inscribed on the headstones.

Below the emblem is the service or regimental number of the individual interred, though this is usually omitted for officers; Then the serviceman's rank, initials, surname and any official abbreviation of any British decorations.

Below this is the name of the service or regiment, date of death, age if known and a religious emblem either a cross or Star of David.

The next of kin could if they so required request a personal inscription of up to sixty letters.

Where a Victoria Cross has been awarded the VC abbreviation is after the recipient's name and an enlarged facsimile of the Victoria Cross may be inscribed rather than a religious emblem.

There are 204,000 unidentified graves from both World Wars. The headstone may simply be inscribed, "A soldier of the Great War " with the word inscribed below, " Known unto God".

Other headstones may be inscribed with, "Buried near this spot", "Buried in this cemetery" or "Known to be buried in this cemetery."

At times remains are still found by chance. In 1981 at Ovillers-la-Boisselle in the Somme, the remains of 49 British soldiers from five regiments and two Germans were discovered following the demolition of farm buildings. None were able to be identified and all the personnel were interred in Terlincthun British Cemetery.

The Stone of Remembrance

It was designed by Sir Edward Lutyens for the Imperial War Graves Commission. It is normally found in cemeteries with over 400 dead.

The altar like point of focus is acceptable to most faiths. The inscription, "Their Name Liveth For Evermore", was chosen by Kipling. It is from Ecclesiastes, Chapter 44, verse 14, which reads, "Their bodies are buried in peace; and their name liveth for evermore".

The aesthetic effect of the Cross and Stone depends upon their setting in relation to the varying levels of the cemetery and surrounding natural features.

The Cross of Sacrifice

The Cross of Sacrifice was designed by Sir Reginald Blomfield for the Imperial War Graves Commission.

There are four sizes ranging from 2.75 m (15 feet) to just over 4.5 m (30 feet high) to suit the dimensions of the cemetery.

It stands on an octagonal block and rests on three steps.

On the face of the cross is a bronze broadsword pointing downwards.

The minimum number of burials to qualify for a cross is generally thirty. There are some exceptions, notably Royal Engineers Grave at Zillebeke in Belgium. Commemorated by name on the base of the cross are an officer, three NCO's and eight men of the 177th Tunnelling Company, Royal Engineers. This is probably the smallest number of dead anywhere to be accorded a Cross of Sacrifice.

The cross represents the faith of the majority of the dead whilst the sword is believed to symbolise its position after the battle is over as well as depicting the military character of the cemetery.

The Victoria Cross

The Victoria Cross was founded by a Royal Warrant issued on 29th January 1856, a single decoration available to the British Army or Royal Navy, "for individual instances of merit and valour". Along with the warrant were fifteen rules and ordinances which had to be met.

Rules were amended and added to consistently up until 1918. By then posthumous VC's could be awarded and open to all services and non-military persons.

*In World War One there were 633 VC's awarded, 188 posthumously.

Three men have been awarded the VC twice. Arthur Martin Leake in the Boer War, Capt Noel Chavasse in the Great War (see Brandhoek Military Cemetery) and Charles Upham of the New Zealand forces in World War Two.

There have up to now been four sets of brothers who have been awarded the Victoria Cross.

During the London Olympics of 2012 I was privileged to view **Lord Ashcroft's collection of VC's in the Imperial War Museum. This is the largest collection of VC's in the world.**

In the Lord Ashcroft Gallery, to which he donated £5 million pounds, one can view his 152 VC's alongside a further 50 owned by the Imperial War Museum.

The first VC bought by Lord Ashcroft was that presented to Ulsterman James Magennis of the Royal Navy which had been awarded in 1945.

In early August 2013 the Government announced that as part of its plans to mark the centenary of the First World War in 2014 that Victoria Cross winners will be recognised for their valour and service.

Special commemorative paving stones will be laid in the home towns of all those in the United Kingdom who had been awarded the Victoria Cross during the conflict.

A national competition is to be held to design specially commissioned paving stones which will be presented to Councils in the areas where Victoria Cross recipients of the First World War were born.

It is hoped these paving stones will ensure there is a permanent memorial to all the Fallen who received this award, "For Valour."

New Commemorative £2 Coin

A new coin for 2014 that commemorates the centenary of the First World War has been produced by the Royal Mint.

It is part of a number of new coins each marking different anniversaries.

The coin marking the outbreak of the First World War features a design depicting Lord Kitchener pointing out from the face of the coin as did the contemporary posters asking people at the time to sign up for the army.

World War One soldiers diaries placed on-line by National Archives.

Diaries from British soldiers describing life on the front line during World War One are being published on-line by the National Archives.

Events from the outbreak of war in 1914 to the departure of troops from the battlefields of France and Flanders were recorded in the official diaries of each military unit.

By mid-January 2014 of the one and a half million diary pages held by the National Archives , a third had been digitised.

The first batch of 1914 digitised diaries detail the experiences of three cavalry and seven infantry divisions in the initial wave of British troops deployed in 1914.

Diaries from soldiers of the 1st South Wales Borderers detail the terror of the opening days of the war during the battles of the Marne and the Aisne.

Other diaries record the experiences of the 4th Dragoon Guards who fought in the battle at Mons , the first major action of the war for the British Expeditionary Force.

There are also diaries from the 5th (Royal Irish) Lancers, a battalion who had the last British soldier to be killed in the conflict. He was Pte G E Ellison who was shot dead on 11th November 1918 and who is buried in St Symphorien Military Cemetery , south-east of Mons , in Belgium.

Thiepval 1st July 2006 - Royal British Legion and French Legion standards

Dead Man's Penny - The Death Plaque

It was in 1916 the Government realised that some form of gratitude should be given to fallen men and women's bereaved next of kin. The following year a competition was launched to design a suitable plaque with the winner receiving a princely sum of £250.

From over 800 entries Mr E Carter Preston of Liverpool was the successful applicant. The selected design was a 12 cm disc made of gunmetal, shown above, which incorporated the following:

An image of Britannia and a lion, two dolphins representing Britain's sea power and the emblem of Imperial Germany's eagle being torn to pieces by another lion. Britannia is holding an oak spray with leaves and acorns. Beneath this was a rectangular tablet where the deceased's individual name was cast into the plaque. No rank was given as it was intended to show equality in sacrifice. On the outer edge of the disk, the words, "He died for freedom and honour".

A scroll 27 x 17 cm made of slightly darkened parchment headed by the Royal Coat of Arms accompanied the plaque with a carefully chosen passage, written in Old English script. (See above).

Beneath the passage, written in the same style was the name, rank and service details of the deceased. To accompany the scroll, again in Old English script was a personal message from King George V.

The plaques were packaged in stiff cardboard wrapping folded like an envelope and sent to the next of kin.

The cost of these was supposed to be financed by German reparation money, began in 1919, with over 1,150,000 issued. They commemorated those who fell between 4th August 1914 and 10th January 1920 for home, Western Europe and the Dominions whilst the final date for other theatres of war was the 30th April 1920.

The Iron Harvest

British and German forces launched more than a billion shells and bombs at each other as they fought in vain to break the stalemate along the Western Front during the Great War.

This lethal ordnance killed millions on both sides during the war and it continues to do so to this day.

It is reckoned 300 millions of unexploded bombs lie under the farmland of Northern France and Belgium.

In March 2014 two construction workers were killed when a shell exploded in Ypres.

In Belgium and France there are teams of army bomb disposal officers , The Belgian officers are stationed permanently in Boesinghe. Over 20 Belgian bomb disposal officers have been killed since 1919.

Bombs designed to kill during the Great War have killed more than 360 people and injured over 500 more around Ypres alone.

The bomb disposal officers are called out on a daily basis by farmers and construction workers.

Not surprisingly people in outlying villages in Northern France and Belgium keep strictly to marked routes when out for an afternoon stroll.

All tourists including British and Irish are constantly reminded that no shell should be touched unless it is by the bomb disposal experts. The fuse for example could suddenly decide to do its work , the shell might be toxic or even the outside of it may be contaminated by chemical weapons that have lain in the soil next to it.

The figures outlined above indicate only too clearly that shells, bombs and ammunition should remain untouched and should you come across any ordnance notify the emergency agencies immediately.

The people who live in Northern France and Belgium do not think of the war as distant history,

It remains a very dangerous factor in their daily lives.

Queen University - WW1 Engagement Centre

Queen's University Belfast has been chosen to help lead a major international research project on World War 1, as part of the Centenary celebrations of the Great war

With four other UK Universities, Queen's is to become a "World War One Engagement Centre", with a remit to supporting community, academic and public research into the events of 1914-1918,

The University will form part of the First World War Centenary Partnership, led by the Imperial War Museum, with the Universities of Birmingham, Kent, Hertfordshire and Nottingham. The Queen's Centre will be headed by Dr. Keith Lilley of the School of Geography, Archaeology and Palaeoecology and based at the Institute of Collaborative Research [n the Humanities (ICRH).

Entitled and "Living Legacies 1914-1918: From Past Conflict to Shared Future", Queen's stands to receive £500,000 from the Arts and Humanities Research Council (AHRC) in partnership with the Heritage Lottery Fund, to establish the Centre.

A key focus of the Engagement Centres will be to provide UK wide support for community groups funded through a range of Heritage Lottery Fund funding programmes, particularly its new £6 million "First World War: Then and Now" community grant scheme.

During the start-up phase ahead of its formal launch on Monday 19th May 2015, the Centres will be extending links with the diverse programmes of community activities already being planned for the centenary as well as developing international links.

For further details of the Queen's Centre contact: livinglegacies@qub.ac.uk.

2

Route 1

The Somme

Preparing your own route

Bearing in mind the casual traveller may be subject to the itinerary on a coach, this publication will prove relatively easy in deciding those places which are of interest to the individual.

For those who wish to explore the battlefields by car, you will quickly realise that I have placed particular emphasis on the exploits of the 36th (Ulster) and the 16th (Irish) Divisions. I have suggested somewhat circuitous routes to encapsulate where Irishmen from all parts of the Island were involved.

In recent years there has been a spate of break-ins to vehicles whilst their occupants have been exploring the battlefield areas in France and Belgium. I would suggest that you do not leave any valuables on view but rather store them under lock and key and well out of sight.

It is important that schoolchildren for example may have a particular interest in sportsmen who were killed in the Great War and the following pages will allow teachers and students to modify their routes to suit their studies.

For those arriving by air into Beauvais Airport, Tille, follow the A16 to Amiens. Take the Amiens ring road eastwards exiting to join the D929 to Albert.

In almost all CWGC Cemeteries you will find a Cemetery Register and a Visitors' Book usually placed in a wall receptacle just inside the entrance gate or in a covered canopy positioned not far away.

The Register is self-explanatory indicating the names and details of the dead and their respective cemetery plot.

Make a point of signing the Visitors' Book as this gives the CWGC an indication of the numbers of visitors over a period of time.

It is illuminating reading some of the comments written therein. One of the most poignant I read was, "*Found you at last, Dad*".

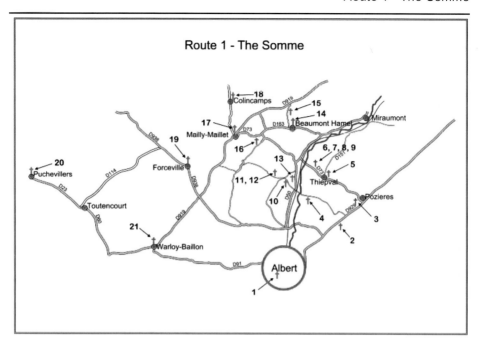

Route 1 - The Somme

1. Albert
2. Baupaume Post Military Cem.
3. Pozieres Memorial to the Missing
4. Authuile Military Cemetery
5. Somme Memorial to the Missing
6. Ulster Tower
7. Connaught Cemetery
8. Thiepval Wood
9. Mill Road Cemetery
10. Martinsart British Cemetery
11. Mesnil Mairie
12. Mesnil Communal Cemetery Extension
13. Hamel Military Cemetery
14. Ancre British Cemetery
15. Newfoundland Memorial Park
16. Auchonvillers Military Cemetery
17. Mailly Wood Cemetery
18. Sucrerie Military Cemetery
19. Forceville Communal Cemetery
20. Puchevillers Military Cemetery
21. Warloy-Baillon Communal Cemetery

Route 1 - The Somme

I have chosen **Albert (1)** formerly known as **Ancre** , as the starting point and the main Albert to Baupaume Road, D929 as the dividing line.

Whilst in Albert make an effort to visit the **Basilique Notre Dame de Brebieres** in the centre of town which gave rise to World War One legends and the interesting **Musee des Arbres** close by.

Take the road D929 towards Baupaume and after 2 km you will reach **Baupaume Post Military Cemetery (2)** on the right hand side of the road. On this particular part of your route the first Portadown casualty you will come across in **Plot 1 D 15 is 2nd Lt James Watson, 2nd Royal Irish Rifles** who lived at Ashfield. Also buried here are men from the 34th (Tyneside) Division of the Northumberland Fusiliers who fell in their hundreds on the nearby Tara and Usna Hills on 1st July 1916.

Continue on the D929 and 4 km further on you will reach the imposing edifice of the **Pozieres Memorial to the Missing (3)**. Here are recorded the names of 14,690 men of the Fifth Army who fell in the Battles of the Somme up to 5th April 1918 and all other casualties up to 7th August who have no known grave. There are nine local men commemorated on its walls including **Pte J. Lamb 1st Royal Irish Fusiliers who had been a player with Portadown Football Club.**

Close by, and whilst not having Portadown connections spend some time exploring **1st Australian Division and Tank Corps Memorial. A few hundred metres along is a Canadian Memorial commemorating their victory at Courcelette.**

Take left on the D159 where you will reach **Authuile Military Cemetery (4),** which is on a back street of the village and down a laneway overlooking the river. Here you will find the last resting places of not one but **two Pte Willie McBrides,** both belonging to the Royal Inniskilling Fusiliers. **Two Portadown men of the 14th Royal Irish Rifles, Rfn G. Tollerton and Rfn T. G. Sloane are interred here.**

The Somme Memorial to the Missing at Thiepval (5) is well signposted and easily spotted. It is an imposing edifice near the south boundary of the former park of the Thiepval Chateau. There is an interpretation centre and bookshop within the grounds. **The Memorial itself commemorates over 73,000 men who died on the Somme battlefields between 1915 and 20th March 1918. Three Ulster recipients of the Victoria Cross are named – Pte W. D. McFadzean, Lt G. S. Shillington and Capt E. N. Bell.**

There are **almost seventy men with Portadown connections** found on the Piers of the Memorial.

Those interested in football should take particular interest in **Pier 6D/7B** which records the names of **four Heart of Midlothian players who fell serving with McCrae's Btn, 16th Royal Scots** , whilst on **Pier 12D/13B** are the names of **men of 17th Middlesex (Footballers') Battalion.**

At the rear of the Memorial is the **Anglo-French Cemetery** which symbolises the joint efforts of the two countries during World War One.

You are now deep into 36th (Ulster) Division territory where you take **"the bloody road"**, from the Somme Memorial to the **Ulster Tower (6).** Again the venue is well signposted. The Tower was unveiled on 19th November 1921 and it is a replica of Helen's Tower at Clandeboye, County Down where the Ulstermen trained prior to setting off to war.

There is a **Memorial Stone** just inside the gates commemorating the **nine Victoria Cross recipients of the 36th (Ulster) Division.**

To the right and behind the Tower is a memorial to the **Fallen Brethren of the Orange Institution**, which saw more of its members serve and make the supreme sacrifice in the First World War than any other single organisation.

Connaught Cemetery (7) some one hundred metres distant sits in No Man's Land over which the Ulster's attacked on 1st July 1916.

Behind is **Thiepval Wood (8)** now owned by the Somme Association. Excavation work here continues and sections of a front line trench and a communications trench have been preserved.

Immediately across from Connaught Cemetery and along a stony 400 metre track you will find **Mill Road Cemetery (9),** which lies on the German front line. There were numerous tunnel systems here during the war and as a result many of the headstones are laid flat on the ground. **Pte W. J. Wilson, 9th Royal Irish Fusiliers from Portadown** is buried here.

Take the D129 in the direction of Aveluy, where 3 km along you will reach **Martinsart British Cemetery (10)**. Here the headstones are made of red Corsehill sandstone. **A row of graves in Plot 1 contain the remains of 14 men of the 13th Royal Irish Rifles who were killed by an enemy shell on 28th June 1916. Several of the dead were from Dromore, County Down.**

Also buried here is Lt L. S. Kelly of the Royal Naval Volunteer Reserve who won an Olympic Gold Medal in 1908 in the coxed eights.

The neighbouring village of **Mesnil** has a memorial plaque to those men of the 13th Royal Irish Rifles whilst also in the **Mairie (11)**– the village hall –are the hands of the village clock taken by the 14th Royal Irish Rifles, (Young Citizens Volunteers) originally taken as it was believed the Germans were using them to send messages. The clock hands were returned to the Mayor of Mesnil on 13th July 1927.

Mesnil Communal Cemetery Extension (12) contains 333 graves including Capt C. M. Johnston, 9th Royal Irish Fusiliers , a member of both Portadown Rugby and Rowing Clubs.

At Aveluy take right for Beaumont-Hamel and head for **Hamel** village. It was here that Lt G. S. Shillington-Cather , Royal Irish Fusiliers won his Victoria Cross and also where Pte R. Quigg gained his Victoria Cross, going out nine times to look for his platoon officer, bringing back a wounded man on each occasion.

Hamel Military Cemetery (13) is on the south side of the village, 25 metres west of the road to Albert. The cemetery has a total of 492 graves including many of 9th Royal Irish Fusiliers from the Portadown area.

Ancre British Cemetery (14) is on the west side of the D 50 road between Beaumont-Hamel and Hamel. Again many soldiers from Portadown are at rest here including **Major T. J. Atkinson, 9th Royal Irish Fusiliers of Eden Villa, Bachelors' Walk.**

Newfoundland Memorial Park at Beaumont-Hamel (15) is now owned by the Canadian government and commemorates the deeds and losses of the **Newfoundland Regiment** on 1st July. The **Caribou Memorial to the Missing** records the names of those who died.

Y Ravine Cemetery contains the grave of **Pte S. McMeekin, 1st Royal Inniskilling Fusiliers** who lies amongst the fallen of The Black Watch.

The park is what it was like in 1916 clearly indicating just how close the British and German front lines were. **The Danger Tree** is where many of the Newfoundlanders fell.

Hawthorn Ridge Cemetery within the confines of the park contains 224 burials from 1st July 1916, killed during the Hawthorn Mine explosion.

Look too for the **"Ours" memorial plaque** at the base of the Caribou Monument. **It is the only commercial monument on the Western Front.**

At the crossroads in Auchonvillers follow the signs for Mailly-Maillet to reach **Auchonvillers Military Cemetery (16).** 2nd Lt R. W. McDermott, 8th Royal Irish

Rifles is buried here, the first officer of the 36th (Ulster) Division to be killed. Also buried here is Sgt W. E. Lynn, 1st Royal Irish Fusiliers who hailed from Coalisland. He is one of four brothers who made the supreme sacrifice.

When you reach Mailly-Maillet, pause and have a look at the church and notice the bullet scars on the building emanating from the First World War. Take the D919 road to Amiens. Well signposted, **Mailly Wood Cemetery (17)** is down a 500 metre mud track. **Pte W. J. Hall , a Seaforth Highlander, originally from Seagoe is buried here.**

Take the road from Mailly-Maillet towards Colincamps. **Sucrerie Military Cemetery(18)** is 3 km east of the village. **Here lies Rfn J. Crozier, 9th Royal Irish Rifles from Battenberg Street, Belfast . His sentence of death has provoked huge controversy in Ulster for many years. Two Portadown soldiers rest here also.**

Head out of Colincamps on the D114 towards Acheux-en-Amienois. Take left on the D938 to Forceville. On the D939 towards Doullens lies **Forceville Communal Cemetery Extension (19).** This was one of the first three permanent cemeteries. **Many Portadown men are buried here.**

Return to Acheux-en Amienois and take the D31 to **Puchevillers British Cemetery (20)**where a **further two Portadown soldiers** have their last resting place.

Follow the D23 to Vadencourt and then left on D919 to **Warloy-Baillon Communal Cemetery Extension (21)**. Here you will find the grave of **Major-General E. C. Ingouville-Williams, Commanding Officer of the 34th Division. Inky Bill lies in the company of two Portadown fallen.**

From Warloy-Baillon it is a leisurely drive back to your starting point at Albert.

Provided you have time on your hands, this overall route would require two days.

An unusual roadblock at St Pierre Divion.

Albert

Albert was the main town in this British sector of the battlefield. In 1914 the French held off the Germans during which time the statue of the Virgin and the infant Christ at the top of the Basilique Notre Dame de Brebieres fell from its base and teetered at an angle of 45 degrees after an enemy bomb had exploded. The statue was secured by French engineers - so the legend began that should the Virgin fall it would mean the end of the war was approaching.

Eventually it did fall but not until 1918 when the Germans had occupied Albert from the period March - August 1918. The Germans then had been using the building as an observation post and - the statue was felled as a result of this, by British artillery.

Paul Reed the celebrated historian tells us that the Australians had christened the Leaning Virgin as "Fanny Durack", a famous Australian swimmer who had won a gold medal in 1912 - they figured the statue of Mary resembled Fanny diving into a swimming pool!

The Basilica today is built and restored on its original base and design and atop a gilt replica of the Virgin and Child.

During the war many British troops were billeted in the town they affectionately dubbed, "Bert". There were several Dressing Stations here as well as ammunition dumps and stores, yet it was still within range of enemy shells.

Musee des Arbris - Museum of the Shelters.

This is an interesting museum and well worth a visit. It is actually encased in a series of subterranean tunnels which stretch under the Basilica and the town.

There are many exhibits of trench life during the First World War.

As you exit the Museum and climb the adjacent series of steps to town level you come across a splendid mural by Irish artist McCartan depicting three soldiers, one of them Irish, walking past the damaged Basilica.

Albert is an excellent base from which to begin your visit to the battlefields of the Somme. It is easily reached from nearby airports at Beauvais and Charles de Gaulle.

There are several hotels in the area and a host of bed and breakfast accommodation.
Details from the Tourist Office of Poppy Country, 9 Rue Gambetta - BP82, 80300 Albert.
Tel: +33(0) 3 22 75 16 42.

Further information may be found on the web: **officedutourisme@pays du coquelicot.com**

Baupaume Post Military Cemetery

The cemetery Is 2 km from Albert on the D929 to Baupaume. It lles to the west side of Tara Hill, south-west of Usna Hill and at times was called by both of these names.

In June 1916 the front line crossed the Baupaume Road between the site of the cemetery and La Boisselle. The attack on La Boisselle on 1st July 1916 was not successful and it was several days before the village was taken.

The cemetery was begun almost at once and used up to January 1917. On 26th March 1918, Albert fell into German hands but it was re-taken by the end of August.

After the Armistice graves were brought in from smaller cemeteries including many of the 34th (Tyneside) Division of the Northumberland Fusiliers , which attacked along the Baupaume Road on 1st July together with many of the 38th (Welsh) Division which recaptured Usna Hill on 23rd August 1917.

There are 410 graves of which 181 are unidentified. The cemetery was designed by Charles Holden.

2nd Lt James Watson 2nd Royal Irish Rifles - 9th July 1916 – 1 D 15. – Ashfield, Cornascriebe, Portadown. He had been a clerk in the Ulster Bank.

Pte E. J. Johnstone 18824 – Royal Scots – 1st July 1916 – 11 M 3. His epitaph reads, " No more with springing feet I'll roam the dear familiar hills of home."

Pozieres Military Cemetery
Pozieres Memorial to the Missing

Pozieres village sits astride the main Albert – Baupaume road, D929. Pozieres was the key to any advance as it sits on the highest point of a commanding ridge. It was the objective for the 8th Division on 1st July 1916, but four attempts by the British during that month failed.

The 1st Australian Division had attacked on 23rd July and within two days had taken most of the village. The 2nd Australian Division renewed the attack on 29th July but was heavily rebuffed. A second attack on 4th/5th August pushed the line beyond the ruined windmill to the north-east of the village. The 4th Australian Division then extended the line north to Moquet Farm. In six weeks the Australians had suffered 23,000 casualties.

The Memorial records the names of 14,690 men of the Fifth Army who died in the Battles of the Somme up to 5th April 1918 and all other casualties in further battles up to 7th August, who have no known grave.

Pozieres Military Cemetery is on the site of Red Cross Corner as it was known in 1916. It was a place for Field Ambulances to bury their dead. The cemetery contains 2,400 graves of which about half are unidentified. It was designed by W. H. Cowlingshaw.

The memorial records the names of 398 Royal Irish Rifles, 276 Royal Inniskilling Fusiliers, 244 Royal Dublin Fusiliers, 163 Royal Irish Regiment, 110 Royal Munster Fusiliers, 86 Royal Irish Fusiliers, 58 Connaught Rangers, 58 Leinster Regiment, 31 Royal Irish Lancers and 13 6th Royal Inniskilling Dragoons.

In the cemetery lie 19 members of the Royal Irish Rifles and one Royal Inniskilling Dragoon.

Many of those named on this memorial were killed during the German Spring Offensive , Operation Michael which lasted from 21st March 1918 until 29th April 1918.

Royal Irish Fusiliers Panels 76/77

Pte J. Lamb 4626 1st Btn 21st March 1918. Member of Portadown Football Club. Lived in Foundry Street.

Pte J. Tedford 25204 1st Btn. 21st March 1918. Margaret Street.

Pte R. E. Watt 24853 1st Btn 24th March 1918 Drumannon, Portadown.**The 1st Btn Royal Irish Fusiliers on 21st March 1918 had one officer and ten other ranks killed, fifty five other ranks wounded and 275 men missing.**

Royal Irish Rifles - Panels 74/76

Rfn T. E. England 130 11th/13th Btn 27th March 1918, Church Street. Two of his brothers served.

Rfn T. J. Smyth 1795 12th Btn 21st March 1918, Foundry Street.

Rfn W. J. Topping 995 16th (Pioneer) Btn 21st March 1918, Fowler's Entry 1 F 15 - Cochrane's Hill, Laurelvale.

Rfn S. S. Woodhouse 20593 12th Btn 21st March 1918 - Breagh

Royal Munster Fusiliers - Panels 78/79

L/Cpl G. M. Smyth 18022 21st March 1918. Church Street**.** His father was Principal of Park Road National School.

36th Machine Gun Corps Panels 90/93

Pte. R. Fulton 17788 21st March 1918 Henry Street.

Graves

Rfn J. McCagherty 5452 Royal Irish Rifles 8th August 1916. 1 F 15 - Cochrane's Hill, Laurelvale

Sgt C. C. Castleton VC, 5th Australian Coy, Machine Gun Corps 29th July 1916, 4 L 33

Pte D. J. Carlson, 49th Canadian Btn, 8th September 1916 – 3 E 48. Found in May 2000 and re-buried.

2nd Lt Edmund de Wind VC

15th Royal Irish Rifles

21st March 1918

Panel 74-76

Edmund de Wind was born in Comber. His father was the Chief Engineer of the Belfast and County Down Railway. After his education at Campbell College, Belfast, he began work in County Cavan with the Bank of Ireland.

He emigrated to Canada in 1910 and worked in banking in Edmonton. He arrived in France with the Canadian Expeditionary Force in September 1915. He saw action in the later stages of the Battle of the Somme in 1916 and at Vimy Ridge in 1917.

He earned a commission in September 1917 and was posted to 15th Royal Irish Rifles (North Belfast Volunteers.)

He won his Victoria Cross in the Kaiser's Spring Offensive 1918, " for most conspicuous gallantry and self-sacrifice on 21st March at the Race Course Redoubt, near Grugies, south-east of St. Quentin For seven hours he held a most important post and though twice wounded, and practically single-handed he maintained his position. On two occasions, with only two NCO's, under heavy machine-gun fire, he cleared the trench, killing many. He eventually was mortally wounded."

L/Sgt William Manning, 26238, 10th Royal Dublin Fusiliers, 27th March 1918 - Panel 79-80.

Willie was an All-Ireland hurler and footballer and was reckoned to be one of the finest defensive players to have represented Antrim in both Provincial football and hurling. He was widely respected throughout the Gaelic Athletic Association.

He played for Antrim in the All-Ireland football final in 1915.

BELFAST GAELIC PLAYER KILLED.

In Gaelic football and hurling circles throughout the country, especially in Belfast, the news of the death in action of Sergt. Wm. Manning, Royal Dublin Fusiliers, the well-known and popular Shauns-Antrim All-Ireland hurler-footballer, will be hailed with feelings of deep regret. In his 26th year "Willie," as he was affectionately known, was one of the finest

A newspaper cutting of the death of Antrim player William Manning.

Authuile Military Cemetery
Somme

Authuile is a village 5 km north of Albert on the D159. The cemetery is approached down the back street of the village and then down a narrow track

Authuile was held by British troops from the summer of 1915 until March 1918 when it was lost during the German Offensive. In March 1916, 108th Field Ambulance set up a marquee to the north of the church and painted it in an attempt to disguise it. The 9th Inniskillings and the 12th and 15th Royal Irish Rifles were involved in various conflicts including hand to hand fighting in the trenches in this area and this is reflected in the number of graves within the cemetery.

On 8th May 1916, on the decision of Major Peacocke, men of the 9th Inniskillings (The Tyrones) left Sunken Road at 11.00 p.m. After clearing several German trenches they returned to the Sunken Road. They then suffered heavy German fire for an hour and a half. The Tyrones' losses the next morning were 18 dead and 84 wounded. All the dead were buried in Authuile later the same evening. This raid had been rehearsed for eight days at the dummy trenches at Clairfaye.

There are now 66 Inniskillings buried here together with almost 50 men of the Royal Irish Rifles.

This is a particularly pleasant cemetery which stretches down the hillside towards the river.

Rfn G. Tollerton 6050, 14th Royal Irish Rifles, 6th May 1916 - D 48 - Mary Street

George worked for The Great Northern Railway Company in Portadown Railway Station where he was employed as a fireman. He was on duty in the trenches as part of a machine gun team when they came under heavy bombardment from the enemy. He was killed instantly when a trench mortar shell exploded beside him.

The Portadown News of 20th May 1916 printed part of a letter penned by Lt R. Renwick, Machine Gun Officer in 14th Royal Irish Rifles who had written to George's widow, "During the bombardment, he stood by his gun with great courage and his name has since appeared in battalion orders for gallantry."

Rfn T. G. Sloane 14th Royal Irish Rifles, 6th May 1916 D 50 - Bridge Street.

Thomas was employed by Messrs Young and Hyde Ltd of Bedford Street, Belfast. His aunt Miss McDowell owned the Albert Hotel in Portadown.

His mother received a letter explaining how Thomas had died which was published in the Portadown News on 20th May 1916.

"The platoon to which he belonged had the honour of holding the most difficult and dangerous portion of our line, and your boy was on sentry duty during the whole of the bombardment. How he held to his post under a positive shower of high explosive, shell and shrapnel will never be understood. The place where he was stationed was comparable only to an inferno and the finger of death was pointed at every man in that platoon. Knowing this as they did they never flinched and refused to retire, thus proving themselves as brave as any heroes whose names and deeds we have been taught to glorify. Your son was one of these and the post which he held was blown to pieces by a shell containing 200 lbs of explosive."

2nd Lt M. R. L. Armstrong 150th Field Coy, Royal Engineers, 22nd April 1916 - D 69 - He hailed from Armagh.

Capt H. G. Barber MC, Yorks and Lancs Regt, 7th July 1916 - G 3. The inscription on his headstone reads, "Death is only an incident in life".

The graves of 33 men of the Dorset Regiment who died on 6th May 1916 are in the front row of the cemetery nearest the river.

One of the most popular folk songs written about the Great War is, " The Green Fields Of France", also known to some as "No Man's Land" or "Willie McBride". It was composed by renowned folk artist Eric Bogle.

In Authuile Military Cemetery there are two Pte Willie McBride's buried. One is in Plot D 67 and the other in A 36.

Pte W McBride 12/23965, 9th Royal Inniskilling Fusiliers 22nd April 1916 - D 67. He was the son of Joseph and Lina McBride of Roan Cottage, Lislea, Armagh.

Pte W McBride 21406, 2nd Royal Inniskilling Fusiliers - 10th February 1916 - A 36

Thiepval Village
Somme

As early as 1914 the Germans chose the site as a place of very strong, if not impenetrable defence on the heights of the Ancre valley, from which they could not be budged. The extensive cellarage provided safe billets for the German troops. A group of these cellars was interconnected and formed a position known as Thiepval Fort.

The machine-guns of the forts as well as those set up in a post in the ruins of a chateau were excellently sited for defence purposes as they commanded the British trenches to the north and in front of Thiepval Wood. They could also sweep the entire western face of the spur and to the south and could bring a withering enfilade upon any forward movement from Authuille. In the Battle of the Somme, the Germans were to hold on to this fortress for nearly thirteen weeks.

1st July 1916
The First Battle of the Somme

The centenary of the carnage inflicted on 1st July 1916 is almost upon us. It is rumoured that hotels, bed and breakfast houses and campsites around the Albert area and further afield have been booked out two years in advance, mainly by folk from the Province of Ulster who wish to pay tribute to the courageous deeds of the men of the 36th (Ulster) Division who gained such glory and who paid the supreme sacrifice on what is generally referred to as Britain's bloodiest day on a battlefield.

Over the passing years Thiepval, St Pierre-Divion, Beaumont-Hamel and Ginchy are hamlets etched in Ulster history where hundreds of Ulstermen, scores of whom hailed from Portadown, so valiantly gave their lives.

The objective of the Division that fateful day was to take the impregnable Schwaben Redoubt and progress to Grandcourt. The Germans were well dug in and the preliminary bombardment which lasted eight days failed to cut the swathes of barbed wire or destroy enemy defences.

At dawn on 1st July every gun on a twenty five mile front was firing. At 7:30 a.m. waves of British infantrymen , moved forward with their bayonets glistening in the sun. Despite the German machine guns creating havoc on the 8th, 9th and 10th Royal Irish Rifles those that had survived to date unfalteringly moved on.

A few members of 107th Brigade managed to reach the German fourth line , their main objective. One patrol actually entered Moquet Farm, the main German Headquarters but they found it vacated.

Few crossing that open countryside of No Man's Land lived to tell the tale. The Germans introduced reinforcements to halt the progress of the Ulstermen. The rest of the British line didn't move forward as expected and as a result the promise of a great victory was lost. The few remaining in German territory were forced to retreat and soon the Schwaben Redoubt was back in German hands.

For the next two days depleted troops tried to fight off the enemy suffering even further casualties. On the evening of 2nd July the 36th (Ulster) Division was relieved by the 49th Division.

The Ulster Division lost 5,553 officers and men in the two day carnage. There wasn't a town or village in Ulster that wasn't affected.

Of the 15th Royal Irish Rifles only 70 men answered their names following the battle. Total British casualties were over 60,000 men.

In the following pages are the names of Portadown dead who fell at the Somme and who are commemorated on the Somme Memorial to the Missing at Thiepval. Scores more lie in the surrounding war cemeteries and all along the Western Front.

The Somme Memorial to the Missing Thiepval

The Somme Memorial to the Missing at Thiepval commemorates over 73,000 soldiers who died on the Somme battlefields between July 1916 and 20th March 1918. Not surprisingly a high proportion of the casualties are those who died on 1st July 1916.

The memorial was designed by Sir Edward Lutyens and unveiled on 31st July 1932 by the Prince of Wales. It is the largest memorial to the missing on the British sector of the Western Front and beneath is a labyrinth of trenches which formed the Leipzig Redoubt.

Almost every regiment and corps of the British army is found here. Every rank from Lieutenant-Colonel to Private is recorded including that of Pte Reginald Giles, Gloucestershire Regiment, aged 16 years.

The London Regiment with 4,340 has the greatest number of names. Next is the Northumberland Fusiliers with 2,502. The names are listed on huge panels , mounted on 16 piers , in regimental order and then within each regiment by rank and then name in alphabetical order.

The site was chosen because it was an open ridge with a suitable historical background and the memorial would be seen from all sides.

When it was nearing completion, it was decided that an **Anglo-French** cemetery should be made in front of the Memorial to symbolise the joint efforts of the two countries in the First World War.

Each country provided 300 of its soldiers. The cemetery is practically astride the German front line. Of the 300 selected only 61 could be identified and **Rfn James Ritchie, 14th Royal Irish Rifles (Young Citizens Volunteers)** who was killed on 1st July 1916 definitely came from the Thiepval area, so the cemetery represents all of the British parts of the Somme battlefields.

On the Somme Memorial to the Missing the names of men from the Portadown area are numerous as can be seen as follows:

Royal Irish Fusiliers - Pier 15A

All the names below are from the Portadown area who were killed on 1st July 1916 and from the 9th Battalion of the Royal Irish Fusiliers. Those not in the 9th Battalion are indicated as well as those who fell later in the war.

Lt Robert T. Montgomery, High Street

Sgt Robert McLoughlin 3880, West Street, 12th October 1916, 1st Btn. He worked for ten years in Glasgow with Post Office Telephones. He was a member of the Orange and Black Institutions.

L/Sgt Denis Moran 17164, Woodhouse Street, 4th September 1916, 8th Btn. He was killed supporting 95th Infantry Brigade at Leuze Wood.

Cpl William Hull 14268, Victoria Terrace.

Cpl William J. Wilson 17070, Baltylum.

Cpl William Robb 14626, Garvaghy Road.

L/Cpl James Hewitt 16423, Clounagh.

L/Cpl Thomas J. Russell 14630, Park Road. He enlisted in 2nd Princess Victoria's (Royal Irish Fusiliers) in 1893. He served in Royal Field Artillery in South Africa. He enlisted again in 1914. His brother W G Russell was awarded the DCM in 1914 whilst serving with the Irish Guards.

L/Cpl Joseph A. Webb 6151, Mary Street, 12th October 1916, 1st Btn. Killed during the Battle of Le Transloy.

L/Cpl David Woods 17662, Portadown

Pte Absalom Abraham 13974, Charles Street. His brother Pte T. R. Abraham died of wounds 17/4/17 at Vimy Ridge, 102nd (North British Columbia) Regt.

Pte James W. Abraham 20292, Charles Street. Brother of Absalom.

Pte William J. Allen 20531, Joseph Street - He came from the USA to enlist.

Pte Hugh Beattie 43190, Church Street, 5th September 1916. He was a local postman. He was killed during the Battle of Guillemont.

Pte William H. Best 13977, Clounagh. He worked for the Portadown Co-operative Society.

Pte William Bowles 13976, Montague Street.

Pte David J. Burrows 14028, Thomas Street. His brother Pte W. Burrows served with Princess Patricia's (Royal Irish Fusiliers) with 10th (Irish) Division.

Pte Henry Donaghy 10509, Fowler's Entry, 12th October 1916, 1st Btn - Killed at the Battle of Le Transloy

Pte James Fulton 14170, Mary Street.

Pte James Gordon 14217, Carrickblacker Road. A member of Clounagh LOL No.9. On the Clounagh lodge banner with Pte Ephriam Sherman unfurled on July 1921.

Pte Albert Graham 11984, Carrickblacker Road, 12th October 1916. Killed during the Battle of Le Transloy. He worked as a bootmaker. A member of Edenderry Pipe Band.

Pte Henry Graham 7513, King Street, 12th October 1916, 1st Btn. Killed at the Battle of Le Transloy.

Pte James Gregg 17556, John Street.

Pte Joseph Hall 17386, Battlehill.

Pte William Harpur 14247, Montague Street.

Pte William Hayes 6042, Sarah Street, 12th October 1916, 1st Btn. Killed during the Battle of Le Transloy. Brother of Pte John Hayes killed at the Somme.

Pte James Hewitt 14309, Kilmoriarty. Brother of Thomas, Ballinteggart.

Pte Thomas Hewitt 22755, Ballinteggart. Brother of above.

Pte Thomas Hewitt 14315, Bridge Street. Attended Seagoe School.

Pte Thomas H. Holmes 14250, Killicomaine Road. His brother Driver N. S. Holmes was killed in action on 21/3/18 whilst serving with 15th (Scottish) Division Ammunition Column.

Pte Andrew Johnston 14349, West Street.

Pte Thomas J. Joyce 16114, Portmore Street.

Pte Arthur Lennon 14424, Bleary. He was a Bangalore torpedo carrier on 1st July.

Pte James Magee 14460, Kilmoriarity.

Pte Alexander McCabe 14573, Seagoe.

Pte Francis McKerr 14542, Drumgor.

Pte Joseph Parks 14599, Clounagh.

Pte William Patterson 18610, Park Road.

Pte George Patton 14618, West Street.

Pte William H. Pentland 17842, Mary Street. He was a Lewis Gun ammunition carrier on 1st July.

Pte John Phillips 18246, Park Road.

Pte William J. Simpson 18053, Portadown.

Pte Joseph Stothers 14683, Bright Street. Brother of Ptes Jackson, Maxwell and William Stothers, all of whom were in 9th Royal Irish Fusiliers. Maxwell died on 7th October 1916 as a result of an accident when a branch of a tree fell on him. Jackson died on 7th January 1917. His body was found at Portobello Lock, Grand Canal, Dublin.

Pte Moses Teggart 14712, Union Street.

Pte Thomas G. Troughton 14196, Mulladry. Member of LOL 371

Pte John Vallelly 16428, John Street.

Pte William J. Walsh 17912, Derrycoose, Annaghmore.

Pte William J. Wilson 17070, Portadown.

Pte Frederick J. Woods 14796, Derrybroughas. Worked as a clerk in Parkside Weaving Company.

Pte William S. Wylie 18104, Derrymacfall. He was a member of a bombing team on 1st July.

Royal Inniskilling Fusiliers - Pier 4D/5B

Pte Thomas Green 14871, Ormonde Street, 11th Btn

Pte George Montgomery 10867, Castle Street, 23rd November 1916 2nd Btn

Royal Irish Rifles - Pier 15A/15B

Again I have indicated date of death where it did not occur on 1st July 1916.

2 Lt William O. Green, Bridge Street, 10th Btn

Rfn William J. Boyd 1069, Derrymacfall, 11th Btn

Rfn Thomas J. Cole 2841, Castle Avenue, 9th September 1916, 7th Btn

Rfn Joseph A. Gregg 17773, Atkinson's Avenue, 14th Btn

Rfn William Hutchinson 1031, South Street, 2nd July 1916, 8th Btn

Rfn Joseph Lappin 1851, Obin's Street, 7th September 1916, 7th Btn

Rfn William J. McGrattan 249, Knocknamuckley, 7th July 1916, 16th (Pioneer) Btn

Rfn David McKinley 317, Carleton Street.

Machine Gun Corps - Pier 5C/12C

Sgt Major William J. Brown 17775, Jervis Street, 108th Coy

Cpl David Orr 17778, Bridge Street, 108th Coy

Pte John Courtney 17783, Mulladry, 108th Coy

Argyll and Sutherland Highlanders - Pier 15A/16C

Pte James Redmond 5007, Curran Street, 29th July 1916, 1st/6th Btn

Irish Guards - Pier 7D

Pte Joseph Thompson 7039, Obin's Street, 15th September 1916, 1st Btn

Pte James Magee 14460

9th Royal Irish Fusiliers, 1st July 1916, Pier 15A

As you drive out of Portadown via the Loughgall Road into the countryside you will soon reach a neat, attractive Orange Hall on the right hand side belonging to Kilmoriarty Bible and Crown Defenders LOL 31. The Lodge received its warrant on 6th August 1796.

It is here in the rural hinterland of County Armagh that Pte James Magee, a former member of the Lodge is remembered annually by the brethren. During my visit on St. Patrick's Day 2015 Past Worshipful Master Adrian Branyan proudly showed me the portrait of Pte Magee which is prominent in the lodge room alongside his Death Penny and scroll. There too is the last letter received from Pte Magee from the front line. It reads:

> *"Dear Emily,*
>
> *Just a few lines to let you know I received your last letter. Glad to hear you and Victor is in good health.*
>
> *You say that Eva wants you to go down for a day or two, you can go if you like and tell Eva I am doing alright and was asking for her and Christy too.*
>
> *I got a letter from Annie and Mary which I was glad to hear from them. I was glad to hear --- is a lot better.*
>
> *You can tell them this is wild country and no ----- in it. Tell him to stay at home as long as he seen. You can tell my mother I am not drowned yet and will not be accept I get drowned in a dish of water.*
>
> *I was sorry to hear of Tom McNally being dead. It is a pity of the wife and children.*

You say you wish I was home but what about the good money you get. If I was at home I could not give it to you.

I heard you were all drunk on the 12th night and the 13th too, but I did not believe it as I was not drunk myself. I think this is about all at present.

From, Jim

To: Emily x, Eva x, Victor x

When the fields are white with daisies I return. Good by for the present. God bless you all."

As will be mentioned later, the Orange Institutions saw more of its members make the ultimate sacrifice than any other single organisation in the First World War.

(Thanks to LOL No 31 for permission to publish Pte Magee's memorabilia.)

Victoria Cross Recipients from 36th (Ulster) Division named on the Somme Memorial to the Missing.

Pte W. D. McFazdean VC, 14th Royal Irish Rifles, Pier 15A/15B

Born in Lurgan, he later moved to Belfast. On the morning of 1st July 1916, in Thiepval Wood, a box of bombs fell into a trench dislodging two safety pins. Showing great courage Pte McFadzean immediately threw himself on top of the box , blowing himself to pieces. As a result of his heroics he had saved the lives of several of his colleagues.

Pte W D McFadzean VC

Capt E N Bell VC

Lt. G. Shillington-Cather VC

Capt E. N. Bell VC, 9th Royal Inniskilling Fusiliers, Pier 4D/5B

Capt Bell came from a military family, his father being stationed in Omagh. On the first day of the Battle of the Somme, he advanced with his infantry. Coming under heavy machine-gun fire he crept forward and killed the machine-gunner. On three further occasions he advanced alone and threw trench mortar bombs amongst the enemy. When out of bombs he stood on a parapet and used his rifle with great coolness. He then began rallying and organising infantry parties who had lost their officers. It was at this point, he was killed.

Lt Geoffrey Shillington-Cather VC, 9th Royal Irish Fusiliers, Pier 15A

Geoffrey was the son of a Belfast clergyman. His grandfather was Thomas Shillington of Tavanagh House, Portadown. On the evening of 1st July 1916, following the carnage which had resulted during the day, he spent five hours searching for wounded men in No Man's Land. He rescued three, dragging them back to safety. On the following morning, he rescued another, all these feats taking place in full view of the enemy. As he continued his search, he too was killed.

King George V presented his Victoria Cross to his mother on 31st March 1917. His brother Capt Dermot Cather then presented it to the Regimental Museum in Armagh in 1979.

McCrae's Battalion - 16th Royal Scots Pier 6D/7B

This "Heart of Midlothian Battalion", raised in Edinburgh was a fraternity of sportsmen whose loyalty was to the famous Gorgie "Hearts."

During the 1914 – 1915 season, Hearts looked certain to win the league title. However the entire Hearts team and 400 shareholders enlisted in McCrae's 16th Royal Scots.

During the war years seven players were killed and eleven gassed or wounded. On 1st July 1916, Duncan Currie, Ernest Ellis and Harry Wattie were killed at the Somme. James Boyd died on 3rd August.

A commemorative Battalion Cairn has been erected at Contalmaison.

Duncan Currie, Ernest Ellis, Harry Wattie and James Boyd

Sgt Duncan Currie 18999

He was born in Kilwinning, into a footballing family. His father was a goalkeeper and his brother Robert played for Hearts and Bury whilst another brother played for Leicester Fosse.

Duncan played as a full back and made 45 times for Hearts, 35 of these during the 191/1915 season.

Pte Ernest Ellis 19009

He was born in Norwich on St Andrew's Day 1885. He worked as a boot operator. He had played for Norwich and Bury before signing for Hearts. He left for France on 8th January 1916 never to see his daughter who was born after this date.

Pte Henry Wattie 19112

Harry was born in Edinburgh and was the youngest of five brothers. Playing as an inside forward Harry scored two goals against Glasgow Rangers in a 2 – 1 victory. Later against Aberdeen, two players tackled him, one was taken off with a broken leg and the other never returned after the interval. He was seen to fall at the Somme but his body was never recovered. He had made almost 60 appearances for Hearts.

L/Cpl James Boyd 18976

He was born in a small mining village in East Lothian. He worked in the shale mines. His brother Archie had been the Hearts goalkeeper for some time and James signed for the Club on 24th August 1914. He was the last Hearts man to be killed on the Somme.

17th Middlesex Regiment (The Footballers Battalion) Pier 12D/13B

Following the outbreak of war in August 1914, a heated debate took place about the continuation of English professional football during a time of national crisis. In response, a Footballers' Battalion, the 17th Middlesex, was raised in Fulham Town Hall in December 1914 with some 35 professional players enlisting. From these, eleven players were from Clapham Orient.

Pte William Jonas F/32

Born in Blyth, Northumberland he worked as a miner in Chambois Colliery and played for several amateur clubs before signing for Clapham Orient in 1912. As a centre forward he made 74 appearances scoring 23 goals.

He was reported as being a popular figure with the ladies receiving over 50 letters a week. The club programme had to remind the fans that William had married his childhood sweetheart five years earlier.

On 27th July 1916 he lost his life in action with his battalion in Delville Wood.

Sgt Norman Wood F/663

Born in Streatham, Norman was a talented inside left who had played for Spurs and Plymouth Argyle. In 1913 he played for Stockport County making 58 appearances and scoring 31 goals.

On 4th October 1913, in his sixth game for Stockport County, he scored an own goal, conceded a penalty and missed a penalty at the other end. Like his colleague William Jonas, Norman fell in action at Delville Wood on 28th July 1916.

Pte William Gerrish F/936

William joined Bristol Rovers in 1905 for whom he made 49 appearances, scoring 18 goals in the Southern League. In 1909 he joined Aston Villa where he made 59 appearances, scoring 18 goals and winning a Football League Championship medal. In 1912 he made 6 appearances for Preston before joining Chesterfield Town.

During an engagement at Guillemont on the Somme, the Middlesex Battalion lost 51 officers and men, with William's legs being shattered by a shell which had exploded nearby. He succumbed to his wounds.

Pte Oscar Linkson F/1723

Born in New Barnet, Hertfordshire, he played at full back.

Oscar signed for Manchester United in 1908. He went on to make 55 league appearances and 4 F A Cup matches. He won an F A Cup winners medal in 1909 and a League Title in 1911.

He later joined Irish club Shelbourne with whom he won the Gold Cup in 1914 and the Leinster Senior Cup the previous year.

He also made the supreme sacrifice at Guillemont on 8th August 1918.

Royal Fusiliers - Piers 8C, 9A, 16A

L/Cpl Leigh Roose (served as Rouse) PS/10898

Roose was a Welsh goalkeeper who was on loan at Glasgow Celtic in 1910. He had 24 caps for Wales before joining the 9th Royal Fusiliers in 1914. He was awarded the Military Medal.

He died on 7th October 1916 during the Battle of Montauban. His regiment was sent to attack the enemy line and it is believed he died as a result of heavy machine-gun fire and shelling.

On that day the records show that the Royal Fusiliers had 25 men killed, 165 missing and 132 wounded.

The Ulster Tower
Thiepval

The Ulster Tower is a memorial to the men of the 36th (Ulster) Division, located near the Schwaben Redoubt which the Ulstermen attacked on 1st July 1916.

The tower is a replica of Helen's Tower in Clandeboye, County Down where the men trained prior to setting off to war.

The architects chosen for the work were Messrs Bowden and Abbott, Craven Street, London. The work itself was carried out by Fenning and Company Limited, Hammersmith, London.

The Ulster Tower is 70 feet high and was unveiled on 19th November 1921 by Field Marshal Sir Henry Wilson. The plaque inside shows it was opened by Sir Edward Carson but due to ill health, he could not attend.

A plaque on the outside of the tower commemorates its re-dedication and was unveiled by HRH Princess Alice of Gloucester on 1st July 1989. The tower is maintained by the Somme Association whose President is currently HRH Duke of Gloucester.

The main chamber inside the tower has an inscription: **"This Tower is dedicated to the Glory of God, in grateful memory of the officers, non-commissioned officers and men of the 36th (Ulster) Division and of the Sons of Ulster in other Forces who laid down their lives in the Great War and of their comrades-in-arms, who, by divine grace, were spared to testify to their glorious deeds."**

In golden letters around the walls of the chamber are the words:

"Helen's Tower, here I stand

Dominant over sea and land

Son's love built me and I hold

Ulster's love in letter'd gold."

These words with only one alteration had been written by Alfred Lord Tennyson in 1861 and they had been inscribed on the walls of the original Helen's Tower in Clandeboye.

In 1994 a visitors' centre was opened. Annually on 1st July, an Order of Divine Service is held in the grounds of the Ulster Tower.

Just before the 75th Anniversary of the Battle of the Somme, two paintings by Ulster artist Bob Beattie were taken from the inside of the building, only a matter of hours after they had been hung on the wall.

One picture, **"The Bomber"** (see above) featured men of the 10th Royal Inniskilling Fusiliers in action.

The other picture, **"Comrades",** depicted the men of the 14th Royal Irish Rifles and the 10th Royal Irish Rifles, during a moment of respite in the trenches.

Despite an exhaustive search by the French authorities neither picture was recovered. The four other remaining pictures by Bob Beattie were removed from the walls of the Ulster Tower for security and placed in the safe hands of the Commonwealth War Graves Commission.

On the morning of Thursday 21st November 2013 at approximately 11:15 a.m., a large track digger unearthed human remains close to the Ulster Tower during preparations for the centenary of the Great War whilst major roadworks were ongoing to improve the parking area and the provision of a cobbled area towards nearby Connaught Cemetery.

Work was immediately suspended whilst the necessary steps were put in place to recover the remains which were treated with the utmost respect at all times. A cap badge (see overleaf), was found with the remains indicating that the soldier was probably a member of the Royal Irish Rifles. From the manner the remains

were distributed it appeared that the soldier may have been killed by shellfire rather than by gunfire.

The remains of a second soldier were found close to Connaught Cemetery on the 27th/28th November 2013. It is believed he was a member of the Royal Inniskilling Fusiliers.

Victoria Cross Memorial Stone

Just inside the gates of the Ulster Tower, on the left, is a Memorial Stone commemorating the nine VC winners of the 36th (Ulster) Division. It was placed on 1st July 1991.

Memorial to Fallen Brethren

To the right and behind the Ulster Tower is the Orange Memorial. It is an historical fact that the Orange Institutions saw more of its members serve and make the supreme sacrifice in the First World War than any other single organisation. The memorial is a black stone obelisk with the insignia of the Orange Order on it. An inscription on it commemorates those of the Orange Institution worldwide who fought and **"finally passed out of the sight of men."**

The word **"Boyne"** is on the base of the memorial. Thiepval Memorial Loyal Orange Lodge No. 1916 was founded in 1966 and its members are responsible for the upkeep of the memorial.

Grand Lodge of Free and Accepted Masons of Ireland

Many masons within the Irish Constitution had strong links with the armed forces and the majority of the 29 warrants issued during the Great War had military connections. Many lodge meetings were held under repeated shellfire.

In 1919 Grand Lodge issued a Roll of Honour of all Irish Freemasons who had served in the army, navy or Royal Flying Corps. This roll totalled 5,119 masons. This Roll was reprinted in recent years and published by the Naval and Military Press.

In his academic book, "The Hounds of Ulster", Banbridge historian Gavin Hughes pays tribute to the members of the Masonic Order, of whom 2,781 came from the province of Ulster of which 469 were killed, gassed or wounded.

Of the 118 Freemasons from the Provincial Grand Lodge of Armagh, 11 died and 14 were wounded. Portadown lodges provided 40 members who enlisted.

Lodge 83 Newry, provided 17 doctors, who received commissions in the forces, of which two made the ultimate sacrifice.

Connaught Cemetery

Connaught Cemetery is found on the D73 about 100 metres from the Ulster Tower.

Prior to the Battle of the Somme, Thiepval was in German hands, garrisoned by the 160th Regiment of Wurtembergers. It sits in No Man's Land over which the 36th (Ulster) Division attacked on 1st July 1916. The headstones face the infamous Schwaben Redoubt . To the rear of the cemetery is Thiepval Wood in which the Ulstermen sheltered waiting on the order to attack. They took the first and second lines easily.

Buried here are many members of the Royal Inniskilling Fusiliers and also those of the 14th Royal Irish Rifles (Young Citizens Volunteers). It was not attacked again until the 26th September when Thiepval village was captured by the 18th Division. On 25th March 1918 it was lost again to the enemy during the great German Offensive. It was retaken the following 24th August by the 17th and 38th (Welsh) Divisions. The cemetery was greatly increased when graves were brought in from smaller cemeteries and battlefields in the surrounding areas.

Pte James Rountree 18697, 103rd Coy, Machine Gun Corps (Inf), 1st July 1916 - II B 5. He lived at Clonroot.

On 19th April 1988, a group of pupils from Bocombra Primary School, Portadown visited the cemetery and laid a wreath on Pte Rountree's grave following a short memorial service.

Seventeen years later on 1st July 2005, the former Principal of Bocombra Primary School, Ronnie Harkness, planted a simple wooden cross on Pte Rountree's grave in memory of the school visit made in 1988.

Pte R Fowler 26694, 9th Royal Inniskilling Fusiliers, 1st July 1916 - I C 23. He came from Lisnamallard, Omagh. His epitaph reads, "He died for Ulster. Gave his best."

Thiepval Wood

Behind Connaught Cemetery is Thiepval Wood from which many of the men of the 36th attacked on 1st July 1916.

In 2003 the then Secretary of State for Northern Ireland, Paul Murphy announced, when attending the annual Somme Service at the Ulster Tower, that the government had offered the Somme Association a grant of £400,000 to aid the purchase of Thiepval Wood.

The Wood itself is the Bois d'Authuille, named after the nearby village, but for the Irish it will always be known as Thiepval Wood.

The Somme Association now owns 58 acres of the wood. Excavations have been taking place for a number of years and the work continues.

A section of the front line trench known as Whitchurch Street has been preserved. A communication trench portion of George Street has been made permanent. Crozier's Bunker was unearthed at a later date.

Tours of the private wood can be arranged through the staff of the Ulster Tower.

Mill Road Cemetery

Mill Road Cemetery is 400 metres up a lane alongside Connaught Cemetery and lies adjacent to the Ulster Tower.

The German army took the area around Thiepval at the end of September 1914. It established a line through the area with troops from 26th Reserve Division.

On 1st July 1916 the 36th (Ulster) Division were detailed to attack the positions known as the Hansa Line and the Schwaben Redoubt. Launched from Thiepval Wood, with scores of Portadown men in their ranks, the attack was initially successful and some reached the second line of defence known as Stuff's Redoubt. Due to other units not taking their objectives the Ulstermen had to retreat.

The cemetery was made in the Spring of 1917 when the German withdrawal to the Hindenburg Line allowed the battlefield to be cleared. After the Armistice the number of graves was significantly increased.

Some of the graves have been laid flat, because the area behind the cemetery formed the German Front Line in 1916 and there were numerous tunnel systems throughout the entire area.

On a clear summer's day it is still possible to see chalklines across the countryside, indicating the old trench systems.

The path walked up from Connaught Cemetery is the route taken by the 109th Brigade in their advance to storm the Schwaben Redoubt. Looking back to Connaught Cemetery, these two cemeteries were more or less the opposing front lines, so this gives the idea as to how far the 36th Division lads had to advance on the 1st July.

In the far corner of the cemetery, one can still find the remnant of the Schwaben Redoubt, a wire stand complete with a small portion of barbed wire remains.

Pte W. J. Wilson 17070, 9th Royal Irish Fusiliers, 1st July 1916, VI C 3 - Portadown

Martinsart British Cemetery

Martinsart is two kilometres south-west of the Ulster Tower on the D129 leading to Aveluy. The village was close to the front line until September 1916 and again from March to August 1918.

The cemetery on the edge of the village was started in 1916 by the Royal Irish Rifles and after the war it was used as a concentration cemetery.

The graves are marked by red Corsehill sandstone, instead of the usual white Portland, an unusual feature, from the Borders area of England. These headstones were used by the War Graves Commission in their early days, to test for the effects of weathering.

In Plot 1, Row A lie the bodies of 14 men of "C" Coy, 13th Royal Irish Rifles (1st County Down Volunteers), who died instantly on 28th June 1916 as a result of an enemy shell. Further along in the same row is the grave of Col H. C. Bernard , Commanding Officer of 10th Royal Irish Rifles who died on 1st July 1916, after disobeying orders not to lead his men into battle.

Lt F. S. Kelly DSO Royal Naval Volunteer Reserve 13th November 1916 1H25

Educated at Sydney Grammar School he was then sent to Eton College. He was part of the **school eight which won The Ladies Challenge Plate at Henley Royal Regatta in 1899.**

Frederick Septimus Kelly was awarded **a Lewis Nettleship musical scholarship at Oxford** and attended Balliol College where he obtained B.A; M.A; He became President of the University Musical Club.

He took up sculling at Oxford and **won the Diamond Challenge Sculls at Henley in 1902. He rowed but lost in the Boat Race for Oxford in 1902. In 1905 he again won the Diamond Sculls in a time that stood for over thirty years.**

In 1908 he was a member of the coxed eight which won a Gold Medal at the London Olympics.

Frederick studied the piano under Iwan Knorr in Frankfurt and on his return to London acted as an adviser to The Classical Concert Society.

He enlisted in the RNVR in 1914 to be with his friend, the poet, **Rupert Brooke** and others of what became known as The Latin Club.

He was **wounded twice at Gallipoli** where he was awarded a DSO and promoted to Lt. Commander. In 1915 he wrote his tribute to Brooke, **"Elegy for a string orchestra"** and was among the party who buried him in Skyros.

Mesnil Mairie
Somme

The village of Mesnil is adjacent to that of Martinsart. At the Mairie a memorial tablet has been erected to commemorate the 23 men of "C" Coy, 13th Royal Irish Rifles who were killed or died later as the result of an enemy shell on 28th June 1916.

The plaque is due to the efforts of Banbridge District Council and especially the tireless work given by Cllr Joan Baird MBE, who is a regular visitor paying her respects to the war dead on an annual basis.

In the Mairie itself are the old village clock hands taken by the 14th (YCV) Royal Irish Rifles as it was believed the Germans were using them on the clock to send messages.

The hands were later restored to safekeeping to the Mayor of Mesnil on 13th July 1927 by Col Mulholland together with a gold mounted regimental stick.

These are looked upon by the villagers as the Mesnil Crown Jewels.

Mesnil Communal Cemetery Extension

The cemetery adjoins the French civilian graveyard. It contains the graves of 333 men, 240 known by name. It was started in 1916 but was extended after the war.

Capt. C. M. Johnston, 9th Royal Irish Fusiliers, 15th July 1916 (30), Carrickblacker Road, Portadown. Plot III B 7.

He played a leading role in the formation of the Portadown Battalion of the Ulster Volunteer Force. He was also a member of Portadown Rowing Club, Portadown Rugby Club and Portadown Unionist Club.

Hamel Military Cemetery
Beaumont Hamel

Hamel is a small village 6.5 km north of Albert. Take the D929 out of Albert towards Baupaume. When you reach La Boisselle take left on the D20 to Aveluy. At Aveluy take right for Beaumont-Hamel and head for Hamel village. The cemetery is behind a house and set back from the road and therefore difficult to spot.

Hamel was well known to the 36th Division and the trenches were given names originating from Ulster. On 1st July the main attacking troops in the Hamel sector, west of the Ancre, were 9th Royal Irish Fusiliers, 12th Royal Irish Rifles, both 108th Brigade. Little progress was made but it is here that Lt G. St G. Shillington-Cather, 9th Royal Irish Fusiliers won his posthumous VC. (Top left).

Here too, Pte R. Quigg, 12th Royal Irish Rifles also won a VC after going out seven times to look for his platoon officer, each time bringing a wounded man back under heavy shell and machine gun fire. (Bottom left)

The village of Beaumont was captured by British troops in November 1916. Hamel however had been in British hands from the summer of 1915 until 27th March 1918.

Field Ambulances began the cemetery in August 1915. It had formerly been known as " Brook Street Trench" and "White City". After the Armistice the cemetery was greatly enlarged. It was designed by Sir Edward Lutyens.

73

There are 33 Royal Irish Rifles buried here, 27 Royal Irish Fusiliers and 10 Royal Inniskilling Fusiliers.

Not surprisingly many of the 9th Royal Irish Fusiliers are from Portadown and surrounding areas.

Sgt William Gordon, 14221, Castle Street - 1 B 6 - See next page.

Cpl William Robb, 14626, Garvaghy Road, 1st July 1916 - 1 B 7. William trained as a carpenter and was an excellent sportsman. **He was interested in athletics but was also a member of Portadown Football Club and Portadown Rowing Club.**

Pte c. Kelly, 13898, 1st July 1916 - 11 C 33. He lived at Battlehill. The Portadown News of 9th September 1916 reported that his body had been recovered.

Pte W. J. Cordy, 14048, 26th June 1916 - 1 C 9. He came from Lower Seagoe. He had been wounded by shellfire at Hamel.

Pte S. J. Forde, 47671, 22nd February 1916 - 1 B 18. He originally hailed from Cloncarrish. He had been spotted in a patrol near the mill at Hamel.

Cpl J. Hamilton, 14288, 1st July 1916, Avenue Road, Lurgan - **1 B 7**

Pte A. Hamilton, 14287, 1st July 1916, Avenue Road, Lurgan - **Sp. Mem.B 2**

Pte J. A. Hutchinson, 22151, 25th April 1916, Drummond, Richhill - **1 E 24**. Killed by shellfire at Hamel.

It is interesting to note that five members of the Royal Irish Rifles who died on 6th April 1916 are buried in this cemetery, side by side.

The total number of graves is 492 of which 487 are UK.

Sgt William Gordon, 14221, (27), "D" Coy Royal Irish Fusiliers,1/7/16, 1 B 7

Sgt W. Gordon with wife Elizabeth and children, Hannah, Mary and George (Victor Gordon)

William was a member of Armagh Road Presbyterian Church, Portadown and was a tenor in the church choir. His sister Mrs Phoebe Cooke lived in Cecil Street. William enrolled in the local UVF.

William managed to spend a few months home on leave prior to the fateful battle. He predicted the worst, telling his mother he would never see her again.

An account of William's death was given by Eddie Leeman of Mandeville Street, Portadown. Eddie had seen William lying wounded on the battlefield. Eddie went to help him, but Bill as he was known told him to go on or he would be shot for cowardice. Eddie was possibly the last person to see Bill alive.

William or Bill had been born in Ballylisk but lived in Mourneview Street in the town. When he married he moved to Castle Avenue and he worked as a tenter in Tavanagh Factory.

In the Portadown News published on 22nd July 1916 a tribute was printed from Parkmount Temperance Flute Band of which he was a member. Part of it read, "We the members of the Committee of Parkmount Temperance Flute Band having heard with regret the death of three esteemed members of our band, viz Sgt W. Gordon, Cpl W. Hull and Rfn G. Hull offer our sincere and heartfelt sympathy with their parents, wives and families in their sorrow and bereavement."

Ancre British Cemetery
Beaumont - Hamel

Ancre British Cemetery is about 2 km south of the village of Beaumont Hamel, on the D50 between Albert and Achiet le Grand.

The village was attacked on 1st July 1916 by the 29th Division and two battalions of the 36th (Ulster) Division. The 9th Royal Irish Fusiliers enjoyed some initial success but at a considerable cost.

The 12th Royal Irish Rifles were less fortunate running into a salient on the brow of a small hill around which the barbed wire was virtually intact. Raked by machine gun fire they were beaten back. Two further attempts were similarly repulsed under withering hail.

Five battalions of the 39th Division tried again on 3rd September suffering 1,850 casualties. The successful attack on 13th November by the 63rd (Royal Naval) Division made up of eight naval battalions returned from Gallipoli and four army battalions, attacked from an advanced trench and captured all of its objectives including Beaumont village, one and a half miles distant, although the casualties amounted to 3,500 men.

A large number of men from 9th Royal Irish Fusiliers from the Portadown area were killed on 1st July 1916 and are buried here.

Major Thomas Joyce Atkinson, 9th Btn Royal Irish Fusiliers, V111 A 5 - Eden Villa

He was a member of the well known and respected Atkinson family of Eden Villa, Bachelors' Walk. Born in 1878 , he attended Trinity College, Dublin. He became a partner in Messrs Carleton, Atkinson and Sloan , Solicitors in Church Place. He was a member of Portadown Rowing Club.

Thomas organised the signing of the Ulster Covenant in Seagoe Church on Ulster Day 28th September 1912. He was second-in-command to Major Stewart Blacker, Commanding Officer, Portadown Battalion, Ulster Volunteer Force.

He served as Major in the 9th Royal Irish Fusiliers. During the attack on 1st July Major Atkinson's company penetrated three German lines and a small body of men reached Beaucourt Station but were unable to hold the position due to a lack of support.

He was killed in action on 1st July though his body was not recovered until mid-August by men of the Durham Light Infantry.

His epitaph reads, "A Son of Ulster, your memory hallowed ,in the land you loved."

Pte D. J. Burrowes 14028, Thomas Street, 2 D 2

David worked for James Walsh, High Street, Portadown prior to enlisting. His brother Pte William Burrowes served in Royal Irish Fusiliers (Princess Victoria's) in 10th (Irish) Division.

Pte John Campbell 20024, Foybeg, V111 A 10

Pte J. Hayes 14303, Sarah Street, V111 A 4. Both his brothers served and were killed in the war. Pte William Hayes on 12th October 1916 in the Battle of Le Transloy whilst serving with 1st Battalion. Pte Alexander Hayes died in France on 31st July 1918 whilst serving with 2nd (Garrison) Battalion, Royal Irish Regiment.

Pte Wesley Hayes 18558, Clonroot, V111 A 16

L/Cpl W. G. Henry 14276, Charles Street, V111 A 11

The Portadown News of 9th September 1916 read, "L/Cpl W G Henry, Corcrain who was wounded at the Battle of the Somme is reported missing. Since 1st July every effort has been made to trace him but in vain and his wife and children still hope he may turn up."

Pte J. Joyce 14355, Drumnakelly, IV D 17

His father made an impassioned plea in the Portadown News on 6th July 1916 saying that he would be grateful for any information regarding the fate of his son at the Battle of the Somme.

Sgt Robert Magee 14466, Coronation Street, VIII A 36

Sgt Magee was one of many Portadown soldiers who "went over the top" and became a casualty on 1st July.

When the pupils from Bocombra Primary School Portadown visited Ancre British Cemetery during a school trip on 19th April 1988 , they placed flowers on the grave of Sgt Magee on behalf of the Magee, Vance and Robinson families from the town.

Pte Joseph Parks 14599, Clounagh Cottages, VIII A 90/93

Joseph was a talented sportsman excelling as a sprinter. On one occasion he won the Portadown News Challenge Cup for flat racing.

The Portadown News of 2nd September 1916 reported, "Pte Joseph Parks, Clounagh has been reported missing and a notification from the War Office led his mother to believe he was a prisoner, but the words were partly obliterated. His anxious mother still awaits anxious news."

Pte W. H. Pentland 17842, Mary Street, VIII A 7

He was a Lewis gun ammunition carrier on 1st July. One of his comrades wrote a letter to his mother which was published in the Portadown News of 26th August 1916. *"Words fail to express how sorry I am at the loss of William. He was like a father to us out here and the good advice he gave us was the means of keeping a lot of us out of danger. There was not a braver soldier in the ranks and he was loved by all his comrades. We who are left of his platoon tender you our deepest sympathy and pray that God may comfort you in your trouble."*

Pte Andrew Rowan 14655, Coronation Street, VIII A 8

He was a weaver in the linen trade. He is buried in the same grave as Pte W H Pentland.

Pte Robert Totten 17554, Sarah Street, VIII A 4

Also buried in this cemetery is:

Lt Hon Vere Sidney Tudor Harmsworth, Hawke Battalion, Royal Naval Division. Died 13th November 1916. V E 19 - Son of newspaper magnate Lord Rothermere.

The majority of those buried in this cemetery died on 1st July, 3rd September or 13th November 1916.

There are now 2,540 Commonwealth casualties of the First World War buried or commemorated in this cemetery. 1,335 of the graves are unidentified, but special memorials commemorate 43 casualties known or believed to be buried among them.

Newfoundland Memorial Park
Beaumont-Hamel

Newfoundland Memorial Park is situated on the D73 between Beaumont-Hamel and Auchonvillers. For anyone visiting the Somme region, it is I believe a must visit as the terrain and trenches remain as they were almost a century ago. It is named after the Newfoundland Regiment of the 88th Infantry Brigade, part of the 29th Division which suffered appalling losses here on the first day of the Battle of the Somme, 1st July 1916.

Nowadays it is a Canadian National Heritage Site and I would suggest that in order to appreciate it fully, you should allow yourself at least 90 minutes to understand its historical significance.

The 1st Newfoundland Regiment was annihilated here in the initial attack which followed the Hawthorn Mine explosion. Being ten minutes too early it enabled the ground to be occupied by enemy troops. Attacking in the second wave along with 1st Essex Regiment the Newfoundlanders were forced to cross 900 metres of exposed land independently and completely on their own.

Of 780 men , casualties numbered 684, of which almost a third of them being fatal – the second highest loss of any battalion during the Somme offensive.

29th Division Memorial

Just inside the entrance of the park is the memorial to the 29th Division which is raised above the level of the park. It was unveiled on 7th June 1925 with a Guard of Honour of men who had served with the 29th Division in the Great War. Before travelling to France , the 29th Division had also experienced action at Gallipoli.

Newfoundland Caribou

The caribou was chosen as the symbol for memorials to the Newfoundlanders. There are several similar memorials located located on a number of other sites on the Western Front where the regiment was in action. The caribou appears to be baying for its lost young.

Set into stones at the base of the mound on which the caribou stands are three bronze panels listing the Newfoundland missing. The central panel lists the missing of the Newfoundland regiment whilst the two lesser panels on either side name the naval and mercantile missing.

Lt Cecil Bayley Clift 505, 1st Newfoundland Regiment, 12th October 1916

He missed the carnage of the 1st July as he had been admitted to hospital on 20th April. He returned with the replacement drafts on 14th July. The 8th Brigade, of which the Newfoundlanders were part, was "loaned" to the 12th Division to assist with the Guedecourt position.

Heavy German shelling occurred on 11th October 1916 causing many casualties. During fierce fighting the battalion took Rainbow Trench and then Hilt Trench. They achieved their objectives and went forward to take Grease Trench.

Lt Clift was killed in the attack on 12th October. He attempted to advance beyond Rainbow Trench but his party was practically wiped out.

Lt Clift was a member of Whiteway Masonic Lodge No.3541

A farewell gathering of Freemasons took place in the Temple in St. John's to bid farewell to the brethren going in the first contingent to England. A similar event took place in 1915 when the brethren were presented with a special form of prayer word book to be used during the war. The brethren of all Masonic lodges in Newfoundland contributed to the establishment of the "Newfoundland Freemasons' Ward", of ten cots in a hospital in southern England.

Y Ravine Cemetery

This cemetery contains 366 burials many of which 38 belonged to the 1st Newfoundland Regiment decimated on 1st July 1916. There are 61 special headstones of soldiers believed to be buried here. Over one third of the graves are unidentified.

This was a German position from which their machine-guns wreaked a devastating fire. This naturally formed crevasse provided a deep fortified position just behind the German front line and was crammed with machine-guns and barbed wire.

One member of the 1st Royal Inniskilling Fusiliers is buried in this cemetery – Pte J. McMeekin 22447, 1st July 1916 – D 47.

The Danger Tree

The petrified Danger Tree rises in front of the German trenches. Many of the Newfoundlanders gravitated towards the tree as their advance was halted by a hail of bullets and shrapnel.

More than 13,000 men were killed during the carnage of the 1st July 1916.

It took three days to clear the wounded from No Man's Land thanks to the agreement of a temporary truce.

Hunter's Cemetery

The attractive Hunter's Cemetery contains 46 men buried in what had been a large shell hole. They are mainly men of The Black Watch of the 51st Division who died when the area was captured by the Division in the Autumn of 1916.

The headstones are not grave markers and they are set in a central wall.

51st Division Cross

This Celtic Cross was moved here from nearby High Wood and commemorates the 51st Division's losses sustained between July – August 1916.

51st Highland Division Memorial

The kilted highland soldier of the 51st Highlanders looks over in an eastern direction towards Beaumont-Hamel which was taken on 13th November 1916.

The inscriptions are in three languages, Gaelic, French and English. The memorial was unveiled in September 1924 by Marshal Fochs.

Hawthorn Ridge Cemetery No. 2

It was made by V Corps in early 1917. This cemetery contains 214 burials from 1st July 1916. A quarter of these are unidentified. They are mostly of the 29th Division.

"Ours" Memorial

Below is the little known "Ours" Memorial Stone at the side of the Caribou Monument. The small circular plaque reads :

"In Honoured Memory of "Ours", First Newfoundland Regiment, from the staff of Imperial Tobacco (Nfld) Ltd."

The term "Ours" was commonly used by the press to designate the Newfoundland Regiment and the bond between the people at home and the boys in the regiment. The Imperial Tobacco Company supplied cigarettes and tobacco to the troops during the war. It is the only "commercial" memorial in France and Belgium.

Newfoundland Memorial Park was opened on 7th June 1925 by Field Marshal Earl Haig. Newfoundland became a province of Canada in 1949.

Newfoundland Park is one of only two Canadian National Historic Sites outside Canada. The other is at Vimy Ridge.

The Visitors' Centre was opened on 1st July 2001. It covers the history of the Royal Newfoundland Regiment. Free guided tours are provided by Canadian students , trained and sponsored by Veterans Affairs, Canada.

Auchonvillers Military Cemetery

The cemetery is situated about 10 kilometres north of Albert. At the crossroads in the village follow in the direction of Mailly-Maillet and the cemetery is 200 metres further along on the right hand side. From the outbreak of the war to the summer of 1915 this part of the front had been held by French troops.

It continued to be used by field ambulances and fighting units. In October 1915, 108th Field Ambulance, 36th (Ulster) Division opened a Dressing Station here. The village was known to the Tommies as "Ocean Villas". Some of the earlier graves are those of men of 36th (Ulster) Division. There is also a communal grave of the 252nd Tunnelling Company, Royal Engineers who worked on the Hawthorn Mine.

Sgt John Martin 10261, 1st Royal Irish Fusiliers, 15th July 1916 II D 2 - Water Street. Died at No. 10 Field Ambulance.

Pte Ephriam Sherman 4777, 1st Royal Irish Fusiliers, 6th July 1916, II E, 34 Montague Street. On 6th July the battalion suffered from shell fire, one starry shell falling amongst a fatigue party and another wrecking the orderlies' dug-out at Battalion Headquarters. A member of LOL No. 9, The Earl of Beaconsfield Primrose League, Clounagh. The lodge unfurled a banner on 8th July 1921 featuring portraits of Ptes Sherman and James Gordon.

Sgt W. E. Lynn, 5700, 1st Royal Irish Fusiliers, 17th July 1916 II F 4. From Mousetown, Coalisland. He was one of four brothers who made the supreme sacrifice. - Driver R. Lynn, Royal Field Artillery, Hop Store Cemetery, Belgium , Sgt J. Lynn, Royal Army Service Corps, Haifa War Cemetery, Israel and Pte John Lynn, 1st Royal Inniskilling Fusiliers, Lijssenthoek Military Cemetery, Belgium.

Cpl John Dunlea, 9349, Royal Dublin Fusiliers, 31st October 1915, I A 6. The inscription on his headstone reads, **"An Irish volunteer. He died for the freedom of small nations."**

Mailly Wood Cemetery
Mailly-Maillet

The cemetery is situated in the village of Mailly-Maillet, on the D919. It is well signposted on the road to Amiens and is along a 500 metre mud track.

Whilst passing through the village stop for a moment at the church and notice the bullet marks which are still visible from the time of the Great War.

Mailly-Maillet was in the line taken over from the French in the summer of 1915. The cemetery itself was begun with the burial of thirteen 2nd Seaforth Highlanders who died on 25th June 1916. In November 1916, the 51st (Highland) Division used it for burials after the capture of Beaumont-Hamel. It was not used again until the period May to August 1918.

There are 671 UK burials out of a total of 702.

Pte William J. Hall 4272, 5th Seaforth Highlanders. Killed 14th November 1916 – 1 M 14. Although he had lived in Dee Street, Belfast, he was originally a native of Seagoe.

Sgt H. J. Colley VC, MM 40684 10th Lancashire Fusiliers. Died 25th August 1918 – Q 4. His VC was awarded for most conspicuous bravery and initiative in preventing the enemy from breaking through. His courage and tenacity saved a very critical situation.

Sucrerie Military Cemetery
Colincamps

Take the road from Mailly-Maillet towards Colincamps. The cemetery is 3 km east of the village on the north side.

Colincamps was the last village for soldiers before going into the trenches facing Serre.

Sucrerie is named after a sugar-beet factory which had been nearby.

The cemetery was begun by French troops in the early summer of 1915 and extended to the west by British units from July in that year until with intervals, December 1918. It was called at first 10th Brigade Cemetery until the German retreat in March 1917.

It was less than 2 km from the front line and from the end of March 1918 (when the New Zealand Division was engaged in fighting at the Sucrerie) to the following August it was under fire.

The 285 French and 12 German graves were removed to other cemeteries after the Armistice and in consequence there are gaps in the lettering of the Rows.

There are now 1,104 World War One casualties buried here. Of these 219 are unidentified.

Of these there are 37 Royal Irish Rifles, 34 Royal Dublin Fusiliers and 21 Royal Irish Fusiliers.

Rfn James Crozier 14218, 9th Royal Irish Rifles, 27th February 1916 - 1 A 5. Shot at dawn

He had lived in Battenburg Street, Belfast.

After going absent Crozier walked a considerable distance before being admitted to an RAMC field hospital. He was court-martialled on 14th February 1916. He was them placed under house arrest and visited by the chaplain whilst an execution post was placed in a back garden of a villa in Mailly-Maillet.

A volley of shots rang out and the Medical Officer confirmed that Crozier was not dead. The officer commanding the firing squad fired a single bullet into the victim's head.

His trial was presided over by Major H. G. Barnard, 8th Royal Irish Rifles, Lt H T Blackwood, 8th Royal Irish Rifles and Capt G. H. Gaffikan of Crozier's own 9th Royal Irish Rifles.

The Commanding Officer Lt Col F. P. Crozier witnessed the events. Though not related he had recruited Crozier personally. He was buried in Mailly-Maillet but re-interred in Sucrerie after the war.

Pte J. Moore, 1st Royal Irish Fusiliers 8th December 1915 - 1 C 21 - Henry Street

Sgt J. A. McReynolds 15468 10th Royal Irish Rifles, 22nd December 1915 - III F 9 - Tartaraghan

Sapper A. McKee 150th Coy, Royal Engineers, 21st November 1915 - III E 11
- Richhill

Lt Col The Hon L. C. W. Palk DSO, Commanding Officer, 1st Hampshires, 1st July 1916 - 1 H 14

Sgt Billy Baker MM, F/521, 17th Middlesex Regiment, 22nd October 1916 - I I 26. He made 193 appearances at left back for Plymouth Argyle. He was killed at Serre.

Forceville Communal Cemetery Extension

The cemetery is roughly 10 km from Albert on the D938 to Doullens and is located to the west of Forceville village.

Commonwealth forces took over this section of the front line from the French in 1915.

A number of battalions of the 36th (Ulster) Division had their headquarters here. In fact the 108th Brigade Field Ambulance used Forceville as its main dressing station leading up to the Somme battle of 1st July. At 08.30 hrs the Field Ambulance received a message from a runner that there were about 400 dead in No Man's

Land. At first the message was not believed, but after confirmation a group of orderlies was sent to Thiepval Wood to set up a first aid station.

It was one of the first three Commission sites to be built after the First World War by designer Sir Reginald Blomfield.

The 36th Division account for over 25% of the graves in this cemetery, with over 40 of the Royal Irish Rifles, 18 Royal Inniskilling Fusiliers, 8 Royal Irish Fusiliers, 5 Royal Dublin Fusiliers and one member of the Royal Irish Regiment.

L/Cpl J. J. Hutchinson 14272, 9th Royal Irish Fusiliers, 26th June 1916 - I E 6 - Drummond, Richhill. Wounded by shellfire at Hamel and died of wounds. His brother Pte Alex Hutchinson, 9th Royal Irish Fusiliers is buried in Hamel Military Cemetery.

Pte J. Magowan 22142, 9th Royal Irish Fusiliers, 2nd July 1916 - II B 11 - Ballybreagh. John was wounded on 1st July and died on 2nd July.

Pte T. Nicholson 16425, 9th Royal Irish Fusiliers, 13th February 1916 - I D 2 - West Street. Hit by shellfire at Mesnil Ridge the previous day. One of the earliest casualties of the 9th Battalion.

L/Cpl D. Woods 17662, 9th Royal Irish Fusiliers, 1st July 1916 - II A 2 - Ballinary, Birches. Wounded at Hamel and died of wounds.

Sgt A. Devlin 153, 13th Royal Irish Rifles, 8th April 1916 - I B 3 - Knockagon, Gilford

Rfn James Walker 4642, 14th Royal Irish Rifles, 6th May 1916 - I C 14. He came from Clady, Dunadry. **He had played for Linfield Football Club** and had won County Antrim Shield and Charity Cup medals.

Pte J. Lewis 15094, 6th Dorsetshire Regiment, 19th April 1917 III E 2. - Shot at Dawn.

Ninety years after their death, 306 of the 346 soldiers who were executed for military offences during World War One were granted posthumous pardons from the British Ministry of Defence. These soldiers were executed during hostilities for breaches of military discipline that included desertion, cowardice, quitting their posts striking a Senior Officer, sleeping at their post and casting away their arms.

The remaining group of 40 soldiers were not granted a pardon, because of the nature of their crimes which included murder and mutiny.

Puchevillers British Cemetery

From Forceville continue on the D938 to Acheux-en-Amienois and then turn left on D114 as far as Toutencourt. Take right on the D23 which leads to Puchevillers. The cemetery is west of the village and is well signposted at the church.

In June 1916 just before the opening battles of the Somme, the 3rd and 44th Casualty Clearing Stations came to Puchevillers. It was then described as a very lively place, champagne, games and horseplay were available to tempt soldiers into spending their pay.

At the beginning of the battle it was not only one of the principal railheads for ammunition, but it was also a place for trains to take away the wounded expected from the first days of the battle, including those of the 36th (Ulster) Division.

In Row A1 of the cemetery are the graves of some of the first men to be buried here including eight who died as a result of a gas raid, that blew back on the men of the Royal Irish Rifles. All told there had been 23 casualties.

There are 1,152 UK graves out of a total of 1,763.

Rfn G. Hull 6959, 16th (Pioneer Battalion) Royal Irish Rifles. Killed 4th June 1916 – Grave 1 C 3. He lived in Garvaghy Road with his wife and was a member of Parkmount Temperance Flute Band. The 16th Battalion was part of 2nd Co. Down Volunteers, UVF.

Pte R. H. Taylor 141789, Canadian Infantry (Quebec Regt.), 21st September 1916, Grave 4 D 28. He came from Derrycarne. He had been employed by Hamilton Robb Ltd as a clerk prior to emigrating to Canada. He received a gunshot wound to his cheek on 9th June and recovered after a few weeks. On 21st September he received a gunshot wound to his right arm which led to a compound fracture. He died at the 44th Casualty Clearing Station.

Capt Marcus Goodall, Yorks and Lancaster Regiment – 14/7/16 – 1 B 55. He was a friend of **Siegfried Sassoon** and attended Marlborough College with him. Two nights after the 36th (Ulster) Division attack at Thiepval, Goodall took out a party of twenty volunteers to assess the strength of the Bosche line. The patrol was fired on as they tried to cut the German wire. Goodall and one other man was hit. He took eleven days to die. A son of a vicar, Sassoon was so upset at the death of his friend he wrote a poem, **"Elegy – for Marcus Goodall".** His epitaph reads, **"Tell England that we who died serving here, rest here content."**

Row A I, the graves of the Royal Irish Rifles killed in a gas raid.

Warloy - Baillon Communal Cemetery Extension

This is a particularly beautiful cemetery that may be reached from Albert by taking the D938 to Hedauvllle, then left along D919 to Warloy - Baillon where the cemetery is signposted towards the eastern end of the village.

The first Communal burial took place in October 1915 and the last on 1st July 1916. By that date Field Ambulances had come to the village in readiness for the attack on the German front some 8km distant. The extension was then begun on the eastern side of the cemetery.

The fighting on the Somme from July to November 1916 accounts for the majority of the burials in the extension. There are 18 German graves.

The cemetery was designed by Sir Reginald Blomfield.

The extension contains 1,331 First World War graves and two from the Second World War.

Sgt Joseph Doak 6935, 2nd Royal Inniskilling Fusiliers, 15th July 1916 - III E 25 - Mourneview Street. A member of the Prince of Wales Lodge LOL No. 56 and also Parkmount Flute Band. A local footballer who played for The Commercials. He served throughout the South African War 1899-1902.

On 21st September 1914 he helped to capture 42 German prisoners. In February 1915 he was evacuated to No. 13 Southern Hospital in France and later to England. He returned to duty and was wounded on 13th July but died two days later.

Pte Samuel Fleming 11257, 6th (Cameronians) Scottish Rifles, 3rd August 1916 - VIII E 8 - Drumcree. He enlisted in Hamilton, Scotland.

Major-General Edward Charles Ingouville-Williams, CB, DSO, General Officer Commanding 34th Division, The Buffs, (East Kents), 22nd July 1916 - D 13

Inky Bill had been reconnoitring the ground in the vicinity of Mametz Wood. He was killed on the bank of Queen's Nullah, south-west of Mametz Wood, after having walked back from Contalmaison to meet his car in Montauban.

His funeral hearse was drawn by black horses of the 34th Division and his burial was attended by many officers.

Lt Col P W Machell CMG, DSO, 11th (S) Border Regiment (Lonsdales), 1st July 1916 - A 17. He was killed leading his battalion attack on the Liepzig Salient.

Capt Oswald Brooke Webb 11th Royal Irish Rifles, 4th July 1916 - III B 2. The son of the founder of Old Bleach linen factory in Randalstown.

Shot at dawn

L/Cpl G. E. Hughes 11257, 7th Royal Lancaster Regiment (The King's Own), 23rd November 1916 - VI D 18. No record of his execution has ever been found.

3

Route 2 - The Somme

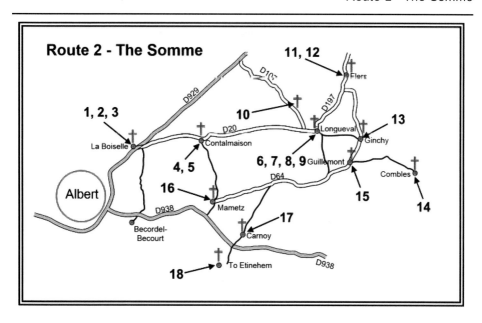

1. La Boisselle Memorial Seat

2. Lochnagar Crater, La Boisselle

3. Gordon Dump Cemetery

4. McCrae's Redoubt, Contalmaison

5. Bells' Redoubt, Contalmaison

6. Pipers' Memorial, Longueval

7. South African National Mem, Longueval

8. Delville Wood Cemetery, Longueval

9. Footballers' Memorial, Longueval

10. London Cemetery Ext, Longueval

11. World War 1 Football Mem, Flers

12. AIF Burial Ground, Flers

13. Ginchy

14. Combles Comm. Cem. Ext.

15. Guillemont

16. Devonshire Cemetery, Mametz

17. Carnoy Military Cemetery

18. Grove Town Cem. Etinehem

Route 2 - The Somme

Again using Albert as a starting point take the D939 in the direction of Baupaume.

At the Routiers Restaurant turn right on to the D20 for **La Boisselle** and immediately you will see a **Memorial Seat to the memory of the Tyneside Irish and Tyneside Scottish, Northumberland Fusiliers, 34th Division (1). They were decimated crossing the Tara Usna line on 1st July 1916 with 70% of their ranks becoming casualties within the first ten minutes of the assault beginning.**

Follow the D20 and you will reach a signpost indicating **"La Grand Mine"** known as **Lochnagar Crater(2).** This mine exploded at 07.28 on 1st July along with 16 others. This site is now privately owned and there is a remembrance service held annually to coincide with the time the mine exploded.

Keep on D20 and you will shortly reach **Gordon Dump Cemetery (3). Here you will find the grave of 2nd Lt Donald Bell VC. He became the first professional footballer to enlist in the British army. (See Bell's Redoubt).**

The D20 leads you to **Contalmaison** where you will come across **McCrae's Memorial Cairn (4). It reminds us of the exploits of the 16th Royal Scots, especially the players and supporters of Heart of Midlothian Football Club in Edinburgh.**

Walk 200 metres along the road and a small lane on the left , a short way down is **Bell's Redoubt (5), a memorial to 2nd Lt D. Bell VC, the first professional footballer to enlist. (See Gordon Dump Cemetery).**

Continue to **Longueval** where in the village square stands the **Pipers' Memorial (6), commemorating all the pipers who fell in the Great War.**

Outside of Longueval on the Ginchy road is the **South African National Memorial at Delville Wood (7)**.Take a walk and tour of the grounds. There is a stone tablet indicating the last remaining tree – **La Derniere Arbre** whilst another tablet records the deeds of two Victoria Cross recipients of the Royal Welch Fusiliers. **The museum itself is one of the best on the Western Front.**

On the road side opposite the National Memorial is **Delville Wood Cemetery (8)**. There are over 5,500 graves here including that of **Sgt W. H. Lewis, 7th Royal Irish Rifles from Carrickblacker Road**. Three hundred metres along on the left of the cemetery is the **Footballers' Memorial (9) unveiled in October 2010, in memory of the men of the 17th and 23rd Middlesex Battalions.**

Take the D6 out of Longueval in **the direction of High Wood and travel 2 km further along to London Cemetery and Extension (10)**. This is the third largest cemetery in the Somme region and contains the grave of **Pte A. Graham, 1st Royal Irish Fusiliers who had lived on the Carrickblacker Road.**

Now take the D197 towards **Flers**. **Here on 21st July 2011, the O's World War One Memorial (11) was unveiled to commemorate the players of Clapton Orient, now Leyton Orient Football Club. It is situated in the grounds of the village church.**

On the D74, 2 km north of Flers is the **AIF Burial Ground (12).**There are several members of the 36th (Ulster) Division buried in this cemetery. One of them is **Cpl W. H. Gracey, 7th South Lancashire Regiment who hailed from Burnbrae Avenue.** Also interred here is **Lt Col C. W. R. Duncombe, 2nd Earl of Feversham and Sgt H. Jackson VC, 7th East Yorkshire Regiment.**

Travel on the D20E towards Ginchy (13), a village in which the 16th (Irish) Division sustained over 2,000 casualties.

Now take the D10 to **Combles,** one of the larger villages in the area. On the D172 **is Combles Communal Cemetery Extension (14). Two Portadown servicemen lie here, CSM Robert Gilpin, 6th Northamptonshire Regiment of Annaghmore and Pte John O'Neill, 7th Royal Inniskilling Fusiliers, Obin's Street.** There is also a pair of brothers buried close together.

Return on the D20 in Ginchy direction and follow the D64 to **Guillemont (15).**The village is situated on the junction of the D64 and D20. **Guillemont will be forever associated with the 16th (Irish) Division. There is a Celtic Cross commemorating the division adjacent to the village church. There are three plaques on the outside of the church wall commemorating the exploits of three recipients of the Victoria Cross whilst fighting in the immediate area.**

Leaving Guillemont head along the D64 to **Mametz Devonshire Cemetery (16)** is situated 800 metres south of the village. There is a small roadside car park. **This cemetery has a poignant story attached to it. It is where the men of 8th and 9th Devons were buried by their chaplain. A stone tablet at the entrance tells the visitor, "The Devonshires held this trench – The Devonshires hold it still."**

Take the D938 between Mametz and Maricourt to reach **Carnoy Military Cemetery (17). It is here, history tells us that footballs were kicked across the battlefield and where Capt W. E. Nevill, 8th East Surrey's, who inaugurated the idea, is buried. Here too is the last resting place of Lt Col J. S. M. Conynham, 6th Connaught Rangers , Springhill, Moneymore.**

Follow through Bray-sur-Somme and take the C6 towards Etinehem. Drive past the first CWGC sign at the edge of the airfield and **the second CWGC sign will guide you down a dirt track to Grove Town Cemetery (18)**. **Two men from Portadown both members of 1st Royal Irish Fusiliers, Pte Patrick Gorman of Curran Street and Pte Samuel Fox, Bridge Street lie buried. Also interred here is the noted war poet Sgt Leslie Coulson, 12th London Regiment, Royal Fusiliers.**

To return to base travel through Meaulte on D42 to Albert.

The 16th (Irish) Division Memorial Guillemont, France

Thursday 3rd September 2009

THE S●MME
REMEMBRANCE
ASSOCIATION

Order of
Divine Service

'They went with song to the battle; they were young, straight of limb,
true of eye, steady and aglow. They were staunch to the end
against odds uncounted. They fell with their faces to the foe.
They shall grow not old as we that are left grow old,
age shall not weary them, nor the years condemn.
At the going down of the sun and in the morning
we will remember them.'

Tyneside Irish and Tyneside Scottish Memorial Seat.

Take the road from Albert towards Baupaume and about 3 km along take off the D929 to the right in the direction of **La Boisselle**. You will reach the **Tyneside Irish and Tyneside Scottish Memorial Seat**. It is a memorial to the men of the **Northumberland Fusiliers, 34th Division** who had the task on 1st July 1916 of storming La Boisselle. At 07.30 hrs, 3,000 men of the Tyneside Irish and Tyneside Scottish set off from the Tara Usna line across completely open ground. As their bayonets glistened in the sun they became a perfect target for the German machine-guns.

About eighty per cent of them became casualties within ten minutes of the assault beginning.

The Memorial Seat was approved by Presidential decree on 13th October 1921. It was erected by the Trustees of the Col Joseph Cowan Fund and opened by Marshal Foch on 20th April 1922.

On the front the central plaque depicts a classical mounted warrior battling a dragon, whilst a weeping maiden looks on.

The inscription, written in both English and French reads:

"Greater love hath no man than this that he lays down his life for his friend. In front of this monument on 1st July 1916 the Tyneside Irish and Tyneside Scottish Brigades attacked the enemy. For many hours the fortunes of war fluctuated but ere night had fallen the two Tyneside Brigades with the aid of other units of the 34th Division attained their objective. Think not that the struggle and the sacrifice were in vain."

Lochnagar Crater
La Boisselle

On the D20 at La Boisselle, signposted "La Grande Mine".

The mine here exploded with 16 other British mines along the Somme front at 07.28 on 1st July 1916.

The crater at La Boisselle is now privately owned by Englishman Richard Dunning. The crater was caused by two charges of ammonal of 26.8 tons. It measures 91 metres across and 21 metres deep.

The Tynesiders were repulsed here on 1st July but the Worcesters took the area two days later.

An annual remembrance ceremony takes place at 07.28 on the 1st July.

There are several memorials at the site.

Bob McKinlay (Somme Association), Richard Dunning and myself.

There is a cross to the memory of Pte George Nugent, Tyneside Scottish, Northumberland Fusiliers whose remains were found here on 31st October 1998 and later interred on 1st July 2000 in Ovillers Military Cemetery 1 A 26.

There is also a memorial seat to L/Cpl Harry Fellows of the 12th Northumberland Fusiliers 1896 - 1967. A poet in later life, the seat was donated by his son Mick.

On the morning of 30th June 2012 I had the privilege of meeting Richard Dunning at Lochnagar, as he was making final preparations for the Annual Service the following day.

Gordon Dump Cemetery
Ovillers -La –Boisselle

On 1st July 1916, 8th Division attacked Ovillers and the 34th Division La Boisselle. Although the villages were not captured, ground was won. On 4th July the 19th (Western) Division cleared La Boisselle and on the 7th July the 12th (Eastern) and 25th Divisions gained part of Ovillers, the village being cleared by the 48th (South Midland) Division on 17th July.

The two villages were lost during the German advance in March 1918 but were re-taken on 24th August by the 38th (Welsh) Division.

It is called Gordon Dump or Sausage Valley Cemetery from the name given to the broad, shallow valley that runs down to it from Becourt.

2nd Lt Donald Simpson Bell VC, 9th Yorkshire Regiment
10th July 1916 - Grave IV A 2

Prior to the war Donald played as an amateur footballer with Crystal Palace and Newcastle United. In 1912 he signed professional forms with Bradford Park Avenue. He became the first professional footballer to enlist in the British army.

He was awarded his VC for his actions on 5th July 1916 at Horseshoe Trench at the Somme. He lost his life five days later performing a similar act of bravery.

On 25th November 2010, his Victoria Cross was bought in a London auction for £252,000 by the Professional Footballers' Association.

McCrae's Battalion Cairn - 16th Royal Scots Contalmaison

The cairn was dedicated on 7th November 2004 and it is made of Elgin stone. It commemorates the 16th Royal Scots battalion who on 1st July 1916 captured the German strongpoint known as Scots Redoubt and in doing so lost around 250 men. The full story of Sir George McCrae's battalion and the sacrifice made by those belonging to Heart of Midlothian Football Club is told in Jack Alexander's splendid book entitled, "McCrae's Battalion".

The inscription on the cairn reads: **"In honoured memory of the players, ticket holders and supporters of Heart of Midlothian Football Club who took part in the advance on Contalmaison on 1st July 1916."**

One of the plaques on the memorial is to the 15th Royal Scots, the City of Edinburgh Battalion who lost roughly the same number of casualties in the attack on Contalmaison.

> **"Come pack up your footballs and scarves of maroon**
>
> **Leave all your sweethearts in Auld Reekie town**
>
> **Fall in wi' the lads for they're off and away**
>
> **To take on the bold Hun with old Geordie McCrae."**

Bell's Redoubt
Contalmaison

Walk along the road from McCrae's Battalion Cairn for about 200 metres and you will see a narrow road , the C 4 on the left hand side. A short distance along you will come upon a memorial to 2nd Lt Donald Bell VC, 9th Yorkshire Regiment who won his citation for his actions in Horseshoe Trench on 5th July 1916 destroying

a nest of German machine-guns. Five days later he was killed in action. The monument was unveiled on 9th July 2000.

2nd Lt Bell was the first professional footballer to enlist in the war. He played professional football for Bradford Park Avenue. He is buried in Gordon Dump Cemetery, to which the reader can refer for further details.

Pipers' Memorial
Longueval

In 20th July 2002 in Longueval a memorial was dedicated to commemorate all the pipers who had been killed in the Great War.

It takes the form of a remembrance wall to which has been added the crests of the Irish Guards, Royal Irish Regiment, Royal Inniskilling Fusiliers, Royal Irish Rifles, Royal Irish Fusiliers, Connaught Rangers, Leinster Regiment, Royal Munster Fusiliers, London Irish Rifles, Liverpool Irish, Tyneside Irish and the Royal Dublin Fusiliers.

A memorial sculpted by Birmingham artist Andy de Comyn and taking the form of a piper in full battledress emerging from a trench.

Longueval was selected as the site as the men of the 9th (Scottish) Division fought there in 1916.

The South African National Memorial Longueval

Delville Wood was a tract of woodland nearly one kilometre square, the western end of which touched Longueval. On 14th July 1916 the greater part of Longueval village was taken by the 9th (Scottish) Division and on 15th July, the South African Brigade of that Division captured most of Delville Wood.

The wood now formed a salient in the line, with Waterlot Farm and Mons Wood on the south flank still in German hands and owing to the height of the trees no close artillery support was possible for defence.

The three South African battalions fought continuously for six days and suffered heavy casualties. On 18th July they were forced back and on the evening of the 20th July, the survivors, a mere handful of men, were relieved.

On 27th July the 2nd Division re-took the wood and held it until 4th August when the 17th Division took it over. On the 18th and 25th August it was finally cleared of all German resistance by the 14th (Light) Division. The wood was then held until the end of August 1918 when it was re-taken during the German advance , but was re-taken by the 38th (Welsh) Division on 28th August.

In the battle the South Africans lost over 2,300 men and in October 1926, the South African National Memorial was unveiled in Delville Wood.

Today it commemorates not only the 10,000 South African dead of the First World War but other major conflicts as well including the Second World War and Korea. In 1986 a museum and visitors' centre were opened.

La Derniere Arbre - The Last Tree

A stone tablet commemorates the last remaining tree from the 1916 conflict.

A separate stone tablet and tree commemorates Cpl Joseph Davies VC and Pte Albert Hill VC, 10th (Service) Battalion , Royal Welch Fusiliers, who were awarded their VC's for conspicuous gallantry near this spot.

Delville Wood Cemetery

The cemetery is immediately across the road from the South African National Memorial. It contains 5,523 graves of which 3,593 are unidentified, of the men who contested this sector.

Sgt W. H. Lewis, 13385, 7th Royal Irish Fusiliers, 9th September 1916 - XV E 9. He lived in Jervis Street.

Footballers' Memorial – 17th and 23rd Middlesex Regiment

On 21st October 2010 at Longueval close to Delville Wood, a monument was unveiled to commemorate the Footballers' Battalions of the 17th and 23rd Middlesex Regiment.

More than 8000 officers and men were engaged in heavy action here, many having played with well known football clubs.

On the above date Gareth Ainsworth, a player with Wycombe Wanderers, blew a whistle and the crowd which had gathered began a silent tribute to association footballers who had lost their lives during World War One.

After an outcry that professional footballers were not enlisting, the Conservative MP, William Joynson Hicks oversaw the creation of the 17th (1st Football) Battalion of the Middlesex Regiment.

A second footballers' battalion was raised in June 1915, which became the 23rd Battalion of the Middlesex Regiment.

At the unveiling of the monument were representatives of more than 20 clubs and members of the Footballers Supporters Federation.

Players such as L/Sgt Walter Tull, Pte Bob Whiting, Pte William Jonas, Sgt Norman Wood, Pte William Gerrish and Pte Oscar Linkson are all mentioned elsewhere in this compilation of heroes who did not return.

London Cemetery and Extension
High Wood
Longueval

The cemetery is found on the D6 out of Longueval. High Wood was fiercely fought over during the Battle of the Somme until cleared by 47th (London) Division on 15th September 1916. It was lost during the German Advance of April 1918, but re-taken the following August. The original London Cemetery at High Wood was begun when 47 men of the 47th Division were buried in a large shell hole on 18th and 21st September 1916.

Other burials were added later, mainly of officers and men of the 47th Division who died on 15th September 1916 and at the Armistice , the cemetery contained 101 graves. The cemetery was then greatly enlarged when remains were brought in from the surrounding battlefields, but the original battlefield cemetery is preserved intact within the larger cemetery , now known as London Cemetery and Extension.

The cemetery, one of five in the immediate vicinity of Longueval which together contain more than 13,000 graves, is the third largest cemetery on the Somme, with 3,871 First World War burials 3,112 of them unidentified.

Pte Albert Graham, 11984, 1st Royal Irish Fusiliers, 12th October 1916 - VI B 21. He lived on Carrickblacker Road. He was killed at Le Transloy.

Flers

Flers is on the D197 between Longueval and Ligny-Thilloy. On 15th September 1916 the village was the objective of the New Zealand and 41st Divisions.

This action was when tanks were first used on the battlefield.

O's World War One Memorial

On 21st July 2011 a memorial funded by Leyton Orient Football Club supporters commemorating East London footballers who fought and died in the Great War was unveiled in the grounds of the village church in Flers.

It recalls the sacrifice of the players, staff and fans of Clapton Orient – as the O's were originally known up until the 1940's. It was the first monument to an English Football League side to be erected on the Somme.

After an outcry that professional footballers were not enlisting in 1914, Clapton Orient led the way and three of its rising stars – CSM Richard McFadden, Pte William Jonas and Pte George Scott were later to pay the ultimate sacrifice at the Somme in 1916.

All three were members of 17th Middlesex (Footballers') Regiment. Jonas killed on 27th July 1917 is named on the Somme Memorial to the Missing at Thiepval, McFadden died later on 23rd October 1916 and is buried in Couin British Cemetery on the Somme whilst Scott who died on 16th June 1916 is interred at St Souplet British Cemetery.

AIF Burial Ground

The cemetery is found 2 km north of Flers on the D74 in the direction of Guedecourt.

Flers was captured on 15th September 1916 in the Battle of Flers - Courcelette. It was entered by the New Zealand and 41st Divisions accompanied for the first time by the use of tanks.

The village was lost in March 1918 and re-taken the following August. The cemetery was begun by Australian Medical Units in November 1916 - February 1917. It was enlarged after the Armistice.

The graves include many men from the 36th (Ulster) Division.

During my visit here in early April 2009, extensive renovations were being carried out.

Several notable graves are located here.

Cpl W. H. Gracey 7599 7th South Lancashire Regiment – 23rd October 1915 150 31 - Lived at Burnbrae Avenue, Portadown.

Lt Col C. W. R. Duncombe, 2nd Earl of Feversham, 215. Yorkshire Hussars Yeomanry, Att. King's Royal Rifle Corps – 15th September 1916 3 L 29. Lord Feversham died in action. Anthony Eden, a future Prime Minister, of the same battalion, supervised the search for his Commanding Officer's body which was missing on the battlefield. It was found over a month later.

Sgt Harold Jackson 18474 VC, "C" Coy 7th East Yorkshire Regiment, 24th August 1916, XV A 21/30 – "For most conspicuous bravery and devotion to duty. He volunteered and went through the hostile barrage and brought back valuable information. Later when the enemy had established themselves in our line, he rushed them and single-handedly bombed them out into the open. Then he stalked an enemy machine gun, threw Mills bombs and put the gun out of action. He later withdrew the Company under heavy fire. He repeatedly carried in wounded."

Ginchy

The village stood on the high plain which defended Combles, an important forward position in the German defence line.

The 16th (Irish) Division attacked Ginchy on 15th September 1916 without success. The Royal Munster Fusiliers , in particular received heavy casualties.

When the village was taken on 9th September, the seven Irish battalions involved lost eight officers and 2,200 men.

The Royal Dublin Fusiliers lost six officers and 61 men. One of the fallen was Lt Tom Kettle, killed during the clearance of, the houses in the village. He was a poet, writer and a professor in Dublin University. He had previously been a Member of Parliament. His name is recorded on the Somme Memorial to the Missing.

Also lost during the Battle of Ginchy were Lt Col H. P. Dalzell-Watson, 8th Royal Inniskilling Fusiliers and Capt W J Murphy, 9th Royal Dublin Fusiliers.

Combles Communal Cemetery Extension

The cemetery is on the D172 just outside the large village of Combles and the Extension is at the back of the Communal Cemetery.

The village was entered in the early morning of 26th August 1916 by units of the 56th (London) Division and the French Army. The Allies held it until 24th March 1918 despite a stubborn stand by the South African Brigade at Marrieres Wood. Then on 29th August it was in the hands of 18th Division.

The cemetery was begun in October 1916 by French troops, but the original 96 French graves have now been moved to another cemetery. The first British burials took place in December 1916.

Later 194 German soldiers were buried here but their graves too have been removed elsewhere.

After the Armistice 944 graves were concentrated here, taken from the surrounding battlefields and smaller cemeteries.

CSM Robert Gilpin 43753, 6th Northamptonshire regiment, 30th August 191 - II F 7 - Blackisland House, Annaghmore.

Pte John O'Neill 18692 7th Royal Inniskilling Fusiliers, 5th September 1916 - IV F 28 - Obin's Street

Two brothers lie in this cemetery - Pte F R G Rockall 50929, 11th Royal Fusiliers (City of London) Regiment 30th August 1918 - II D 15 and Gunner P R W Rockall 31290 "B" Battery, 77th Brigade, Royal Field Artillery, 11th September 1916 - II B 14 - Thornton Heath, Surrey.

Guillemont

The village is approximately 12 kilometres east of Albert at the junction of the D64 and D20 roads.

Guillemont was an important point in the German defences at the beginning of the Somme battles. It was situated on high ground between Longueval and Combles and was in the second line of German defence. On several occasions it had been entered by British forces but these had been repulsed.

Twice during August, the 2nd Leinster Regiment had attempted to storm the village but suffered heavy casualties.

During what was known as the Battle of Guillemont, 3rd – 9th September 1916, the village was eventually captured by the 20th (Light) Division and 47th Brigade of the 16th (Irish) Division which included 7th Leinster Regiment, 6th Connaught Rangers, 8th Royal Munster Fusiliers and 18th Royal Irish Regiment.

At 12.00 hours the British artillery opened up with a heavy bombardment. The leading companies went over the top giving the Germans no time to come out of their dug-outs.

It was here that Lt J V Holland, 7th Leinster Regiment won his Victoria Cross. After bombing an enemy dug-out, he led his bombers, twenty six of them, to clear a great part of the village. Only five returned, the rest being killed or wounded.

The Connaught Rangers suffered 200 casualties from their own mortars.

Lt Lenox-Conynham, carrying only his cane, his pistol in his holster was in the first line trench. He called out, "That Connaught Rangers is what you have to take." He then fell dead. By 12.55 hours the Connaught Rangers third objective had been taken.

Pte Tom Hughes, 6th Connaught Rangers, despite being wounded, single-handedly captured a German machine gun. Again being wounded he brought in three prisoners. For these actions he was awarded a Victoria Cross.

The village was lost again in March 1918 during the German Offensive but re-taken on 29th August by the 18th and 38th (Welsh) Divisions.

The village church is the focal point of the village outside of which stands the Celtic cross memorial of the 16th (Irish) Division, the inscription on which reads, "**1914 1918 - In commemoration of the victories of Guillemont and Ginchy** ,

September 3ʳᵈ – 9ᵗʰ 1916. In memory of those who fell there and of all Irishmen who gave their lives in the Great War. RIP."

The people of Northern Ireland and particularly The Somme Association have a close affinity with the village. The local church, the Eglise Saint Pierre de Guillemont has received pews from some of the churches in Ulster.

On 6ᵗʰ September 2008, a plaque was unveiled inside the church in memory of the gallant men of the 16ᵗʰ (Irish) Division.

The following day, Mayor Didier Samain re-named a street, **"Rue de la 16eme Division Irlandaise"**. A little further up from the church, a street was named in honour of **Hauptman Junger of the 73ʳᵈ Hanoverian Fusiliers**. He had written the classic war novel, **"Storm of Steel"**, relating his adventures and experiences around Combles and Guillemont.

Almost a year later on 3ʳᵈ September 2009, a plaque was unveiled on the outer wall of the church, to commemorate three winners of the Victoria Cross.

Lt. J. V. Holland VC   Pte. Thomas Hughes VC

Lt John V. Holland VC, 3rd Leinster egiment, attached 7th Battalion. He led his bombing team through an artillery barrage, taking 50 prisoners and losing 19 of his own men. **Pte Thomas Hughes VC 6th Connaught Rangers.** Despite being hit four times, he went over the top at Guillemont and captured a German machine-gun post and brought back four prisoners.

Sgt D. Jones VC, 12th Liverpool Regiment. After his officer in charge had been killed going forward at Guillemont, he took command and led the advance on. He and his men held the Germans off for two days until relief arrived.

Devonshire Cemetery
Mametz

Devonshire Cemetery is situated 800 metres south of Mametz, 450 metres west of the D938 Albert to Peronne road. There is a small roadside car park, go up the steps along a dirt pathway to reach the cemetery.

Mametz was within the German lines until 1st July 1916 when it was captured by 7th Division and the 8th and 9th Devonshire battalions of the Devonshire Regiment near a plantation called Mansell Copse. They buried their dead in a section of their old front line trench.

"The Devonshires held this trench

The Devonshires hold it still"

On 1st July 1986 HRH The Duke of Kent unveiled a new memorial in memory of the 8th and 9th Devonshires.

Capt D. L. Martin, Devonshire Regiment, 1st July 1916, A 1 .He had made a plasticine model of the area and had forecast a German machine gun position at the Shrine, the crucifix in the village cemetery. It happened as Capt Martin had predicted.

The machine gun post survived the bombardment and caused heavy casualties to the Devonshires, although all their objectives were eventually taken.

9th Devonshires - 123 dead: **8th Devonshires - 38 dead:**

Most of the 161 men of the Devonshire Regiment were buried by the **Regimental Chaplain**, the **Rev E C Crosse**. He later said to an officer, **"I buried all I could collect in our front line trench. Nearly all the casualties were just by the magpie's nest."**

Lt W. N. Hodgson MC, 9th Devonshire Regiment, 1st July 1916, A 3 - One of the war poets - Son of the Vicar of Thornbury. A few days before the Big Push he wrote his last poem, **"Before Action"**, from which the last line, **"Help me die, 0 Lord"**, has immortalised him.

2nd Lt P. F. Gethin, 8th Devonshire Regiment, 28th June 1916, B4 - An artist.

Carnoy Military Cemetery

Carnoy is a village north of the D938 Albert to Peronne road. The cemetery is found on the road to Maricourt.

It was started in August 1915 by 2nd King's Own Scottish Borderers and 2nd King's Own Yorkshire Light Infantry. It was closed in March 1917.

It has just over 20 Irish graves representing 10 different regiments but the variety in ranks of those interred makes it particularly interesting.

It is one of the most visited in the area.

Identified: 826   Total: 855

Captain Wilfred P Nevill, 15th East Yorkshire Regt, att: 8th East Surreys, 1st July 1916, E 28. He devised a plan to dribble footballs across No Mans Land to relieve the strain on the men. On the eve of battle two footballs were printed with the message:

The Great European Cup - The Final

East Surreys v The Bavarians,

Kick Off at "Zero

No Referee."

Nevill was shot through the head as he reached the German wire.

Lt Col J S M Lenox-Conynham – 6th Connaught Rangers, 3rd September 1916, R 33 .Son of Sir William Lenox-Conynham, Springhill, Moneymore. He died during the taking of Guillemont by elements of the 16th (Irish) Division. The wooden cross that originally marked his grave is in Armagh Church of Ireland Cathedral. According to Ray Westlake in his book, "British Battalions on the Somme", Lenox-Conynham's last words were, "That Connaught Rangers is what you have to take". Pte T. Hughes (see Guillemont) won his VC in the same action that Lenox-Conynham was killed.

Lt Col F. E. P. Curzon, 6th Royal Irish Regiment, 9th September 1916, R 34. He died after the taking of Ginchy and had been Mentioned in Despatches for the DSO, two months after his death.

Rev C. B. Plummer, Chaplain to the Forces 4th Class, 12th March 1917, A 5

Captain B. P. Ayre, 8th Norfolk Regiment, 1st July 1916, DA10 - one of four brothers who died in the war. Originally from Newfoundland.

Cpl E. Dwyer VC, Cross of St George, 1st East Surrey's, 3/9/16, III J 3 - won his VC at Hill 60 in Belgium 20th April 1915. He found himself alone in a trench. He collected all the grenades he could find and threw them at the enemy. He kept the Germans at bay until reinforcements arrived and the trench was saved.

Capt C. R. J. R. Dolling MC, 2nd Btn Royal Welsh Fusiliers, 20/8/16, 1 D 39, Maralin, Co. Down.

Lt Col A. P. Hamilton MC, Att: 1/19th London's, 15/9/15, 7 I 2

Lt Col J. Mortimer, 1/5th Yorkshires, Att Machine Gun Corps, 15/9/16, 4 J 5

Grove Town Cemetery
Meaulte

Travelling from Mametz direction join D938 and shortly afterwards take left on D147 for Bray-sur-Somme. Take D1 out of the village and then left on D1 F towards Etineham. **Follow the C6 just after seeing the first CWGC sign at the edge of the airfield. A short distance down is a second CWGC sign indicating a right turn down a dirt track . Carry straight on for 4 km to reach Grove Town Cemetery.**

In September 1916, the 34th and 2/2nd London Casualty Clearing Stations were established at this point, known to the troops as Grove Town, to deal with casualties from the Somme battlefields. They were moved in April 1917 and except for a few burials in August and September 1918, the cemetery was closed.

Pte Patrick Gorman 17632, 1st Royal Irish Fusiliers, 17th October 1916 - I N 6 - Curran Street. He enlisted in Glasgow. He and his wife had lived in Partick, Glasgow for a time.

Pte Samuel J. Fox 11664, 1st Royal Irish Fusiliers, 12th December 1916 - II E 15 - Bridge street. Worked as a compositor in the Portadown News. He was a member of Seagoe Harriers. He had been posted to the Balkans and had fought in Salonika. After suffering frostbite he was invalided home via Alexandria. His letters home were published in the Seagoe Church magazine. On 11th December he was struck in the spine and died the next day at No. 2 Casualty Clearing station.

Sgt Leslie Coulson, 12th London Regiment, Royal Fusiliers, 7th October 1916 - I J 24

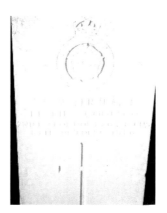

A noted war poet, Leslie was born in a street off Kilburn High Road. He entered journalism and later became **assistant editor of, "The Morning Post".**

He enlisted in September 1914 and joined the 2/2nd London Regiment known as, **"The two and twopennies"**, because so many of them came from the big London stores.

He saw service in Malta, Gallipoli and Egypt.

After promotion to Sergeant he became a member of the 12th London's, "The Rangers". On 1st July he was involved in a diversionary attack at Gommecourt.

On 7th October he was involved in action at Dewdrop Trench, east of Lesboeufs. They were subject to heavy machine-gun fire. Coulson was shot in the chest and died the following day at Grove Town Casualty Clearing Station.

Two poems were found on his body, "From the Somme" and "Who made the law?".

In 1917, "From an outpost and other poems", were published and 10,000 copies were sold in less than twelve months.

Route 3 - Cambrai
and its surrounds

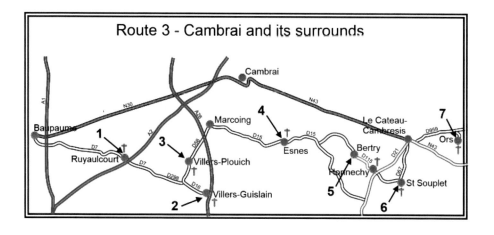

Route 3 - Cambrai and its surrounds

1. Ruyaulcourt Military Cemetery

2. Villers Hill British Cemetery

3. Fifteen Ravine British Cemetery

4. Esnes Communal Cemetery

5. Honnechy British Cemetery

6. St. Souplet British Cemetery

7. Ors Communal Cemetery

Route 3 - Cambrai and its surrounds

Battle of Cambrai - 20th November 1917

Haig approved the general idea of a tank and infantry attack near Cambrai, in the hope that the Bourlon Ridge would be seized which would therefore hamper the German's use of Cambrai as a railway communications centre.

The Cavalry Corps would be held in reserve ready to sweep through the gaps in the German lines.

A total of 216 tanks each supported by 200 infantry advanced along unbroken ground each supported by 200 infantry. On the first day the British took its early objectives.

However on the second day impetus began to fade. The Cavalry was too far back to maintain the momentum gained on the first day.

After several days fighting Bourlon Wood was taken. However, a week later, Cambrai was still a couple of miles distant.

Many consider the Battle of Cambrai a failure. Both sides lost roughly 40,000 men each.

This area of France is sometimes largely forgotten, as the Somme and Passchendaele rightly take priority.

However the 36th (Ulster) Division and the 107th, 108th and 109th Brigades were heavily involved in the battle, especially around the Canal du Nord and in the heavy fighting in Bourlon Wood.

Whilst the route to be outlined is relatively short, nevertheless those who made the supreme sacrifice in this area, and especially those who hailed from the Portadown area should not be forgotten.

From Albert take the D929 in the direction of Baupaume. Just short of Baupaume take right on the D7 to Bertencourt and from there follow the signs to Ruyualcourt. **Ruyaulcourt Military Cemetery (1)** lies 500 metres north of the village along an unmarked road, but it is signposted to the left by the village church as you enter the village from the Baupaume direction.

Here you will find the grave of Rev Alex Stuart, 12th Royal Irish Rifles who was the son of Rev J. C. Stuart of Tandragee. He was the first Irish Presbyterian casualty of the First World War.

Leave Ruyualcourt and proceed on the D7 to Gouzeaucourt where you join the D16 to **Villers- Guislain. Villers Hill British Cemetery (2)** is 1 km south-east of the village.

Pte P. J. McVeigh, 2nd Argyll and Sutherland Highlanders who originated from Obin's Street is interred here. Note the mis-spelling of his name on his headstone.

From Villers-Guislain take the short trip northwards to **Villers-Plouich. Fifteen Ravine British Cemetery (3)** is east of the village on the road to La Vacquerie.

Rfn George Flavelle of 8th/9th Royal Irish Rifles is buried here. He hailed from Corbrackey.

Leave Villers-Plouich and take the D17 to Marcoing and join the D15 to **Esnes. Esnes Communal Cemetery (4)** is north-east of the village on the road to Langsart. Esnes witnessed fighting in the Battle of Le Cateau on 26th August 1914. **It was here that Pte Robert McShane, 1st Royal Irish Fusiliers was killed on the following day. He had lived in West Street.**

From Esnes follow the D15 and join the D16 via **Bertry to Honnechy.** Honnechy was also part of the Battle of Le Cateau in August 1914. **Honnechy British Cemetery (5)** is north-east of the village on the road to Reumont.

Buried here is Pte George Neill, 1st Royal Irish Fusiliers who had lived in Park Road. He had been a member of Parkmount Temperance Flute Band.

Travel out of Honnechy on the D115 via Escaufourt to St Souplet where you will reach **St Souplet British Cemetery.(6)** Here lies Pte J. Black, 6th Royal Inniskilling Fusiliers who was a member of Drumnahuncheon LOL No 371. He had served in Gallipoli, Salonika, Egypt and France. He lived at Artabracka.

Also found here is the grave of Pte George Scott, 17th Middlesex (Footballers') Battalion. He played 205 times for Clapton Orient, now Leyton Orient and had scored 33 goals.

Follow the D21 to Le Cateau and take the D59 in the direction of Landrecies. Nearing Landrecies take off right to the small village of Ors. **You are visiting Ors Communal Cemetery (7) so be careful not to confuse it with Ors British Cemetery.**

There are only 63 graves here, of which 29 are men of the Lancashire Fusiliers. However there is a host of notable servicemen, two have won the Victoria Cross and several others have either the Military Cross or Military Medal.

The cemetery is mainly noted for the grave of Lt Wilfred Owen MC, 2nd Manchester Regiment who like so many others in this cemetery was killed on 4th November 1918. Lt Owen was recognised as the most important and original poet of the period. Probably his most famous poem is entitled, "Strange Meeting."

Follow the D463 to Cambrai, using the ring road to join the D630/ D930 to Baupaume. If your base is in Albert travel on the D929 to reach the town.

Ruyaulcourt Military Cemetery

From Albert once again take the D929 in the direction of Baupaume. Just short of Baupaume turn right on to the D7 to Bertencourt and from there follow the signs to Ruyaulcourt.

The cemetery lies 500 metres north of Ruyaulcourt village along an unmarked road, but it is signposted to the left by the village church as you enter the village from Baupaume direction.

The village was attacked by the 7th D C Light Infantry on the 28th/29th March 1917, found unoccupied the following night by 7th Somerset Light Infantry, lost on 23rd March 1918 and then cleared by the New Zealand Division on 4th September 1918.

Ruyaulcourt German Cemetery once contained 405 German graves, 2 Royal Air Force officers, 2 United Kingdom and one New Zealand soldier. It was removed in 1928 and two of the British graves were brought into the Military Cemetery.

Ruyaulcourt Military Cemetery was begun in April 1917 and used by fighting units and field ambulances, mainly of 42nd (East Lancashire) Division until March 1918. It was re-opened again in September 1918.

There are now over 300 First World War casualties commemorated on this site. Of these ten are unidentified and special memorials are erected to the two airmen buried in the German Cemetery, whose graves could not be found.

Wheelchair access is impossible at this cemetery.

Some of the casualties of the Battle of Cambrai are buried here.

Rev Alex Stuart, 12th Royal Irish Rifles, 4th Class Chaplain to the Forces, 24th October 1917 - F 5. Alex was the son of Rev J. C. Stuart of Clare, Tandragee. He was a minister in the Presbyterian Church in Ireland.

He was Assistant Minister of Agnes Street Church, Belfast and had been ordained in May 1915 in Bessbrook.

In early 1916 he was with the YMCA in Egypt. After becoming a temporary chaplain to the forces, he was killed in action, just two weeks after having arrived in France.

He was the first Irish Presbyterian casualty of the First World War. He is commemorated on Aldershot Memorial.

Lt Col T. Best DSO and Bar, Ist/2nd Royal Inniskilling Fusiliers, 20* November 1917 - F 8. He was a native of Clonmel, County Tipperary.

He was killed on the first day of the Battle of Cambrai.

Lt The Hon. Arthur Kinnaird MC, 1st Scots Guards, 27th November 1917 - F15. Son of the 11th Baron of Kinnaird, of Rossie Priory, Inchture, Perthshire. His brother The Hon Douglas Arthur also fell and is buried in Godezonne Farm Cemetery, Belgium.

Pte T. Dennison 306878,1^/8* Lancashire Fusiliers, 13th June 1917 - B 3. He was one of three brothers killed in the war.

Villers Hill British Cemetery

Villers Guislain

Leave Ruyualcourt and follow the D7 to Gouzeaucourt where you join the D16 to Villers-Guislain. Villers Hill British Cemetery is one kilometre south-east of the village.

Villers-Guislain was occupied by Commonwealth forces from April 1917 until the German counter attacks at the end of November 1917, in the Battle of Cambrai. It was lost on 30th November and retained by the Germans on 1st December in spite of the fierce attacks of the Guards Division and tanks. The village was finally abandoned by the Germans on 30th September 1918, after heavy fighting.

The cemetery was originally known as Middlesex Cemetery, Gloucester Road and begun by the 33rd Divisional Burial Officer on 3rd October 1918 and used until the middle of October. The original cemetery, now Plot 1, contained 100 graves, of which 50 belonged to 1st Middlesex and 35 to the Argyll and Sutherland Highlanders. More graves were added after the Armistice, many of whom are officers and men who died in April 1917, November - December 1917, March 1918 and September 1918.

Pte P. J. McVeigh 3/6960 2nd Argyll and Sutherland Highlanders 24th September 1917 - 7 C13 Pte McVeigh lived in Obin's Street. He had enlisted in Glasgow. He had taken part in the Retreat from Mons in August 1914. He had previously been wounded on three occasions.

Notice the mis-spelled surname on his headstone - it reads McVey.

Fifteen Ravine British Cemetery

Villers-Plouich

From Villers-Guislain take the short trip northwards to Villers-Plouich. Fifteen Ravine British Cemetery is east of the village on the road to La Vacquerie.

Fifteen Ravine was the name given by the army to the shallow ravine, once bordered by fifteen trees, which ran at right angles to the railway about 800 metres south of Villers-Plouich, but the cemetery is in fact "Farm Ravine", on the east side of the railway line, nearer the village.

It was begun by the 17th Welsh Regiment in April 1917, a few days after the capture of the ravine by the 12th South Wales Borderers. It continued in use during the Battle of Cambrai and until March 1918.

On 22nd March, the second day of the great German Offensive, the ground passed into their hands after severe fighting. It was not regained until the following September. The cemetery was enlarged after the Armistice.

Rfn George Flavelle, 175 Royal Irish Rifles, 5th December 1917 - 4 D 20. He lived at Corbrackey and had enlisted in Belfast.

Esnes Communal Cemetery

From Villers-Plouich join the D17 to Marcoing, then take the D15 to Esnes. The cemetery is northeast of the village on the road to Langsart.

Esnes witnessed fighting in the Battle of Le Cateau on 26th August 1914 and it was captured by the New Zealand Division on 8th October 1918.

In the corner of the cemetery, left of the entrance are five graves, one (marked also by a French memorial) contains the bodies of 112 soldiers of the 4th Division who fell in August 1914 and in the others are buried *four other* United Kingdom soldiers who died later in the war. Of the 116, 62 are unidentified.

The majority of the graves belong to men of the Lancashire Fusiliers, Essex Regiment and the Royal Inniskilling Fusiliers.

Pte Robert McShane 8751, 1st Royal Irish Fusiliers, 27th August 1914 - Grave 1. Robert lived in West Street. He was a member of Portadown Rechabites. He is interred in the same grave as another soldier.

Honnechy British Cemetery

From Esnes follow the D15 and join the D16 via Bertry to Honnechy. The cemetery is north-east of the village on the road to Reumont.

Honnechy was part of the battlefield of Le Cateau in August 1914 and from that time it remained in German hands until 9th October 1918, when the 25th Division and the 6th Cavalry Brigade captured it.

It had been a German Hospital centre, and from its capture until the end of October it was a British Field Ambulance centre.

The village was inhabited by civilians during the whole of the war.

The cemetery stands on the site of a German Cemetery begun in the Battle of Cambrai 1917 and used by German troops and then by British until 24th October 1918.

The 300 German graves were removed to another burial ground, leaving 44 British graves. The cemetery was re-made in 1922 and 1923 by the concentration of British graves almost entirely from German cemeteries.

Pte George Neill 10772, 1st Royal Irish Fusiliers, 27th August 1914 - 1C19.
George lived in Park Road. He was a member of Parkmount Temperance Flute Band. The British Expeditionary Force met the full force of the German army at the Battle of Mons on 23rd August 1914. By the 26th it had withdrawn to Le Cateau after having been attacked by 8 German Divisions.

The British lost 8,000 men, killed, wounded or missing.

St Souplet British Cemetery

Take the D115 out of Honnechy via Escaufourt to St Souplet. It is about an 8 minute drive.

St Souplet village was captured by the American 30th Division on 10th October 1918. The American troops made a cemetery of 371 American and 7 British graves on the south-west of the village, on the road to Vaux-Andigny and a smaller British cemetery was made alongside. The American graves were removed after the Armistice, one being taken to the British cemetery with the seven British graves, and other British graves were brought in from various burial grounds and from the battlefields.

Pte J. Black 19209, 6th Royal Inniskilling Fusiliers, 5th November 1918 - 11 B1. Lived at Artabracka. He was a member of Drumnahuncheon LOL No 371. He had enlisted in Airdrie and had seen action in Gallipoli, Salonika, Egypt and France.

Pte George Scott F1583, 17th Middlesex Regiment, 16th August 1917 - 2 AA 19. George was a professional footballer who signed for Clapton Orient in 1908. He made 205 appearances and scored 33 goals. He was injured at Guillemont on 8th August.

L/Cpl J. Doherty 6426 1st Royal Irish Fusiliers, 24th March 1918 - 1G 20. He came from Cruit Island, Kincasslagh, Co. Donegal. His epitaph reads, "Tis ever so the good, the beautiful, the brave, are first to go."

Ors Communal Cemetery

Take the D21 to Le Cateau and follow the D59 in the direction of Landrecies. Nearing Landrecies take off right to the small village of Ors.

Be careful not to confuse Ors Communal Cemetery with Ors British Cemetery.

This is a small cemetery which contains 63 burials. The village was cleared by the 6th Division on 1st November 1918.

There are 2 Victoria Cross recipients, Military Cross winners and those with Military Medal awards interred here.

Lt Wilfred Owen MC, one of the best known war poets is buried here. Most of the burials are men of the Lancashire Fusiliers of whom 29 are resting here.

2LT James Kirk VC, 10th Batt. Attd. 2nd Manchester Regiment, 4th November 1918 - A 22. He was awarded his Victoria Cross, "For most conspicuous bravery near Ors on 4th November 1918 whilst attempting to bridge the Oise Canal."

Lt Col J. N. Marshall VC: MC and Bar, Officer Order of Leopold: Croix de Guerre (Belgium), Irish Guards, attd. 16th Lancashire Fusiliers, 4th November 1918 - - Grave in line with A 22

" For most conspicuous bravery, determination and leadership in the attack on the Sambre-Oise Canal, near Catillon on 4th November 1918."

141

Lt Wilfred E. S. Owen MC 2nd Manchester Regiment, 4th November 1918 - A 3.

He had enlisted in the Artists' Rifles in October 1915. Commissioned into the Manchester Regiment in June 1916. In June when he was posted home on sick leave he met Sassoon whose influence had a profound effect on him.

Now almost universally recognised as the most important and original poet of the period. Though born in Oswestry, near the Welsh border and with a Welsh name, he was not in fact Welsh. His apprentice work was much influenced by W B Yeats.

He returned to active service in September 1918. **A month later he was awarded the Military Cross, "for conspicuous gallantry and devotion to duty." He was killed in action a week before the Armistice.**

One of his finest poems was, "Strange Meeting"

Pte T. E. Cliffe MM, 311115,2nd Manchester Regt, 4th November 1918 - A10

L/Sgt A. E. Hall MM 57558, Lancashire Fusiliers, 4th November 1918 - A1

Capt C. H. J. Hulton MC, 16th Lancashire Fusiliers, 4th November 1918 - B15

Capt A. McKenzie MC and Bar, 2nd Manchester Regiment, 4th November 1918 - A 5

Cpl C. Syrett MM, 2nd Manchester Regiment, 4th November 1918 - A14

5

Route 4 - Bapaume to Bethune

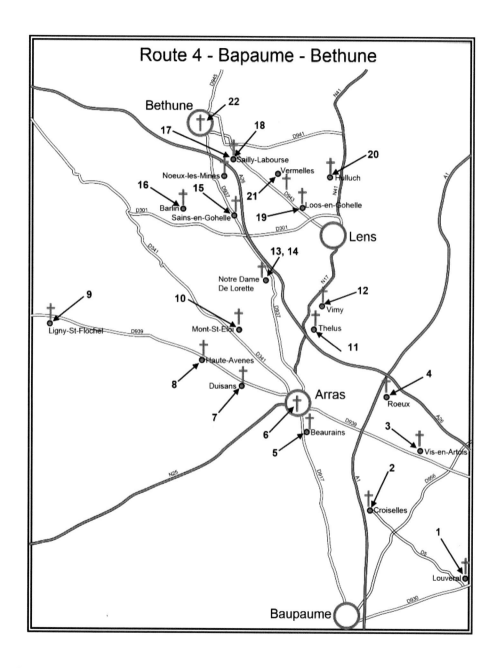

Route 4 - Bapaume to Bethune

1. Cambrai Memorial, Louverval
2. Croiselles Railway Cemetery
3. Vis-en-Artois British Cemetery and Memorial, Harcourt
4. Brown's Copse Cemetery, Rouex
5. Beaurain's Road Cemetery, Beaurain
6. Arras Memorial and Faubourg d'Amiens Cemetery
7. Duisans British Cemetery, Etrun
8. Haute Avenses British Cemetery
9. Ligny St Flochel British Cemetery, Averdoingt
10. Ecoivres Military Cemetery, Mont St Eloi
11. Nine Elms Military Cemetery, Thelus
12. Vimy Ridge
13. Notre Dame de Lorette
14. Ring of Remembrance
15. Fosse No. 10 Communal Cemetery Extension
16. Barlin Communal Cemetery Extension
17. Noeux-les.Mines Communal Cemetery
18. Sailly-Labourse Communal Cemetery Externsion
19. Dud Corner Cemetery and Loos Memorial
20. Bois-Carre Military Cemetery
21. Vermelles British Cemetery
22. Bethune Town Cemetery

Route 4 - Baupaume to Bethune

The route outlined is somewhat haphazard If you wish to take in all that is suggested. I would recommend if you have time limitations, that you curtail your itinerary accordingly to suit your interests. The route encompasses many of the areas where heavy fighting took place at some time during the 1914-1918 period.

Battle of Armentieres 13th Nov - 21st Nov 1914

Troops from the BEF – British Expeditionary Force – moved northwards from the Aisne front in early October and joined with the French forces to push the Germans back towards Lille.

However German reinforcements arrived towards the end of that month and began to attack the British-Franco lines from Arras to Armentieres. The Germans pushed back the Allies on several occasions .

The **1st Royal Irish Fusiliers** were engaged in heavy combat at **La Ruage (19th Oct) and Frelinghiem (20th Oct)** . They eventually had to withdraw to **Houplines** where they suffered heavy shelling and infantry assaults. It was late November before these attacks subsided.

Battle of Arras 9th April - 16th May 1917

This was a major British offensive when troops from the four corners of the British Empire attacked trenches held by the Germans, east of Arras. Although most of the battlefield area around Arras was flat, **Vimy Ridge** to the north, held by the Germans, dominated the countryside and therefore British lines were under constant observation.

The Battle of Vimy 9th - 14th April, involved heavy fighting by the Canadian and British forces and they ejected the German army off the ridge. In Canada, the Battle of Vimy Ridge, in their eyes was when Canadians recognized that their national conscience was forged.

Following the capture of Rouex on 13th - 14th May and the Battle of Bullecourt, the Arras Offensive came to an end.

The British sustained 160,000 casualties, killed, wounded, missing or taken prisoner.

As you progress via the route outlined **it will become very evident that many men who originally resided in the Portadown district had emigrated prior to the First World War beginning.**

Some of them later enlisted in the Canadian, Australian and New Zealand forces, later to fight on the Western Front, where many made the ultimate sacrifice.

From Baupaume take the D930 towards Cambrai where at **Louverval** you will reach the **Cambrai Memorial (1)** which commemorates more than 7,308 servicemen of the United Kingdom and South Africa who died in the Battle of Cambrai 1917. Note especially the name of **2nd Lt J. S. Emerson VC, 9th Royal Inniskilling Fusiliers, 36th (Ulster) Division,** on Panel 5/6. There are also two Portadown men named on the memorial.

From Louverval take the D5 to Croisilles. **Croisilles Railway Cemetery (2)** lies off a track, approximately 2 km long, on the D9 Ecoust-St-Mein road. **Lt J. H. Grayson, Royal Irish Regiment,** who lived in High Street is buried here. **There are numerous soldiers from several Irish Regiments buried in this cemetery.** There is also a number of German graves.

From Croisilles take the D9 to Vis-en-Artois. Here you will find the **Vis-en-Artois British Cemetery and Memorial (3)** which commemorates those who fell during the Advance to Victory in 1918. There are over 9,000 men named, who have no known grave. They include **Pte W. Partridge of the 13th King's Own Rifle Corps who was born in Drumgor.**

To reach our next destination we have to travel across the country to **Rouex**. Take the D9E out of Haucourt towards Boiry-Notre-Dame. Join the D34 to Hamblain-les-Pres. Now follow the D33 E1 in the direction of Roeux.

Brown's Copse Military Cemetery (4) is about one km north-west of Rouex on the eastern outskirts of the neighbouring village of Fampoux. It is signposted from Fampoux village. **Two Portadown men both serving in the 1st Royal Irish Fusiliers lie here. Pte James Falloon lived in Jervis Street and Pte J. H. Weir in Meadow Lane. Aslo buried here are Sgt J. Allan, 16th Royal Scots and a member of the Heart of Midlothian Football Club and Lt D. Mackintosh VC of 3rd Seaforth Highlanders.**

From Fampoux take the D42 in the direction of Arras. Filter right on the D60 and take the turn off for Beaurains. **Beaurains Road Cemetery (5)** is on the D17, north of the village.

Here you will find the grave of Pte Samuel Robinson, 72nd Canadian Infantry, (British Columbia Regiment), a native of Drumheriff.

Entering Arras, take the Boulevard General de Gaulle and near the Citadel, two km from the centre of town is the **Fauberg d'Amiens Cemetery and Arras Memorial (6).** The memorial commemorates those who fell in the Arras sector from Spring 1916 until August 1918 from the United Kingdom, South Africa and New Zealand.

The Flying Services Memorial records the names of almost a 1000 men from the Royal Flying Corps, Royal Air Force and Royal Naval Air Service. **2nd Lt John Collen, 7th Squadron, Royal Flying Corps had lived in Stewart Avenue. A further four Portadown soldiers are named on the Arras Memorial whilst another has a known grave.**

Bay 7 will be of interest to football followers, as here are recorded the names of those who have no known grave from the **17th Middlesex (Footballers) Battalion. Take note especially of Walter Tull of Northampton Town, the first black footballer and that of Sandy Turnbull, 8th Surreys, who won two league championships and an F A Cup winners medal with Manchester United after winning an F A Cup winners medal with rivals Manchester City.** There are other famous footballing personalities of this era commemorated here also.

Leave Arras and take the N39 towards Etrun. **Duisans British Cemetery (7) lies in Etrun** but takes its name from the nearby village. The cemetery is one km off the N39 in the angle of the Arras-Habarcq road on a track leading to Haute-Avenses.

Driver N S Holmes, 15th Division Ammunition Column, Royal Field Artillery, a Killycomain man is buried here.

Continue to Haute-Avenses, where north of the village on the C2 road leading to Habarcq you will reach **Haute-Avenses British Cemetery(8).**

One of the smaller cemeteries in the area with only 150 graves, one of which is the last resting place of **Pte P. Gilmore, 1st Royal Irish Fusiliers, who had lived in Curran Street.**

Return to the main N39 Arras to St Pol road and drive onwards to Ligny-St Flochel. South of the village on on the D81 is **Ligny-St Flochel British Cemetery (9). You will realise we are now in an area where the Canadians were involved in heavy fighting. Many Portadown men had emigrated only to enlist later in the Canadian forces to pay the supreme sacrifice and lie forever in the silent cities of the Western Front.**

Pte W. H. Preston, 5th Canadian Mounted Rifles (Quebec Regt) was originally from Henry Street.

To save time return towards Arras on the N39 and when you reach Aubigny-en-Artois, take the D75 and shortly afterwards take right on D49 towards **Mont St Eloi.**

Ecoivres is a hamlet on this road, south-west of Mont St Eloi and you will reach **Ecoivres Military Cemetery (10).**

Pte J. Benson, 52ⁿᵈ Canadian Infantry, (Manitoba Regt) hailed from Drumherriff.

Continue on the D49 as far as **Thelus. Nine Elms Military Cemetery (11)** is south of the village on the main Arras to Lens road.

Pte George Brownlee, 60ᵗʰ Canadian Infantry (Quebec Regt), who lived in Carleton Street, lies here. There are also two brothers, who died on the same day, Pte W. West and Pte A. West, 14ᵗʰ Canadian Infantry, lie in the same grave.

Follow the N17 towards **Vimy Ridge (12)** where the Spirit of Canada weeps for her fallen countrymen. **It is a memorial to 11,285 Canadian officers and men who have no known grave. Pte T. Thompson, 1ˢᵗ Canadian Infantry, named here was formerly a member of Mullavilly Church Lads' Brigade. Also named on the memorial is Pte W. J. Todd, Royal Canadian Regiment from Clonmacate. The 9ᵗʰ April is now a National Day of Remembrance in Canada to mark the anniversary of the 1917 battle.**

There are guided tours of the trenches and tunnels which have remained undisturbed since that time.

Nearby, take the D937, north of Arras and you will reach the **French National Memorial at Notre Dame de Lorette (13).** The contains over 40,000 burials whilst a marked tomb in the floor of the crypt indicates a further 23,000 soldiers.

In the chapel is a memorial to **Louise de Bettignes, a British agent,** whilst on the pulpit there is a plaque which honours **Francois Faber, 1909 winner of the Tour de France.**

On **11ᵗʰ November 2014, French President, Francois Hollande unveiled architect Philippe Prost's, "Ring of Remembrance"(14) , which includes the names of 580,000 who died in northern France during the First World War, and they are listed alphabetically without nationality or rank.**

Take the D937 to **Sains-en-Gohelle.** When you reach the village, **Fosse No. 10 Communal Cemetery Extension (15)** is signposted towards the left.

The grave of Pte Joseph Annesley, 15th Canadian Infantry, (Central Ontario Regiment), can be located. He originated from Ballyfodrin.

Take the D188 to Barlin. **Barlin Communal Cemetery Extension (16)** is north of the village on the D171 to Houchin.

Pte J. Cunningham VC, 2nd Leinster Regiment, lies alongside Pte Willie Chapman, 54th Canadian Infantry, (Central Ontario Regiment) who came from Portadown and Pte T. R. Abraham, 102nd Canadian Infantry, (Central Ontario Regiment), whose home was in Henry Street.

Follow the D179 to **Noeux-Les-Mines where the Communal Cemetery (17)**, is found north of the town on the D65 to Labourse.

There are two Victoria Cross recipients lying here as well as Sgt S. Gracey MM, Canadian Army Medical Corps, who lived on the Carrickblacker Road.

Continue on the D65 to **Sailly-Labourse where the Communal Cemetery Extension (18)** is found on the N43 road to Lens.

Buried here is Pte James McKeown, 5th Royal Irish Fusiliers who came from Obin's Street.

It is necessary now to backtrack on the N43 , taking the D165 to Loos-en-Gohelle.

Here the **Loos Memorial (19)** records over 20,000 officers and men who fell in the area from the River Lys to west of Grenay, including **Capt The Hon Fergus Bowes-Lyon** brother of the late Her Majesty the Queen Mother. The adjoining **Dud Corner Cemetery** has roughly 1800 burials. **Four Portadown fatalities are named as is Pte James Speedie, 7th Cameron Highlanders, a member of the famous Heart of Midlothian side, all of whom had enlisted "en masse."**

Continue on the D165 to join the D947 towards Haisnes. At **Hulluch** take the D39 towards Vermelles. You will reach **Bois-Carre Military Cemetery (20) which is situated in the middle of fields where Pte Patrick Monaghan, 7th Royal Irish Fusiliers, a native of Marley Street is buried alongside Sgt H E Nunn, 1st Norfolk Regiment from Woodside Street.**

Continue towards Vermelles and **Vermelles British Cemetery (21)** is found at the junction of the D75 to Mazingarbe. Buried here is **Gunner George Rodgers, 59th Siege Battery, Royal Garrison Artillery who came from Ballygargan.**

Continue on the road to Mazingarbe and join the N43 to enter Bethune. **Bethune Town Cemetery (22)** can easily be found from any point in Bethune, by following the French sign for **"Cimetiere Nord".**

The cemetery contains the graves of over 260 servicemen from a range of Irish regiments.

Cambrai Memorial
Louverval

The Cambrai Memorial commemorates more than 7, 038 servicemen of the United Kingdom and South Africa who died in the Battle of Cambrai in November and December 1917 and whose graves are not known. Sir Douglas Haig described the objectives of the Cambrai operations as the gaining of a "local success by a sudden attack at a point where the enemy did not suspect it."

Here, tanks would be used to break through the German wire, with no preliminary artillery bombardment. The attack began on the morning of 20th November 1917 and initial advances were remarkable. A halt was called for rest two days later. This allowed the Germans to bring forward reinforcements. From 23rd – 28th November the fighting was concentrated around Bourlon Wood.

Fighting ensued for several days and the initial ground gained, was lost.

The memorial was designed by Sir Chalton Bradshaw and the sculptor was C. S. Jagger.

The chateau at Louverval was taken by the 56th Australian Infantry Battalion on 2nd April 1917. It was regained by the Germans during their advance in 1918 until it was re-taken in the following September.

2ⁿᵈ Lt J S Emerson VC, 9ᵗʰ Royal Inniskilling Fusiliers, 6ᵗʰ December 1917 - Panel 5-6. He was born in Collen, Co. Louth. His Victoria Cross was won for his actions on 6ᵗʰ December 1917, on the Hindenburg Line, north of La Vacquerie in France.

"He led his company in an attack and cleared 400 yards of trench. Though wounded, when the enemy attacked in superior numbers,, he sprang out of the trench with eight men and met the attack in the open, killing many and taking six prisoners. For three hours after this, all other officers having become casualties, he remained with his company, refusing to go to the dressing station and repeatedly repelled bombing attacks. Later when the enemy attacked again, in superior numbers, he led his men to repel the attack and was mortally wounded."

Sgt T. Clements MM, 17151, 9ᵗʰ Royal Irish Fusiliers, 22ⁿᵈ November 1917 - Panel 10 - Ahorey. He enlisted in Oct/Nov 1914 when he was aged 16. As a Corporal he took part in a fighting patrol on 14ᵗʰ August 1916 with Lt Godson earning a Military Medal. He was wounded in the Battle of Langemarck on 16ᵗʰ August 1917. He was killed in action on 22ⁿᵈ November at Moeuvres.

Pte S. Malcolmson 14454, 9ᵗʰ Royal Irish Fusiliers, 23ʳᵈ November 1917 - Panel 10 - Jervis Street. He suffered from shell shock at the Somme, on 1ˢᵗ July 1916, at Hamel. He was killed in action at Moeuvres

Rev T. J. Shovel, 4ᵗʰ Class Chaplain to the Forces, 2ⁿᵈ/2ⁿᵈ Essex Field Ambulance, 5ᵗʰ October 1918 - Grave A 6

Croisilles Railway Cemetery
Croisilles

The 7th Division attacked Croisilles in March 1917 and took it on 2nd April. It was lost on 21st March 1918 and re-captured by 56th (London) Division on the following 28th August, after heavy fighting.

The cemetery was begun by 21st Manchesters at the beginning of April 1917 and used by units of various divisions until January 1918.

There are a huge number of Irish dead here including 34 Connaught Rangers, 16 Royal Munster Fusiliers and 14 Royal Irish Regiment.

Lt J. H. Grayson 6th Royal Irish Regiment, 20th November 1917 - 1 D 7. Although his parents came from Malahide, his father worked in the Bank of Ireland and the family lived in High Street. He enlisted in Portadown.

This is a particular pleasant cemetery with the railway running alongside. There are also a number of German graves.

Vis-en-Artois British Cemetery and Memorial Haucourt

Vis-en Artois and Haucourt are villages on the road from Arras to Cambrai. From Croisilles simply follow the D9. The villages were taken by the Canadian Corps on 27th August 1918.

The **Cemetery** was begun immediately afterwards and was used until the middle of October by fighting units and field ambulances. It consisted originally of 430 graves (in Plots 1 and 2) of which 297 were Canadians and 55 belonged to 2nd Duke of Wellington's Regiment. It was increased after the Armistice by a concentration of graves from the battlefields of April – June 1917, August and September 1918 and from the smaller cemeteries in the neighbourhood.

The **Memorial** bears the names of over 9,000 men who fell in the period from 8th August 1918 to the Armistice, during the Advance to Victory in Picardy and Artois, between the Somme and the Loos, who have no known grave. They belonged to the forces of Great Britain and Ireland and South Africa: the Canadian, Australian and New Zealand forces being commemorated on other memorials to the missing.

Rfn W. Partridge, 53960, 13th King's Own Rifle Corps, 13th September 1918 - Panel 9 - Sarah Street. He was born in Drumgor. He had previously served with the Royal Irish Rifles.

Brown's Copse Military Cemetery Rouex

Roeux was built over a series of caves which helped make its capture in 1917 exceptionally difficult. It was attacked by the 9th (Scottish) Division without success on 12th April. The chemical works close to the railway station were taken by 51st (Highland) Division on 22nd April and after incessant fighting the village was cleared by the same division on 14th May.

The chemical works were lost again and re-taken on 16th May. The Germans re-entered the village at the end of March 1918 and it was finally re-taken by the 51st Division on the following 26th August.

The cemetery is named after a small copse – Bois Rossignol – on the east side.

There are 134 South African servicemen buried in the cemetery.

Pte James Faloon, 22122, 1st Royal Irish Fusiliers, 11th April 1917 - 2 C 28 - Jervis Street. James was a casualty of the Battle of Arras. He was married with three daughters and later moved to Fowler's Entry.

Pte J. H. Weir 6128, 1st Royal Irish Fusiliers, 11th April 1917 - 2 D 14 - Meadow Lane. Killed in action on the same day as Pte Faloon. He was employed as a linen weaver. He was killed during an attack on the chemical works at Roeux. A brother, George, died in Mesopotamia in October 1918.

Sgt John Allan 270157, 16ᵗʰ Royal Scots, 28ᵗʰ April 1917 - 1 H 3

A member of McCrae's Battalion, 16ᵗʰ Royal Scots and a member of Heart of Midlothian Football Club.

In November 1914 with Hearts comfortably leading the First Division, sixteen players removed their football boots, for those in the army, enlisting to fight in France. They became the first British team to sign up "en masse."

Several prominent players perished at the Somme in early July 1916 - Duncan Currie, Ernest Wallis, Harry Wattie and James Boyd.

A Scots folk song penned by Scottish comedian and artist, Hector Nicol and called "Hearts of Glory", has become extremely popular

Lt Donald Mackintosh VC, 3ʳᵈ Seaforth Highlanders, 11ᵗʰ April 1917 - 2 C 49. On 11ᵗʰ April, north of Fampoux, during the initial advance, he was shot in the right leg, but although crippled, continued to lead his men and captured the trench. He then collected men of another company who had lost their leader and drove back a counter-attack when he was again wounded. Although unable to stand, he nevertheless continued to control the situation.

With only 15 men left he ordered them to be ready to advance to their final objective and with great difficulty got out of the trench, encouraging them to advance. He was wounded yet again and fell.

His dying moments are immortalised on Fette's College War Memorial, which features a statue of him urging his men onwards and bears the legend – "Carry On."

Beaurains Road Cemetery
Beaurains

From Fampoux take the D42 in the direction of Arras. Filter right on D60 and take the turn off for Beaurains. The cemetery is found on the D17, north of the village.

The cemetery was begun a few days before Beaurains was captured by Commonwealth forces on 18th March 1917. It was a month before the Battle of Arras began and the Germans were close by in Tilloy-les-Mofflaines.

The cemetery was used and sometimes called Ronville Forward Cemetery until the beginning of June by the 14th (Light) Division Burial Officer and by fighting units.

It was used again for a short time in August and September 1918, in the Second Battle of Arras. It contained at the date of the Armistice, the graves of 129 British soldiers, 15 French soldiers and four German prisoners.

It was enlarged after the Armistice when graves were brought in from surrounding battlefields and smaller cemeteries. It now contains 331 burials.

Pte Samuel Robinson 2137998, 72nd Canadian Infantry (British Columbia Regiment), 2nd September 1918 - B 31. He lived at Drumheriff. He had emigrated to Canada and enlisted in Vancouver.

The Arras Memorial
Faubourg d'Amiens Cemetery
Arras

The Arras Memorial is in the Faubourg d'Amiens Cemetery which is in the Boulevard General de Gaulle, near the Citadel, about two kilometres west of the railway station.

The French handed Arras over to the Commonwealth forces in the Spring of 1916 and its systems of tunnels were used and developed in preparation for the major offensive planned for 1917.

The most conspicuous events of this period were the Arras Offensive, April to May 1917 and the German attack of the Spring of 1918.

The Commonwealth part of the cemetery began in March 1916 behind the French Military Cemetery established earlier. It was used until November 1918. The French graves were removed after World War One for the construction of the Arras Memorial and the Arras Flying Services Memorial.

The Arras Memorial

This memorial contains the names of 35,000 soldiers from the United Kingdom, South Africa and New Zealand who died in the Arras sector from the Spring of 1916 until 7th August 1918, the Eve of Advance to Victory, and who have no known grave.

The regiments are named by panel or bay numbers.

A large number of wedding photographs usually with a military connection are taken here.

The Arras Flying Services Memorial

This memorial commemorates nearly 1,000 airmen of the Royal Naval Air Service, Royal Flying Corps and Royal Air Force who were killed on the Western Front and who have no known grave. The cemetery and memorial were designed by Sir Edward Lutyens and the sculpture was by Sir William Dick Reid.

2nd Lt John Collen, 7th Squadron, Royal Flying Corps, 25th October 1916

He lived in Stewart Avenue. John originally enlisted in the 7th Leinster Regiment and later received a commission to the 7th Royal Inniskilling Fusiliers. He later attached to 7th Squadron, Royal Flying Corps. He was shot down over Puiseux.

He was one of 190 officials from the Bank of Ireland who enlisted during the war. Of these 33 were killed and a further 47 wounded. He was a member of the "Under Age Four", of Portadown Rowing Club. All four were killed during the war.

Pte J. J. Proctor, 32444, 15th Royal Scots, 28th April 1917 - Bay 1-2. His family lived in Harcourt Street. His brother Archie fought in Gallipoli and died of pneumonia.

Capt S. E. McClatchey, Royal Army Medical corps, 18th Welsh Regiment, 25th March 1918 - Bay 10. His father was Town Clerk in Portadown and the family lived in Woodhouse Street.

Pte J. McKee, 7953, 2nd Royal Munster Fusiliers, 25th June 1916 - Bay 9. Born in Drumcree and lived in Curran Street.

Pte F. Monaghan, 6394, 1st Royal Irish Fusiliers, 11th April 1917 - Bay 9. Employed in Spence Bryson's. Lived in Bann Street.

Pte T. Magowan, 40144, 10th Cameron Highlanders (Scottish Rifles), 21st December 1917, Grave V11 A 15. Lived at Annaghmore.

Capt John George Anderson MC, Mentioned in Despatches, Royal Army Medical Corps, Attached 1/6th Black Watch (Royal Highlanders), 21st March 1018 - Bay 10.

George was a member of Banbridge Hockey Club. He undertook his studies at Edinburgh University and played international hockey for Scotland in 1910.

He came from Roselawn, Banbridge and one of Ulster Hockey Union's oldest cup competition, the Anderson Cup, still played for to this day is in his memory.

Incidentally the first winners of the competition in 1920 was Banbridge Hockey Club.

Banbridge Hockey Club had 27 members who served during the First World War, eight of whom were killed, four of them being international players.

17th Middlesex (Footballers' Battalion) Regiment
Bay 7

L/Sgt Walter Tull F/55

Grandson of a slave, he was of mixed ethnicity. Originally from Barbados, Tull's father Daniel came to England in 1876. He married a local girl Alice Palmer and had five children. After Alice died in 1895 he married Clara Palmer, his wife's niece. Clara died in 1897 by which time a child was born. Unable to support his family, Walter and his brother Edward were placed in a Methodist run Children's Home and Orphanage in East London.

After serving an apprenticeship Walter started playing football for Clapton, an amateur club. In 1909 he signed for Tottenham Hotspur after accompanying them on a tour to South America.

In 1909 - 1910 he played in six of the first seven matches but did not keep his place, his confidence being undermined by racial abuse.

In 1911 he signed for Northampton Town, and as a half-back he made over 100 appearances for the club. In 1914 he enlisted in the 17th Middlesex.

He was killed in action near Favreuil on 25th March 1918. On 11th July 1999, a memorial was erected to Walter by Northampton Town.

Its inscription reads, "Through his actions W. J. D. Tull ridiculed the barriers of ignorance that tried to deny people of colour equality with their contemporaries. His life stands testament to a determination to confront

those people and those obstacles that sought to diminish him and the world in which he lived. It reveals a man, though rendered breathless in his prime, whose strong heart still beats strongly. This memorial marks an area of reflection space in a Garden of Remembrance."

On 28th April 1917 the Middlesex Regiment lost 11 officers and 451 other ranks at Oppy Wood.

Pte Bob Whiting F/74

Bob was the former Brighton and Hove Albion goalkeeper who was blown to pieces whilst tending to the wounded.

Renowned for his phenomenal distance of goal-kicks, "Pom-Pom" was reputed to have cleared the opposing team's crossbar from within his own goal area.

He signed for Chelsea in 1906 making 52 appearances and he helped the club to achieve promotion to the first division in his first season.

In 1908 he moved to Brighton and Hove Albion where he became a firm favourite.

Lt Albert Wade

Albert was a former Scottish rugby international who had been attached to 6th Brigade Trench Mortar Battery since December 1916.

He played against England at Inverleith in 1908. He too, was killed at Oppy Wood.

Pte John "Ginger" Williams F/57

Before becoming a professional footballer John had worked at the Mountain Colliery in Flintshire.

He had played football for Bury, Accrington and Birmingham City before moving to Crystal Palace in 1909. Here he once scored five goals in a match against Southend. He was later capped for Wales.

In 1913 he moved to Millwall where he scored 12 goals in 59 appearances for the Lions.

After his death, his last two clubs Crystal Palace and Millwall played a fund-raising match in 1917 at the Den, attracting 5,000 spectators.

In June 1916 the 17th was rotated in and out of the front line around Souchez. He was killed on 5/6/16 at Vimy Ridge.

9th Royal Scots Bay 1 and 2

Sgt John Allen 351266

Born in Greenlaw in Berwickshire he served his time as a joiner. A member of the famous Hearts of Midlothian side whose playing colleagues joined the 16th Royal Scots, McCrae's Battalion.

John joined the 9th Royal Scots, the only Royal Scots battalion to wear kilts and they formed part of the 51st Highland Division.

They took part in the Battle of Arras in which there was a large percentage of casualties, although in the early stages of the battle, some 13,000 German prisoners had been taken.

A patrol from the 9th Royal Scots had been sent out to reconnoitre a wood near to Roeux. The patrol was engaged in crossfire and John was killed on 22nd April 1917.

He became the last Hearts player to be killed in action.

L/Sgt Alexander (Sandy) Turnbull 28427 8th East Surrey Regiment 3rd May 1917 Bay 7

Sandy was born in Scotland and joined Manchester City in 1903. **He won an F A Cup Final medal with them when they defeated Bolton Wanderers.**

City was forced to sell several payers due to making additional payments and **Sandy was signed by Manchester United.** He scored on his debut on 1/1/07 scoring the only goal of the game against Aston Villa.

He went on to play a total of 220 league games and 25 F A Cup matches for United until 1915.

He scored the winning goal in the F A Cup Final against Bristol City in 1909 at Crystal Palace. He also won two First Division titles with United in 1907/1908 and 1910/1911.

He then became instrumental in setting up a Players' Union.

In 1915 he received a lifelong ban from football along with several other players being accused of match fixing. He was posthumously re-instated in 1919.

He joined the 8th East Surrey Regiment (The Footballers' Battalion) during the First World War. On 3/5/17 he was involved in a muddled unsuccessful night attack, east of Arras. His body was never found. He is commemorated on the Arras Memorial.

A large number of members of the Masonic Order made the supreme sacrifice during the Great War. A number of them were awarded the Victoria Cross but eight of these recipients were killed during the course of the war. Two of them are named on the Arras Memorial.

Arras Memorial - Bay 6

2nd Lt Basil Horsfall VC (30) 3rd East Lancs Regiment, att. 11th Btn.

He was killed in action on 27th March 1918 at Moyenneville, Arras and was awarded his VC for actions at Moyenneville and Ablainzeville on that date.

He was a member of Sphinx Lodge No.107 of the Irish Constitution in Colombo, Ceylon.

His VC was sold at Sotheby's in 1982 for £9750.

Arras Memorial - Bay 8

Sgt Alexander Edwards VC (32) - 265473 1/6th (Morayshire) Btn, Seaforth Highlanders (Ross-shire Buffs) - Duke of Albany's.

He was killed in action on 24th March 1918 but he had been awarded his VC for actions between 31st July and 1st August during the Battle of Ypres.

He was a member of Pltgaveny Lodge No 681 under the Scottish Constitution which met in Lossiemouth. He had been a member of the Order for only three months prior to his death.

Seaforth Highlanders Bay 8

Pte Peter Johnstone 285280

Peter was born in Cowdenbeath. He was employed as a miner and signed for Glasgow Celtic F C in 1908.

He was a pre-war Glasgow Celtic legend who had won the league title six times in a row under Willie Maley.

Peter was at the heart of the Celtic defence in the 1914 double winning team which had conceded only 14 goals.

His last game for Celtic was the Glasgow Cup Final on 7th October 1916 when his side defeated Clyde by three goals to two.

He died on 16th May 1917 when his regiment was told to capture a chemical factory as part of the Battle of Arras. In the two day battle it was reported that 43 of his regiment died, 26 were missing and 51 wounded. Peter was amongst the missing.

In March 2014 a group was set up in the Benarty area of Fife to remember the fallen war hero. This Memorial Committee plan to set up a memorial garden which will be situated at the entrance to the former Glencraig Colliery where Peter had worked from the age of thirteen.

Seven Glasgow Celtic players made the supreme sacrifice in the Great War, whilst another, William Angus, Highland Light Infantry was awarded the Victoria Cross. After the war William became President of Carluke Rovers F C until his death.

Army Chaplains Department

There are three Chaplains remembered on the Arras Memorial. Two have graves and one is named on Panel 10.

One hundred and seventy two Chaplains of all denominations made the supreme sacrifice in the Great War.

Here too within the grounds, during a visit on 3rd July 2009 I witnessed at first hand the excellent work undertaken by the employees of the Commonwealth War Graves commission who in the blazing sunlight, were concentrating on restoration of some of the headstones.

Le Mur de Fusilles - Take the road left of the memorial and around the corner to the rear of the Citadel, you come to Le Mur de Fusilles which commemorates over 200 partisans from the various resistance groups shot by the Germans 1941 - 1944.

Duisans British Cemetery Etrun

The cemetery lies in Etrun but takes its name from the nearby village of Duisans. The cemetery is one km off the N39 in the angle of the Arras-Habarcq road on a track leading to Haute-Avenses.

The area around Duisans was occupied by Commonwealth forces from March 1916, but it was not until February 1917 that the site for this cemetery was selected for the 8th Casualty Clearing Station.

The first burials took place in March and from the beginning of April the cemetery grew very quickly, with burials being made from the 8th Casualty Clearing Station (until April 1918), the 19th (until March 1918) and the 41st (until July 1917).

Most of the graves belong to the Battle of Arras in 1917 and the trench warfare that followed. From May to August 1918 the cemetery was used by divisions and smaller fighting units for burials from the front line. In the autumn of 1918 the 23rd, 1st Canadian and 4th Canadian Clearing Stations remained at Duisans for two months and the 7th was there from November 1918 until November 1920.

Driver N. S. Holmes, 100913, 15th Divisional Ammunition Column, Royal Field Artillery, 31st March 1918 - V F 76. He lived at Killicomain and attended Seagoe School. He was married in Seagoe Church on Christmas Day 1915. His brother Pte Thomas Holmes was killed at the Somme on 1st July 1916.

Haute-Avenses British Cemetery

The British Cemetery is north of the village on the C2 road leading to Habarcq.

The 51st (Highland) Division started the cemetery in July 1916 and it continued to be used by field ambulances of the divisions holding this part of the line.

The cemetery contains 142 Commonwealth burials of the First World War. There are also eight German war graves.

The cemetery was designed by A J S Hutton.

Pte P. Gilmore 3930, 1st Royal Irish Fusiliers, 14th April 1917 - C 11. He lived at Curran Street.

Ligny-St Flochel British Cemetery Averdoingt

The cemetery is south of the village of Ligny-St Flochel on the D81 towards the village of Averdoingt.

It was started at the beginning of April 1918 when the 7th Casualty Clearing Station came back from Tincques ahead of the German advance. At the end of May the 33rd Casualty Clearing Station arrived from Aire and in August, the No. 1 Casualty Clearing Station from Pernes. There are 632 Commonwealth burials and 46 German graves.

Pte W. H. Preston, 3080368, 5th Canadian Mounted Rifles (Quebec Regiment), 14th September 1918 - IV D 24. He originated in Henry Street, prior to emigrating. He enlisted in Montreal, Canada. He was wounded on 28th August and moved to the No. 10 Casualty Clearing Station where he later died.

Ecoivres Military Cemetery
Mont St Eloi

Ecoivres is a hamlet about 1.5 km from Mont St Eloi on the D49 road. The cemetery is really an extension of the communal cemetery where the French had buried 1000 men. The 46th (North Midland) Division took over the extension with this part of the line in March 1916 and their graves are in rows A to F in Plot 1. Successive divisions used the French military tramway to bring in their dead from the front line trenches .

The attack of the 25th Division on Vimy Ridge in May 1916 is recalled in Plots 1 and 11. The 47th (London) Division burials (July to October 1916) are in Plot 111, Rows A to H, and Canadian graves are an overwhelming majority in the rest of the cemetery.

Plots V and VI contain the graves of men killed in the capture of Vimy Ridge in April 1917, After the war eight men of the 51st (Highland) Division were brought into Plot VIII, Row A, from Bray Military Cemetery.

Pte J. Benson, 198631, 52nd Canadian Infantry (Manitoba Regiment), 2nd April 1917 - VI A 3 - He enlisted in Sioux Lookout, Ontario and came from Drumherriff.

Nine Elms Military Cemetery Thelus

Thelus is a village 6.5 km north of Arras and 1 km east of the main road from Arras to Lens. It is 1.5 km south of the village.

"Nine Elms" was the name given by the army to a group of trees 460 metres east of the Arras-Lens main road between Thelus and Roclincourt. The cemetery was begun, after the capture of Vimy Ridge, by the burial in what is now, Plot 1, Row A of 80 men of the 14th Canadian Infantry Battalion who fell on the 9th April 1917; and this and the next row were filled by June 1917. The rest of the cemetery was made after the Armistice by the concentration of British and French graves from the battlefields of Vimy and Neuville-St Vaast and from other small cemeteries.

Pte George Brownlee, 139515, 60th Canadian Infantry (Quebec Regiment), 26th November 1916 - 1 E 15. Lived in Carleton Street. He enlisted in Toronto, Canada. His brother Cpl Albert Brownlee died in France on 23rd April 1918.

Two brothers Pte W. J. West 797116 and Pte A. W. West 797131, 14th Canadian Infantry (Quebec Regiment) were killed on the same day, 9th April 1917 and lie in the same grave - 1 A 3.

Vimy Ridge

Vimy is 8 km north east of Arras on the D17 towards Lens. The memorial was dedicated to the members of the Canadian Expeditionary Force killed during World War One.

All four Canadian divisions made the assault at the Battle of Vimy Ridge which was part of the Battle of Arras.

The attack at Vimy Ridge which was undertaken by the Canadian Corps on **Easter Monday 9th April 1917** is often seen as the first main success gained by British forces during the course of trench warfare.

The Germans had held the heights at Vimy since late 1914 and the French, who had previously held this part of the line, had failed to re-take it in May and September 1915.

On the Memorial, the Spirit of Canada weeps for her fallen countrymen. The twin pillars stand on the summit of Hill 145.

Vimy Ridge is now owned by the Canadian Government. Standing on the memorial one can see for miles across the Douai Plains, the slag heaps of Lens including the slag heaps of the Double Crassier.

It took architect Walter Seymour Allward eleven years to build.

Unveiled by King Edward VIII in the presence of the French President, Albert Lebrun, on 26th July 1936. It is also a Memorial to the Missing and bears the names of 11,285 Canadian officers and men who died in France and have no known grave.

After extensive renovations, the monument was re-dedicated by Queen Elizabeth II on 9th April 2007.

In recognition of the Canadians' achievements here, April 9th was declared a National Day of Remembrance in Canada to mark the anniversary of the battle.

The ground in the memorial park has been left undisturbed and trenches and shell holes are clearly visible. Grange Tunnel is a network of underground passages.

Pte T. Thompson 6615, 1st Canadian Infantry (West Ontario Regiment), 15th June 1915. A former member of Mullavilly Church Lads' Brigade. He sailed with his battalion on the S S Laurentia on 3rd October 1914.

Pte W. J. Todd 401752, Royal Canadian Regiment, 16th September 1916 - Clonmacate.

Notre Dame de Lorette
French National Memorial

One of the major French National Memorials and Cemeteries, the chapel and lighthouse tower dominate the ridge for which the French fought a long bloody battle. Situated just off the D937, north of Arras it can also be seen quite clearly as you travel towards Arras along the A26 from Calais.

The original oratory was raised in 1727 by N. F. Guilbert. It was destroyed in 1794 and rebuilt in 1815, before being transferred into a small chapel in 1880.

The battle for this small hill lasted for twelve months from October 1914.

The Lantern's first stone was laid by Marshal Petain on 19th June 1921 and inaugurated on 2nd August 1925.

The crypt contains the coffins of Unknown Soldiers from World War Two. A marked tomb on the floor indicates that 23,000 soldiers lie here. The cemetery itself contains 40, 057 burials of which 20,000 have individual graves.

Louise de Bettignies

Inside the chapel is a memorial to Louise de Bettignies. After studying English at Oxford, she found herself in Lille in 1914 which was under German occupation.

She became Alice Dubois, a British agent working under Lord Cameron. She also worked for the French Intelligence Services under the name of Pauline.

Her Unit expanded and she helped Allied soldiers escape to Holland. She was arrested in Tournai on 20th October 1915 and in March 1916 was condemned to death. Her sentence was later commuted.

She was transferred to prison in Sieberg. She was later moved to a hospital in Cologne where she died from pneumonia on 27th September 1918.

Her body was brought to France for burial in 1920 and her original wooden cross was brought to Notre Dame de Lorette and placed in the Basilica.

Francois Faber - 1st Regimente Etrangers

Francois won the Tour de France in 1909 and died near Carency in 1915. His memorial plaque has pride of place on the altar in the Basilica.

General Barbot

The first grave on your left as you enter the cemetery is that of General Barbot of the 77th (French) Division whose impressive Divisional memorial is in Souchez village. He was killed there on 10th May 1915.

He is credited with saving Arras from occupation, in 1914, twice.

General Maistre

Opposite the cemetery on the other side of the road is **a statue to General Maistre and the 21st Army Corps** which was erected in 1925. It was he who had stubbornly assaulted the Hill since December 1914 until 12th May 1915 before the area of the chapel was captured.

The Ring of Remembrance
Notre Dame de Lorette

On the 11th November 2014, the Ring of Remembrance was unveiled by French President, Francois Hollande, in the presence of other notable dignitaries, including the Mayor of Craigavon, Cllr Colin McCusker.

The site at Notre Dame de Lorette is known as "colline sanglante" or "bloody hill". The area was razed to the ground in the First World War.

The eight million euro international memorial is different aesthetically and symbolically from the surrounding cemeteries and obelisks.

Parisian architect Philippe Prost was tasked with designing a structure that would honour ALL war dead. His low rise elliptical structure cast in dark concrete, features the names of 579,606 combatants who lost their lives. These names – collated over two years of research are listed in alphabetical order, with no reference to nationality or rank.

The names are packed together on 500 sheets of bronzed stainless steel panels, each standing three metres tall, zig-zagging around the inner wall of the ring. At night they are lit by spotlights embedded in the paving.

The names start with Aa Tet, who was from the French colonies in Indo-China and end with Zyguitz Rudolf.

There are 42 John Robertson's, 72 Karl Schmidt's and 30 men with the name of William Williams.

The memorial seeks to unite the opposing sides.

Fosse No. 10 Communal Cemetery Extension Sains-en-Gohelle

Take the D937 to Sains-en-Gohelle. The cemetery is well signposted as you reach the village. Fosse 10 is by an old mine and group of miners' houses on the southern outskirts of the village.

The Extension is on the South side of the Communal Cemetery. It was begun in April 1916 and used continuously, mostly by Field Ambulances until October 1918.

It is believed that it takes its name from the local Pithead which once stood nearby.

Not surprisingly there is a huge number of Canadian graves, namely 214, found here.

Out of a total of 472 burials, there are 257 United Kingdom graves.

Pte Joseph A. Annesley, 204585, 15th Canadian Infantry (Central Ontario Regiment), 7th February 1918 - 111 A 2. His original home prior to emigrating was Ballyfodrin.

Barlin Communal Cemetery Extension

Take the D188 to Barlin. The Communal Cemetery and Extension lie north of the village on the D171 road to Houchin.

The Extension was begun by French troops in October 1914 and when they moved south in March 1916, to be replaced by Commonwealth forces, it was used for burials by the 6th Casualty Clearing Station.

In November 1917, Barlin began to be shelled and the hospital was moved back to Ruitz, but the Extension was used again in March and April 1918 during the German advance on this front.

L/Cpl H. M. Murray 475951 Canadian Machine Gun Corps, 25th April - 1 A 62 - Ballinary, Birches

Pte T. R. Abraham, 253019, 102nd Canadian Infantry (Central Ontario Regiment), 17th April 1917 - 1 A 34. He lived in Charles Street but had enlisted in Govenlock, Saskatchewan. He had taken part in the attack on Vimy Ridge but died of wounds at No. 6 Casualty Clearing Station. One of three brothers killed in the war - Pte J. W. Abraham and Pte A. Abraham, both killed on 1st July 1916.

Pte Willie Chapman, 645858, 54th Canadian Infantry (Central Ontario Regiment), 1st April 1917 - 1 G 45. He came from Portadown but his army details do not name the street.

Cpl John Cunningham VC 8916, 2nd Leinster Regiment, 16th April 1917 - 1.A 39. He came from Thurles, County Tipperary.

Noeux-Les-Mines Communal Cemetery

Follow the D179 to Noeux-Les-Mines where the Communal Cemetery is found on the north of the town on the D65 to Labourse.

The cemetery was used by Commonwealth forces, in succession to the French from June 1915 until August 1917. The earlier burials were carried out by units and field ambulances, but in April 1917, the 7th Casualty Clearing Station began to use the cemetery.

The Extension was begun in August 1917 and used until December 1918, chiefly by the 6th and 7th Casualty Clearing Stations.

Sgt S. Gracey MM, 8659, Canadian Army Medical Corps, 15th August 1917 - II K 7. Lived on Carrickblacker Road. He enlisted in Valcartier, Canada. He was awarded the Military Medal for excellent work in the field tending the wounded and sick.

There are two Victoria Cross recipients buried here:

Major Okil Massey Learmouth VC, MC, 2nd Battalion Canadian Infantry, 19th August 1917 - II K 9

Pte Harry W. Brown VC, 10th Canadian Infantry (Alberta Regiment), 17th August 1917 - II J 29

There are also the graves of four servicemen, "Shot at Dawn".

Sailly-Labourse Communal Cemetery Extension

Continue on the D65 to Sailly-Labourse. The Communal Cemetery Extension is found on the N43 road to Lens.

The village was used for rest billets and by field ambulances for much of the First World War.

It was close to the battlefield of Loos, but from October 1915 to September 1918, no considerable advance or retirement took place in this sector.

The Communal Cemetery Extension was begun by 2nd/8th Manchesters in May 1917 and used until October 1918.

There are 217 burials of which 210 are United Kingdom.

Pte James McKeown, 4811, 5th Royal Irish Fusiliers, 29th September 1918 - L 11. He had lived in Obin's Street.

Dud Corner Cemetery
Loos Memorial

Loos-en-Gohelle is a village 5 km NW of Lens. The cemetery is about 1 km west of the village on the N43, Lens to Bethune road.

It stands almost on the site of a German stronghold known as Lens Road Redoubt.

The Loos Memorial forms the back and side of Dud Corner Cemetery and commemorates over 20,000 officers and men who have no known grave, who fell in the area from the River Lys to the old southern boundary of the First Army, and west of Grenay.

Half of the graves in the cemetery are unidentified. There are also fifteen special memorials of men believed to be buried here.

Dud Corner received its name from the large number of unexploded shells found in the neighbourhood after the Armistice.

The majority of dead here fell at the Battle of Loos in 1915, others were buried in succeeding years.

On 14th March 2014, there was a re-burial service for Pte William McAleer and 19 unknown British soldiers of the First World War at Loos Cemetery.

184

It is thought the soldiers perished during the Battle of Loos. Up to now Pte McAleer's name had been commemorated on the Loos Memorial.

Pte McAleer, 13766 was a member of the 7th Royal Scots Fusiliers, part of the 15th (Scottish) Division which had only landed in France in early July 1915.

He was killed in action on 26th September 1915 probably during the attack on Hill 70 at Loos.

The servicemen were laid to rest at 10.00 am in Plot 20, Row G, Graves 20-26. The ceremony was open to the public.

There are four Portadown servicemen commemorated here:

Pte T. Conway 16498, 15th Durham Light Infantry, 25th September 1915, Panels 106/107 - Marley Street

Pte J. H. McArdle, S/1925, 10th Gordon Highlanders, 25th September 1915, Panels 108/112 - Killicomain

L/Cpl H. Watson, 19877, 11th Highland Light Infantry, 25th September 1915, Panels 108/112 - Park Road

Pte G. Overend 14751, 6th Btn Royal Scots, 26th September 1915, Panels 46/49 Brackagh

Pte James H. Speedie, S/16102, 7th Cameron Highlanders, 25th September 1915, Panel 119/124. Born in Edinburgh, he later worked as an insurance clerk. In the 1914-1915 season, he played his first game for Hearts at inside-left, defeating Celtic 2 -0 before 20,000 spectators. He made 34 appearances and scored 9 goals.

He took part in the Battle of Loos on 25th September 1915. His regiment swept past Loos and on to Hill 70, where he met his death.

He was one of the famous Hearts team who joined, "en masse". He also became the first Hearts player to make the supreme sacrifice for his country.

There are FIVE Victoria Cross recipients buried or commemorated :

Capt A. M. Read VC, Northamptonshire Regiment, Royal Flying Corps, 25th September 1915 - VII F 19

Sgt H. Wells VC, 2nd Royal Sussex Regiment, 25th September 1915 - V E 2

Lt Col A. F. Douglas-Hamilton VC, Cmdg 6th Cameron Highlanders, 26th September 1915 - Panel 119/124

Rfn G. Peachment VC, R/11941, 2nd King's Royal Rifle corps, 25th September 1915, Panel 101/102

2nd Lt F. B. Wearne VC, 3rd Battalion, Att. 10th Essex Regiment, 28th July 1917, Panel 85/87

Capt The Hon Fergus Bowes-Lyon, 8th Black Watch, 27th September 1915, Panel 78/83 - Brother of Her Majesty The Queen Mother.

2nd Lt C. H. Sorley, 7th Suffolk Regiment, 13th October 1915, Panel 37/38 - a highly regarded war poet.

Bois-Carre Military Cemetery Haisnes

Haisnes is a village just south of Le Bassee, but Bois-Carre Military Cemetery is 2km south of the village, south-west of the village of Hulluch. Take the D39 towards Vermelles and you will find the cemetery in the middle of fields.

Haisnes village remained in German hands until the final advance in the year 1918, but parts of the commune were gained by British troops in the Battle of Loos.

Bois-Carre Military Cemetery is named from a small copse about 274 metres to the South-West.

It was begun in September 1915, and used, largely by the 16th (Irish) Division, until August 1916, one more grave being added in March 1918.

The irregularity of the rows in this cemetery is due to the often extreme circumstances in this area.

There are 227 burials in this cemetery.

Sgt H. E .Nunn 7849, 1st Norfolk Regiment, 8th May 1917 - 1 D 13. He lived in Woodhouse Street

Pte Patrick J. Monaghan, 20541, 7th Royal Irish Fusiliers, 22nd August 1916 - Special Memorial 22. He lived in Marley Street. He was in the act of writing a letter home, when a shell nearby exploded, killing him instantly.

Vermelles British Cemetery

Continue on the D39 towards Vermelles and the Military Cemetery is found at the junction of D75 to Mazingarbe.

Vermelles was in German hands from the middle of October 1914 until the beginning of September 1914, when it was recaptured by the French. The cemetery was begun in August 1915, though a few graves are slightly earlier, and during the Battle of Loos, when the Chateau was used as a dressing station, Plot 1 was completed.

It was laid out and fenced by Pioneers of 1st Gloucesters and known as a time as, "Gloucesters' Graveyard." The remaining plots were made by the Divisions (from the Dismounted Cavalry Division onwards), holding the line 1.6 km east of the cemetery until April 1917, and they incorporated a few isolated French graves of October 1914.

From April 1917, to the Armistice, the cemetery was closed, but after the Armistice graves were brought in from the battlefields to the east.

Gunner George Rodgers, 32466, 59th Siege Battery, Royal Garrison Artillery, 19th September 1915 - 1 F 30. He was born at Knocknamuckley but lived in Ballygargan.

Bethune Town Cemetery

Continue on the road to Mazingarbe and join the N43 to enter Bethune.

Bethune is rich in architectural heritage and history. It has a large paved square with shops and cafes and is a suitable place to take a rest after an exhausting itinerary.

During the war Bethune was mostly defended by British, Canadian and Indian forces. It was an important railway junction and hospital site, holding the 33rd Casualty Station until December 1917.

During the second stage of the Ludendorff Offensive in April 1918, German forces reached Locon, 3 km distant. On 21st May 1918, the Germans launched a bombardment which virtually flattened the town. The whole town has been rebuilt.

There are a number of hotels and guest houses in and around Bethune, should you decide a rest would be welcome.

Bethune Town Cemetery can easily be found from any point in Bethune by following the French sign for "Cimitiere Nord".

For much of the First World War, Bethune was comparatively free from bombardment, and remained an important railway and hospital centre, as well as a corps and divisional headquarters. The 33rd Casualty Clearing Station was in the town until December 1917.

Early in 1918, Bethune began to suffer from constant shellfire and in April 1918, the Germans reached Locon, five kilometres to the north. The bombardment of the 21st May did great damage to the town and it was not until October that pressure from the Germans relaxed.

Buried within the cemetery are 26 men of the 1/8th Manchester Regiment who were killed by a bomb on 22nd December 1917 while marching to rest billets.

There are over 260 servicemen, belonging to various Irish regiments interred in this cemetery.

Royal Munster Fusiliers 56: Royal Inniskilling Fusiliers 45: Royal Irish Fusiliers 41: Irish Guards 32: Royal Dublin Fusiliers 31: Royal Irish Rifles 21: Royal Irish Regiment 18: Connaught Rangers 14: 129th Duke of Connaught's Own Baluchis 2: 8th (King's Royal Irish) Hussars 1.

There are also four soldiers who were, "Shot at Dawn."

L/Cpl Joseph McCourt, 18220, 8th Royal Irish Fusiliers, 27th May 1916 - V D 42. He lived in Obin's Street.

Pte Joseph Mann, 1763, 1st Irish Guards, 19th May 1915 - III D 65. He came from Milford but is related to the Mann and Mullan families in Portadown.

Lt Frank A. De Pass VC, 34th Prince Albert Victor's Own Poona Horse, 25th November 1914 I A 24. His citation reads, "For conspicuous bravery near Festubert, on 24th November, in entering a German sap and destroying a traverse in the face of the enemy's bombs, and for subsequently rescuing, under fire, a wounded man who was lying exposed in the open."

Route 5 - Bethune to Bailleul

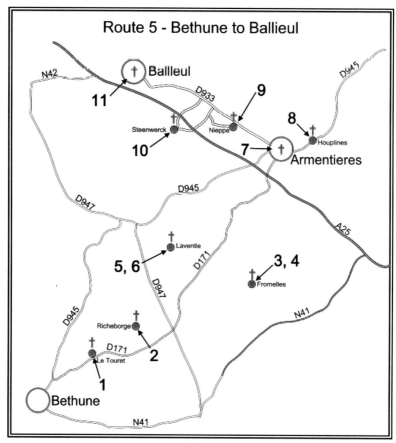

Route 5 - Bethune to Ballieul

1. Le Touret Memorial and Cemetery, Festubert
2. Rue Des Berceaux Military Cemetery, Richebourg L,Avoue
3. Fromelles (Pheasant Wood) Cemetery
4. VC Corner, Fromelles
5. Royal Irish Rifles Graveyard, Laventie
6. Laventie Military Cemetery
7. Cite Bonjean Military Cemetery, Armentieres
8. Houplines Communal Cemetery Extension
9. Nieppe Communal Cemetery
10. Trois Arbres Cemetery, Steenwerck
11. Bailleul Extension

Route 5 Bethune to Bailleul

Leaving Bethune on the D945 in the direction of Estaires, you will shortly branch off via the D171 to Le Touret where approximately 1 km after the village you will find **Le Touret Memorial and Cemetery (1)** on the right hand side of the road.

The Le Touret Memorial commemorates over 15,000 men who fell in the area before 15th September 1915 in the battles at Le Bassee, Givenchy, Aubers Ridge and Neuve Chapelle.

There are four Victoria Cross recipients named as is Pte M. Quinn from Castle Avenue and Pte J. Chambers from Queen Street who both served in 2nd South Lancs Regiment.

Also commemorated is Pte Henry berry, 4th Gloucestershire Regiment who was an English rugby international.

Travel onwards **to Richebourg L'Avou**e and from the church in the village head south on the D166 where 950 metres along you will reach Rue-Des-Berceaux Military Cemetery (2).

One of the greatest tennis champions of all time, Capt Tony Wilding, Royal Marine (Armoured Car Division), is interred in the cemetery.

Continue through the villages of **Neuve Chapelle and Aubers Ridge prior to reaching Fromelles**. The village is signposted off the main N4 Lille to La Bassee road.

Fromelles (Pheasant Wood) Cemetery (3) is the first new war cemetery to be built by the Commonwealth War Graves Commission since the 1960's. In 2008, the remains of 250 soldiers of the 5th Australian and 61st (South Midland) Divisions who fell in the Battle of Fromelles 1916 were found in communal pits. Many were identified using modern DNA techniques and each was buried with full military honours.

The cemetery was officially opened on the anniversary of the battle, on 19th July 2010, in the presence of HRH The Prince of Wales and Her Excellency Ms Quentin Bryce, Governor-General of Australia.

Two km outside Fromelles on the road to Sailly is **VC Corner, Australian Cemetery and Memorial (4)**. Here lie 400 men who died in the **Battle of Fromelles** but who could not be identified. The Memorial commemorates 1,299 casualties.

Alongside, **"The Cobbers"** sculpture depicts an Australian soldier carrying a wounded mate. It was unveiled on 5th July 1988.

Laventie is close by and well signposted. **The Royal Irish Rifles Graveyard (5)** is on a minor road from Fleurbaix to Couture. Here you will find the grave of yet another sportsman, **Capt Wyndham Halswelle, 1st Highland Light Infantry was a 1908 Olympic 400 metres gold medal winner. His medal proved very contentious as having been the only walkover in the history of the Olympics.**

Take the D166 from Laventie and turn right. You will reach **Laventie Military Cemetery (6) where Irish flying ace , Capt George McElroy MC and Two Bars; DFC and Bar lies buried.**

Take the D22 to Armentieres and follow the D95 towards Estaires. **Cite Bonjean Military Cemetery (7)** is signposted just off this road just before Erquinghem-sur-la Lys.

There are over 2000 burials of which one is Pte Thomas J McCann, 1st Royal Irish Fusiliers who lived in Wilson Street. Another Portadown man, Pte John Cordy, 2/5th King's Own, Royal Lancaster Regiment, who came from Carn, is also buried here.

Drive out of Armentieres towards Houplines on the D945. **Houplines Communal Cemetery Extension (8)** is on the north-west of the Communal Cemetery.

Four Portadown men lie here, three from the 1st Royal Irish Fusiliers, Pte T Woodhouse from Breagh, Drumcree, Pte F. W. Todd, Sandy Row and Pte J. Woods, Charles Street. One member of the 2nd Royal Irish Fusiliers, Pte H. Sinnamon came from Mountcharles.

From Houplines head for the D933 and turn on to the D77 to Nieppe. On the south-east side of the crossroads to Coutre-Rue lies **Nieppe Communal Cemetery (9).**

In this small cemetery of 62 burials lies Pte Maxwell Stothers, 9th Royal Irish Fusiliers of Bright Street.

Keep on the D77 to Steenwerck . **Trois Arbres Cemetery (10)** is found midway between the village and the main road from Armentieres to Bailleul.

Buried here is Pte William Hanvey, 1st Royal Irish Fusiliers from Derryanville.

Follow the D38 to join D933 and travel into Bailleul. From Grand Place take the leper road and 400 metres along is a sign indicating **Bailleul Extension (11).**

There are three Portadown casualties. Sgt W. Johnston, 13th Royal Irish Rifles, Drumcree: Sgt J. Dalzell, 1st Royal Irish Fusiliers, Fowler's Entry and Cpl G. Robinson MM from Druminally.

The cemetery contains 4,403 burials.

On leaving the cemetery, note there is a one-way system, which will take **you back to the town centre.**

In Bailleul the Tourist Office is located at 3 Grand Place, tel: 003332843200. There you will be able to obtain information on hotel or bed and breakfast accommodation. There are numerous restaurants.

Le Touret Military Cemetery and Memorial Festubert

Leave Bethune on the D945 in the direction of Estaires, branch off on the D171 to Le Touret and after 1 km you will reach Le Touret Military Cemetery and Memorial.

The Le Touret Memorial commemorates over 15,000 men who fell in the area before 15th September 1915 in the battles of La Bassee, Givenchy, Aubers Ridge and Neuve Chapelle.

Pte M. Quinn, 7655, 2nd South Lancs Regiment, 24th October 1914, Panel 23 - Castle Avenue

Pte J. Chambers, 6621,2nd South Lancs Regiment, 24th October 1914 - Panel 23 - Queen Street

Cpl Henry Berry,5711, 4th Gloucestershire Regiment, 9th May 1915 - Panel 17 - A Gloucester and England rugby international. He played every game in the victorious Five Nations campaign in 1910, scoring two tries in two matches.

Four Victoria Cross recipients are named - Pte A. Acton VC, 10694, 16th May 1915, Border Regiment – Panel 15: Cpl W Anderson VC, 8191, 13th March 1915, 2nd Yorkshire Regiment – Panel 12: Pte E Barber VC, 15518, 12th March 1915 – Panel 2: Pte J Rivers VC, 6016, 1st Sherwood Foresters (Notts and Derby Regiment),12th March 1915 - Panel 26/27.

Rue-des-Berceaux Military Cemetery Richebourg L'Avoue

Richebourg is a village and commune to the north of Bethune. From the church in the village head south on the D166. The cemetery will be found on the right hand side 950 metres from the church.

It was begun in 1915 and used until February 1917. Two German soldiers were buried in it in April 1918 and in September 1918 some further British burials were made.

Plot II was made after the Armistice by the concentration of graves from the battlefields in the area and from other smaller cemeteries.

Captain Tony Wilding Royal Marines (Armoured Car Division) 9th May 1915 2 D 37

Tony was born in Christchurch, New Zealand. He entered Cambridge University in 1902.

He became a champion tennis player and was a Wimbledon Champion on seven occasions, 4 singles and three doubles titles from 1907 - 1913.

He helped Australasia win the Davis Cup and secured two Australasia Open Titles. He won at least 112 singles titles.

He qualified as a barrister and solicitor at the Supreme Court of New Zealand.

In 1912 he won a bronze medal at the Stockholm Olympics in the men's singles for Australia.

In the early 1900's he played for the Canterbury Cricket Club in two first class matches.

He was killed during the Battle of Aubers Ridge at Neuve Chapelle. **He had been dating and was about to marry Hollywood silent screen star Maxine Elliott.**

In 1978 he was named to the International Tennis Hall of Fame.

Wilding Park, the principal venue for tennis in Christchurch is named in his honour.

Pte John Jordan 3525, 2nd Royal Inniskilling Fusiliers, 14/5/15, 2 D 34 - Hammond St, Moneymore.

Dedication of Fromelles (Pheasant Wood) Military Cemetery

Fromelles is a small village in the Nord / Pas de Calais region. It is signposted off the main N4, Lille to La Bassee road. In Fromelles the cemetery is situated opposite the church on Rue de la Basse Ville.

Ninety four years after they were dumped in a mass grave, 250 First World War soldiers were finally honoured.

Men from the 5th Australian and 61st (South Midland) Division had been slaughtered on 19th June 1916 at Fromelles. The finding of their remains in mass graves had occurred between May and September 2008.

Using DNA techniques, the process of identifying the skeletons had been painstakingly slow. DNA had been matched with that of relatives, but also the bodies' heights and age ranges have been compared with the service records of those known to have been lost in battle.

My wife and I had by chance travelled to the small village of Fromelles the day prior to the scheduled dedication, simply to acquaint ourselves with the area.

By good fortune, only a few people were about and we were able to witness at close quarters the rehearsal ceremony for the burial of the Unknown Soldier. Twenty four hours later Fromelles would be besieged by members of Royalty, Government Ministers, top Military brass, the world's media and thousands of everyday folk all wanting to pay their respect to the fallen of Fromelles.

On Monday 19th July 2010, over 1,500 invited guests were in Fromelles as thousands more watched the huge television screens in surrounding fields.

It proved to be a scorching hot day, people of all ages trying to find some shade from the rays of the sun.

Through the narrow streets of Fromelles, the coffin of the final soldier was carried on a First World War wagon from Pheasant Wood .the site of the original communal graves – pulled by horses from The King's Troop Royal Horse Artillery and escorted by soldiers from the British and Australian armies.

HRH Prince Charles walked alongside Her Excellency Ms Quentin Bryce, Governor-General of Australia and other dignitaries behind the coffin as it was drawn through Fromelles on to the site of the new cemetery. The Dedication and Burial Ceremony was solemn and dignified and there was scarcely a dry eye in the congregation gathered.

A Firing Party fired three volleys over the grave, the Last Post was sounded, a One Minute, Silence immaculately observed and Reveille played.

Following the laying of wreaths the ceremony ended with the playing of La Marseillaise, Advance Australia Fair and God Save The Queen.

HRH Prince Charles writing in the Dedication brochure stated, "On this day ninety four years ago, here at Fromelles, the men of the 5th Australian Division and the 61st South Midland Division saw their first major offensive action of the First World War. Tragically, for so many, it was also to be their last. My wife and I are so proud to have come here today to pay our respects to all those who lost their lives in the appalling conflagration that came to be known as the war to end all wars".

Order of Service

Dedication
and
Burial

Fromelles
(Pheasant Wood)
Military Cemetery

19th July 2010

"Almost a century after the Armistice was signed, the First World War may seem a distant memory. Yet its lessons are as relevant today and to today's conflicts as they were at the Battle of Fromelles. Then, as now, the Armed Forces managed somehow to retain their resilience, their patience and fortitude, not to mention an incredible sense of humour in the face of seemingly overwhelming odds.

Then, as now, when the time came they were not found wanting."

Project Manager at the cemetery was a forty seven year old Ulsterman, David Richardson, a former pupil of Dungannon Royal School.

"Over four hundred people travelled from Australia to France for today's service. Fromelles is on a par with Gallipoli in the psyche of the Australians and you could see that at the service in the reaction of the relatives, ninety four years after the battle".

Having experienced memorial services at other sites in France and Belgium over many years and also in Green Hill Cemetery in Gallipoli, I can honestly say on that particular afternoon in Fromelles, when we remembered 250 casualties whose remains were recovered ninety four years after they had been entombed in mass graves, will remain with me for ever.

VC Corner
Australian Cemetery and Memorial
Fromelles

It is situated 2 km north-west of Fromelles on the road to Sailly.

On 19th July 1916 after a preliminary bombardment the 5th Australian and 61st (South and Midland) Divisions undertook what officially is known as the Attack on Fromelles.

The 61st Division attack failed with the loss of over 1,000 officers and men.

The Australian left and centre reached the German trenches and held their second line during the day and night, but the right was held off by fierce machine-gun barrage and only reached the front in isolated groups. **The action was broken off on 20th July after the 5th Australian Division had lost over 5,000 men.**

VC Corner was made after the Armistice. It contains the graves of over 400 Australian soldiers who died in the attack at Fromelles and whose bodies were found on the battlefield, but not a single body could be identified.

It was therefore decided not to mark the individual graves but to record on a screen wall the names of all the Australian soldiers who were killed in the engagement and whose graves were not known.

The memorial, designed by Sir Herbert Baker commemorates 1,299 Australian casualties.

Australian Memorial Park
"Cobbers"
Fromelles

Opened on 5th July 1998, it is on the site of the German strong-point that guarded the spot where the road crossed the German trenches. It was captured by the Australian 14th Brigade and held overnight on July 19th /20th until the attack was called off.

At the entrance is a Ross Bastiaan plaque with explanatory texts. There are the remains of four German bunkers.

The park's centrepiece is the "Cobbers" sculpture of an Australian soldier carrying a wounded mate, based on the real story of Sgt Simon Frazer of the 57th A.I.F. Battalion who rescued many wounded men from the battlefield. Information panels provide a detailed account of the battle. The sculptor was Peter Corlett.

Royal Irish Rifles Graveyard Laventie

The cemetery is 3 km south-west of Laventie on a minor road from Fleurbaix to Couture. The position of the road behind the British front line, during the greater part of the war, made it a natural line of a number of small British cemeteries.

Begun in 1914 the cemetery was first used by 1st Royal Irish Rifles. After the Armistice the graveyard was increased from the battlefields east of Estaires and Bethune.

Capt Wyndham Halswelle 1st Highland Light infantry 31st March 1915 (32) 3 J 2

Wyndham won the Olympic 400 metres Gold Medal in 1908 in a controversial re-run which was the only walkover in the history of the Games. He was a record holder over 200 metres 300 metres and the 400 metres. He was killed by a sniper's bullet at Neuve Chappelle.

Laventie Military Cemetery
La Gorgue

Laventie and La Gorgue are adjoining towns. From Laventie take the D166, and a kilometre further on take the first right turn. The cemetery is 400 m down this narrow road.

Following the Battles of the Lys in April 1918, the Germans occupied both towns until they were retaken by British forces the following September

The cemetery was started in late June 1916 by the 61st (South Midland) Division whose name is synonymous with the Battle of Fromelles on 19th July 1916.

There are almost 550 burials of which 495 are identified.

Captain George McElroy MC and two bars; DFC and bar Royal Flying Corps/ Royal Air Force 31st July 1918 1 C 1

Born in Donnybrook, Dublin, McElroy was a graduate of Trinity College. He served for a period in the Royal Engineers and later received a commission as a Lieutenant in the 1st Royal Irish Regiment.

After attending Woolwich Royal Military Academy he joined the Royal Flying Corps in March 1917. There he came under the tuition of Major "Mick" Manning, also an Irishman from Co. Cork who became Britain's most famous air ace.

In February 1918 he commanded No. 24 Squadron and his air exploits are expertly chronicled in Neil Richardson's, "A Coward if I return; a Hero if I die."

On July 31st he failed to return from a patrol, and the next day a German Atavik dropped a note on British lines to say that McElroy had been killed after being shot down by ground fire.

When he died at the age of 25 years, he had been awarded an MC with two bars and a Distinguished Flying Cross and bar.

McElroy was credited with 47 confirmed kills, the third most successful British air ace of the First World War.

Cite Bonjean Military Cemetery Armentieres

From Armentieres take the D945 to Estaires and the cemetery is signposted just off this road before Erquingham-sur-la- Lys.

Armentieres was occupied by the 4th Division on 17th October 1914 and it remained within Allied lines until its evacuation ahead of the German Advance on 10th April 1918, after a long and heavy bombardment with gas shell. It was occupied by the Germans the next day and was not recovered until 3rd October 1918.

Cite Bonjean Military Cemetery was begun (Plot IX) in October 1914 and during the winter of 1914-1915 it was used for civilian burials, the town cemetery at Le Bizet being too greatly exposed: the civilian graves are now in a separate enclosure.

The cemetery continued to be used by field ambulances and fighting units.

There are 500 German graves in the cemetery.

There are 1,190 UK graves out of a total of 2,604 burials.

Pte J. McCann, 11495, 1st Royal Irish Fusiliers, 16th November 1914 - 1X A 80 - Wilson Street

Pte R. J. Cordy, 241830, 2/5th King's Own, Royal Lancaster Regiment, 22nd August 1917 - VIII D 29 - He lived at Carn, but had enlisted in Barrow. He was killed by a shell whilst sleeping in his dug-out. A member of Tamnificarbet LOL No. 17.

Houplines Communal Cemetery Extension

Houplines is 2 km east of Armentieres on the D945. The Communal Cemetery Extension is located on this road.

Houplines was in Allied hands , near the front line, from 17th October 1914. It fell into German hands in April 1918 during the great advance, but was recovered in September. The village contained four Commonwealth cemeteries in addition to plots in the communal cemetery, but the graves were regrouped after the war and only two cemeteries remain. Houplines Communal Cemetery Extension was begun as "Houplines New Military Cemetery" in October 1914 and used until January 1916, mainly by the 4th and 6th Divisions. It was enlarged after the Armistice when graves were brought in from other burial grounds and from battlefields around Armentieres.

Pte Thomas Woodhouse, 8355, 1st Royal Irish Fusiliers, 21st October 1914 - II C 20 Lived in Breagh, Drumcree.

Pte Francis W Todd,7365, 1st Royal Irish Fusiliers, 22nd October 1914 - II C 21. Lived in Sandy Row.

Pte John Woods, 7445, 1st Royal Irish Fusiliers, 14th November 1914, - II D 11 - Charles Street.

Pte Henry Sinnamon, 18535, 2nd Royal Irish Fusiliers, 1st July 1917 - III A II - Florencecourt.

Nieppe Communal Cemetery Extension

From Houplines head for the D933 and turn on to the D77 for Nieppe. On the south-east side of the crossroads to Coutre Rue lies Nieppe Communal Cemetery Extension.

The village of Nieppe was within the Allied lines from 16th October 1914 until 11th April 1918 when the 34th Division were driven out after hard fighting. Nieppe was recaptured by the 29th Division on 3rd September 1918. Nieppe Communal Cemetery was used by Commonwealth field ambulances and fighting units from October 1914 to November 1917 and again in September and November 1918.

There is a total of 62 burials of which 43 are United Kingdom soldiers.

Pte Maxwell Stothers, 14680, 9th Royal Irish Fusiliers, 7th October 1916 - III B 6. Lived in Bright Street. He died in an accident when a tree branch fell on a guard tent. One brother Pte Jackson Stothers died on 7th January 1917 when his body was found in the Grand Canal, Dublin. Another brother Pte Joseph Stothers was killed at Hamel on 1st July 1916. Another brother Pte William Stothers survived the war although he had been wounded on 1st July. All four brothers were members of 9th Royal Irish Fusiliers.

Trois Arbres Cemetery
Steenwerck

Stay on the D77 to Steenwerck. Trois Arbres Cemetery is situated to the north-east midway between the village and the main road from Armentieres to Ballieul.

Steenwerck village remained untouched for much of the First World War, but on 10th April 1918, it was captured by the Germans and remained in their possession until the beginning of October. Trois Arbres passed into German hands a day later than Steenwerck, after a rearguard defence by the 34th Division. The site for Trois Arbres Cemetery was chosen for the 2nd Australian Casualty Clearing Station in July 1916, and Plot 1 and the earlier rows of Plot II, were made and used by that hospital until April 1918.

A few further burials were made in the cemetery after the German withdrawal at the end of 1918 and after the Armistice, graves were brought in from the battlefields of Steenwerck, Nieppe, Ballieul and Neuve-Eglise.

There are 1,704 burials of which 997 are United Kingdom.

There are four servicemen who were "Shot at Dawn."

Pte W. Hanvey, 11158, 1st Royal Irish Fusiliers, 8th November 1914 - II A 32

He lived in Jervis Street. He was rescued and brought back by a colleague. He died of wounds at No. 10 Field Ambulance. He was killed during the First Battle of Ypres – 18th October – 22nd November 1914.

The Allies held the Salient for the rest of the war although Ypres was virtually, wounded or missing. Germany's losses totalled 130,000.destroyed by artillery fire. British casualties were 55,000 killed.

Bailleul Communal Cemetery Extension

Bailleul is a large town in France, near the Belgian border, 14 km SE of Ieper and on the main road from St. Omer to Lille.

From the Grand Place take the Ieper road and 400 metres along the cemetery is signposted.

It was occupied on 14th October 1914 by 19th Brigade and the 4th Division. It became an important railhead, air depot and hospital centre for a large number of various battalions and divisions.

It was a Corps HQ until July 1917, when it was severely bombed and shelled, and after the Battle of Bailleul (13th – 15th April 1918) it fell into German hands and was not re-taken until 30th August 1918.

In 1915 the space available in the communal cemetery had been filled, the extension was opened up and used until April 1918 and again in September and after the Armistice graves were brought in from the neighbouring battlefields.

There are 4403 Commonwealth burials of the First World War; Eleven of the graves made in April were destroyed by shellfire and are represented by Special Memorials. There are also 7 Commonwealth graves of World War 2 and 154 German burials from both World Wars.

Sgt W. Johnston, 17935, 13th Royal Irish Rifles, 14th February 1917 - III A 51. Drumcree

Sgt J. Dalzell, 5505, 1st Royal Irish Fusiliers, 12th May 1915 - 1 A 138. Born Drumcree but lived at Fowler's Entry. Died of wounds received in the Battle of Frezenburg or St Julian (Second Ypres).

Cpl J. Robinson MM, 17944, 9th Royal Irish Fusiliers, 12th September 1916 - II F 214. Druminally. Wounded in the liver by a machine gun bullet in River Douve area and died of wounds.

Sgt Thomas Motterhead VC, DCM, 1396, 20th Squadron Royal Flying Corps, 12th January 1917 - III A 126. After his aircraft was enveloped in flames, 9000 feet over Ploegsteert, he flew back making a successful landing but he was pinned under the burning wreckage, dying four days later. He saved his observer's life.

Capt Robert B. Burgess, Royal Engineers 9th December 1915 - II B 63. A native of Kingstown, Dublin and an Irish rugby international.

Pte Leslie Houston, 7378, 2nd Royal Inniskilling Fusiliers, 31st October 1915 - C 15. A player with Linfield football Club.

Brigadier General F. Johnston CB, Cmdg 3rd New Zealand (Rifle) Brigade, formerly North Staffordshire Regiment, 7th August 1917 - III C 260

Brigadier General C. Brown DSO, Cmdg 1st New Zealand Infantry Brigade, 8th June 1917 - III C 265

Pte R. Lockhart 18559, 9th Royal Irish Fusiliers, 12th October 1916 - II F 254. Main Street, Tandragee. He was wounded during the attack at Hamel on 1st July 1916. He was wounded at the raid on Le Petite Douve Farm on 12th October 1916 and died later the same day.

Pte G. C. Ensor, 16423, 7th Canadian Infantry (British Columbia Regiment), 28th April 1915 - 1 B 20. A member of Loughgall Masonic Lodge No. 625.

There are also three servicemen buried here who were, "Shot at Dawn."

Route 6 - Bailleul to Ieper

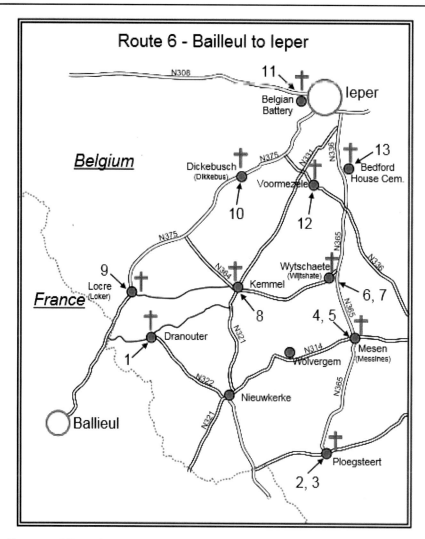

Route 6 - Bailleul to Ieper

1. Dranoutre Military Cemetery, Dranouter

2. Ploegsteert Memorial/Berks Cem./Hyde Park Corner (Royal Berks) Cem

3. Strand Military Cemetery, Ploegsteert

4. Island of Peace Park, Mesen

5. Messines/Frickleton Memorial

6. Irish Divisions Memorial Columns

7. Wytschaete Military Cemetery

8. Kemmel Chateau Military Cemetery

9. Locre Hospice Cem./Major Redmond's grave

10. Dickebusch Old Military Cemetery, Dikkebus

11. Belgian Battery Corner Cemetery, Ieper

12. Voormezeele Enclosure No. 3, Voormezeele

13. Bedford House Cemetery, Ieper

219

Route 6 - Bailleul to Ieper (Ypres)

South of Ieper (Ypres) there is a plethora of cemeteries and interesting places to visit, many with significant connections to both the 36th (Ulster) and 16th (Irish) Divisions. Many are in close proximity and it is difficult to plan a route in circuitous fashion.

Prior to setting off on your journey it would be advantageous to itemise in advance those particular places you wish to visit . The following is merely a suggestion.

From Bailleul travel across the Belgian border on the GR128 to Dranouter. **Dranoutre Military Cemetery (1)** is reached on the Dranouter to Loker road where a CWGC sign indicates off the main road, by means of a track that seems to be leading into a timber yard. You will see the cemetery as you pass the buildings.

Capt R. Jackson, 9th Royal Inniskilling Fusiliers who came from the Birches is buried here.

Now take the D322 towards Ploegsteert via Nieuwkerke. Take the Armentieres road out of Ploegsteert and 1 km further on at the foot of Hill 63 you will reach you will reach the majestic **Ploegsteert Memorial (2) which commemorates more than 11,000 servicemen of the United Kingdom and South Africa who fell in this sector and have no known grave.** The names of five local men are etched on the walls. Within this complex is **Berks Cemetery Extension (2).**

Immediately opposite is **Hyde Park Corner (Royal Berks) Cemetery (2) in which Lt Ronnie Poulton-Palmer, an English rugby international is buried. Close by lies Rfn A. E. French who was sixteen years of age when he was killed.**

Some 300 metres along the road is **Strand Military Cemetery (3)** with over 1000 Commonwealth graves including several men from Ulster. Here you will find the grave of **Pte T. Cordner, 1st Royal Irish Fusiliers who lived in Joseph Street.**

Now head for **Mesen, previously Messines**, on the N365, noted for the battle on 7th June 1917. The immortal words of General Plumer are well remembered, **"Gentlemen, we may not change history tomorrow, but we shall certainly change the geography."** Twenty four mine tunnels containing nearly a million pounds of ammonal were blown.

On the N 365 just before reaching the village of Mesen you will arrive at the **Island of Ireland Peace Park.(4).** The Irish round tower was built as a reconciliation project by young people from all parts of Ireland.

It was officially opened on 11th November 1998 by President Mary McAleece of Ireland in the presence of HRH Queen Elizabeth II and King Albert II of Belgium.

Outside the church in Messines village is a memorial to L/Cpl Samuel Frickleton VC (5) of the New Zealand Rifle Brigade which was unveiled on 7th June 2007.

View the 11th century crypt within the church. The Germans had used there for their Headquarters. It was restored to its original state in 1931.

Take the N365 Armentiere/Ieper road and you will soon reach the village of Wytschaete. Some 500 metres prior to reaching the village you will come across two Memorial Columns (6) unveiled by the King of Belgium on 10th June 2007 to commemorate the exploits of the 36th (Ulster) and 16th (Irish) Divisions, in the taking of the village during the Battle of Messines.

At the village square turn into Wytschaetestraat and Wytschaete Military Cemetery (7) is 500 metres ahead on the north side of the road to Kemmel. Buried in this cemetery is Rfn T. R. Corkin, ,16th (Pioneer) Btn Royal Irish Rifles. He came from Ballygargan and was an uncle of the late Ulster Unionist MP for Upper Bann, Harold McCusker.

Wytschaete was taken by the combined efforts of the 16th (Irish) and 36th (Ulster) Divisions . There is a Celtic cross outside the cemetery in memory of the 16th (Irish) Division.

Travel to Kemmel and on reaching the village drive along Reningelstraat and take first right. At Kemmel Chateau Military Cemetery (8) there are graves from both World Wars. Cpl R Whiteside, 16th Royal Irish Rifles (Pioneers) of Carrickblacker Road, lies here as does Lt Col Guy du Maurier, brother of the novelist Gerald, as well as eleven members of the 250th Tunnelling Company killed at the Petit Bois mine.

Travel to Loker formerly Locre using the N304 and when you reach the N375, take left. reaching the Kemmelbergweg, then immediate right into Godtschalckstraat. Locre Hospice Cemetery (9) is 900 metres on the right hand side of the road. There is a small access path. Outside the right hand wall of the cemetery is the grave of Major Willie Redmond MP, 6th Royal Irish Regiment. He had been carried wounded from the battlefield by Pte John Meeke of the 36th (Ulster) Division. Within the cemetery there is a Brigadier-General and a Lieutenant-Colonel.

Take the N375 to Dikkebus. Turn left of the Dikkebusseweg into a small street called Kerkstraat and 200 metres along, just beyond the village church, turn into Neerplats.

Dickebusch Old Military Cemetery (10) is on this street. In the cemetery is the grave of Pte D. H. Cranston, 2ⁿᵈ Royal Irish Fusiliers who lived in Garvaghy Road.

Take the N 75 out of Dikkebus in the direction of Ieper. When you come to a sharp left hand bend take it and first right into Frezenburgstraat and 200 metres further on is Omloopstraat where **Belgian Battery Corner Cemetery (11) is found. Buried here is Pte W. A. Allen, 2ⁿᵈ Australian Imperial Force who had lived in Carleton Street, prior to emigrating.**

Return via the N375 in the direction from whence you came and when you reach Ruuschaartstraat, take left to reach Voormezele.

Voormezeele Enclosure No. 3 (12) is well signposted. Here is the grave of Rfn J Gracey, 2ⁿᵈ Royal Irish Rifles who lived in Florence Court.

Now travel via Sint-Elooisweg to the N336 and join N365 towards Ieper. **Bedford House Cemetery (13)** is easily located and has ample parking facilities.

Two Portadown men are interred here. Pte W. J. Campbell, 9ᵗʰ Royal Irish Fusiliers who came from Montague Street and Pte James Benson, 19ᵗʰ Canadian Infantry (Central Ontario Regiment), whose family home was Derrykeevan Post Office.

Drive directly to **Ieper (Ypres)** where there is a multitude of shops, restaurants and hotels. It is an excellent stopping off point for overnight stays.

The main attraction is the **Menin Gate Memorial** which bears the names of 54,896 men who have no known grave. **Every night at 20.00 hrs** the traffic is stopped from driving through the archway and the **Last Post** is sounded and wreaths led by many organisations. A moving ceremony and despite how many times you visit , it will still bring a tear to your eye.

Delegates representing The Somme Association, Northern Ireland lay a wreath at the Menin Gate ceremony on 29ᵗʰ June 2006. Cllr Joan Baird MBE, Banbridge District Council is immediate right.

Dranoutre Military Cemetery
Dranouter

When you reach the village of Dranouter look for the CWGC sign which indicates that the cemetery is set back off the road behind a large builder's yard and is difficult to spot until you pass the buildings.

After being occupied by 1st Cavalry Division on 14th October 1914, the village of Dranoutre remained in Allied hands until the Germans captured it from the French in April 1918. The village was finally retaken on 30th August 1918 by the 30th Division.

The military cemetery was opened in July 1915 in succession to Dranoutre Churchyard which had been used for burials up until then.

The cemetery continued to be used by Field Ambulances until March 1918. In 1923 it became necessary to move 19 graves from the Churchyard to enable the rebuilding of the church.

There are several members of the 9th Royal Inniskilling Fusiliers interred in this cemetery.

Cpl R. Jackson, 9/19311, 9th Royal Inniskilling Fusiliers, 1st March 1917 - 1 H 19. He lived in the Birches.

2nd Lt R. J. Sleator, 9th Royal Irish Fusiliers, 8th May 1917 - II H 8. He was a travelling salesman prior to enlisting. He died after shooting himself with his revolver in the Quartermaster's Store. This was after spending several months in hospital suffering from severe depression. A member of Masonic Lodge No. 39 Armagh.

223

Ploegsteert Memorial
Berks Cemetery Extension
Hyde Park Corner (Royal Berks) Cemetery

From Dranouter take the N322 via Nieuwkerke to Ploegsteert. About 1 km out of Ploegsteert on the Armentieres road you will reach the majestic Ploegsteert Memorial to the Missing and associated cemeteries.

The Ploegsteert Memorial commemorates more than 11,000 servicemen of the United Kingdom and South African forces who died in this sector during the First World War and who have no known grave.

The memorial serves the area Caestre-Dranoutre-Warneton to the north, to Haverskerque-Estaires- Fournes to the south, including the towns of Hazebrouck, Merville,Bailleul and Armentieres, the Forest of Nieppe and Ploegsteert Wood.

Most of those named on the memorial did not die in major offensives but were killed in the course of day to day trench warfare which characterised this part of the line, or in small scale set engagements , usually carried out in support of the major attacks elsewhere.

The sounding of The Last Post takes place at the Memorial on the first Friday of every month at 7.00 p m.

Panel 4 - Royal Irish Regiment

Pte T. H. Allen, 3417, 8th Royal Irish Regiment, 6th September 1918 - Mourneview Street.

Panel 7 - Sherwood Foresters

Pte J. Beattie, 646, 2nd Sherwood Foresters (Notts and Derby Regiment), 24th November 1914 - Montague Street

Panel 9 - Royal Irish Fusiliers

L/Cpl W. H. Armstrong DCM, 7599, 1st Royal Irish Fusiliers, 11th May 1915 - Irwin Street. He was killed near Armentieres.

Pte J. Hewitt, 14306, 1st Royal Irish Fusiliers, 4th September 1918 - West Street. He was killed south of Wulverghem.

Pte W. Sharpe, 5851, 1st Royal Irish Fusiliers, 4th September 1918 - James Street. Born in Laurelvale.

Berks Cemetery Extension

Berks Cemetery Extension in which Ploegsteert Memorial stands, was begun in June 1916 and used continuously until September 1917

At the Armistice the extension comprised Plot 1 only, but Plots II and III, were added in 1930 when graves were brought in from Rosenberg Chateau Military Cemetery and Extension, about 1 km to the north-west when it was established that these sites could not be acquired in perpetuity.

Rosenberg Chateau Military Cemetery was used by fighting units from November 1914 to August 1916. The Extension was begun in May 1916 and used until March 1918. Together Rosenberg Military Cemetery and Extension were sometimes referred to as "Red Lodge."

The cemetery now contains 876 burials.

Hyde Park Corner (Royal Berks) Cemetery

Hyde Park Corner (Royal Berks) Cemetery is separated from Berks Cemetery Extension by a road. It was begun in April 1915 by the 1st/4th Royal Berkshire Regiment and was used at intervals until November 1917.

Hyde Park Corner was a road junction to the north of Ploegsteert Wood. Hill 63 was to the north-west and nearby were "The Catacombs", deep shelters capable of holding two battalions, which were used from November onwards.

There are 83 Commonwealth burials plus four German graves.

The cemetery, cemetery extension and memorial were designed by H. Chalton Bradshaw, with sculpture by Gilbert Ledward. The memorial was unveiled by the Duke of Brabant on 7th June 1931.

Lt R. W. Poulton-Palmer

Royal Berkshire Regiment

5th May 1915

Ronald Poulton-Palmer was an English rugby international who had captained the side. He was educated at Balliol College, Oxford and played for Oxford Union RFC and the Barbarians.

He is one of three men to score a hat-trick of tries in the Varsity match. He captained England during the 1913-1914 Grand Slam season, scoring four tries against France in 1914.

He changed his name to Poulton-Palmer after inheriting a fortune from his uncle G W Palmer of Huntley and Palmer biscuit company in 1913.

He was one of twenty six internationals who lost their lives in the Great War.

On the morning of 5th May whilst surveying his newly repaired dug-out, he was killed by a sniper's bullet - to a man his platoon wept at their's and the nation's loss.

He is buried in Plot B 11.

Rfn A. E. French, C/7259, King's Royal Rifle Corps, 15th June 1916 - B 2. He was 16 years of age.

Strand Military Cemetery
Ploegsteert

The cemetery lies on the N365 some 300 metres along from Ploegsteert Memorial to the Missing.

Charing Cross was the name given by troops to the point at the end of a trench called the Strand, which led into Ploegsteert Wood. In October 1914, two burials were made at this place, close to an advanced dressing station. The cemetery was not used between October 1914 and April 1917, but in April-July 1917, Plots I –IV were completed.

Plots VII-X were completed after the Armistice, when graves were brought in from some small cemeteries and from the battlefields lying mainly between Wytschaete and Armentieres.

The cemetery was in German hands for a few months in 1918, but was very little used by them.

There are now 1,143 Commonwealth burials, 354 being unidentified.

Pte T. Cordner, 11254, 1st Royal Irish Fusiliers, 9th November 1914 - IX N 4.
He lived at Joseph Street. He met his death trying to save his friend Pte W. Hanvey. At the base of his headstone his sister has placed a plaque and the inscription,**"A good name is better than fame or riches."** He was killed at Houplines.

Capt D. G. H. Auchinleck, 2nd Royal Inniskilling Fusiliers, 21st October 1914, - VIII Q 6. Served in the South African campaign. A member of Dungannon Masonic Lodge No. 9.

Messines now Mesen
Island of Ireland Peace Park

Follow the N365 to Mesen. Nowadays Mesen is a haven of peace and tranquillity. The Battle of Messines is not one that readily comes to most minds when thinking of the First World War , but it was certainly one of the most successful for the Allied forces. Twenty four mine tunnels filled with a total force of nearly a million pounds of ammonal, were blown.

"Gentlemen, we may not change history tomorrow, but we shall certainly change the geography". – Herbert Plumer, 6th June 1917.

The nearby village of Wytschaete was taken by both the 36th (Ulster) and 16th (Irish) Divisions, fighting side by side.

The 16th (Irish) had 748 men killed whilst the 36th (Ulster) had 700 killed during the Battle of Messines.

For this reason, this site was chosen to build the tower, which is known as the Island of Ireland Peace Park.

A round Irish tower, using stone from Tipperary forms the centre piece of the Park. It was built from July – November 1998, as a reconciliation project by young people from all parts of Ireland. It was the brainchild of Paddy Harte, a former Donegal TD in the Dail and Glenn Barr, a prominent Ulster loyalist.

On 11th November 1998, the Peace Park was officially opened by the President of the Irish Republic, Mary McAleece in the presence of HRH Queen Elizabeth II of the United Kingdom and King Albert II of Belgium.

The gardens are laid out to represent the four provinces of Ireland. It is in memory of Irishmen of the two divisions who fought side by side at Messines.

Many people believe that the Irish Peace Tower at Messines, set to right a great wrong, as soldiers from what is now the south of Ireland who went to war in a British uniform were denied jobs in the new Free State when they returned home. Now they are properly remembered by the Irish Government in Dublin.

There are several columns with writings by Irish soldiers, one of the most poignant being by Patrick McGill, London Irish Regiment,

"I wish the sea were not so wide, that parts me from my love

I wish the things men do below, were known to God above.

I wish that I were back again, in the glens of Donegal

They'll call me a coward if I return, but a hero if I fall."

Mesen Village
Samuel Frickleton VC Memorial

Outside the village church, a memorial to L/Cpl Samuel Frickleton VC of the New Zealand Rifle Brigade was unveiled on 7th June 2007, with two of his grandchildren being present. This was on 90th Anniversary of the Battle of Messines.

Along with Cllr Charlie Chittick and Cllr Ross Hussey of Omagh District Council I was privileged to attend alongside a large number of New Zealand representatives, two of whom voiced the Karanga, a traditional Maori calling, to the official party welcoming them to the ceremony.

He was a third generation of Scottish descent but with some Irish blood in him as well as his grandfather had moved to Scotland from County Armagh.

He and three brothers had been part of the New Zealand Expeditionary Force and all had been in action at Gallipoli. After being found unfit for service for a period, he re-enlisted in 1916 with the 3rd New Zealand Rifle Brigade.

He was awarded the Victoria Cross for destroying two German machine guns and their crews on 2nd August 1917.

He was presented with his Victoria Cross by King George V.

He died in Nannae, in the Hutt Valley, New Zealand on 6th September 1971.

A member of the Masonic Order, he belonged to three lodges - Lodge 152 Westport, South Island: Lodge 5 Napier, North Island and Lodge 229 Wellington, North Island.

In a jam packed itinerary on 7th June 2007, the huge New Zealand contingent present was joined by elected representatives from both Northern Ireland and the Republic of Ireland. After the dedication of the Frickleton Memorial those present paraded to the Ceremony of Remembrance at Messines Ridge New Zealand Memorial to the Missing which adjoins Messines Ridge British Cemetery.

The ceremony was made all the more poignant when one noticed that on each New Zealand grave, a red rose for remembrance had been placed.

Cllrs Harkness, Hussey and Chittick with Royal British Legion standard bearers from Londonderry

The Crypt in Messines Church

The 11th Century Roman crypt is a protected building. The Germans used it as a Headquarters and it is believed to have been visited by Adolf Hitler. It was restored in 1931 to its original state, after the devastation of the Great War.

The church was also the subject of a number of water drawings by Adolf Hitler, then a German infantryman. He was treated at the medical station here in 1914.

The cross which can be found in the crypt is in memory of:

Schnieder Anton 3538, Musk, 17th September 1918.

Irish Divisions Memorial Columns
Wytschaete

Travelling from Menin on the N365 towards Wytschaete, and about 500 metres prior to entering the village, you will **see two Memorial Columns, one on each side of the road, honouring the men of the 36th (Ulster) and 16th (Irish) Divisions in recognition of the two divisions fighting side by side, in the Battle of Messines, in taking Wytschaete.**

Unveiled by the King of Belgium, on Sunday 10th June 2007, in the presence of representatives of the Redmond and Meeke families.

During the battle Major Willie Redmond, Royal Irish Regiment 16th (Irish) Division – an Irish Nationalist MP - was seriously wounded and taken from the battlefield by Pte John Meeke MM, a stretcher-bearer with the Royal Inniskilling Fusiliers, 36th (Ulster) Division, to a dressing station, where Major Redmond, later died.

This memorial is the only one in Belgium, which commemorates the 36th (Ulster) Division.

Wytschaete Military Cemetery

Wytschaete, known to the Tommies as "Whitesheet", was taken by the Germans in early 1914 and it remained in German hands until the Commonwealth forces took it on 7th June 1917, during the Battle of Messines.

It will go down in the annals of Irish military history as having been taken by the combined efforts of the 36th (Ulster) Division and the 16th (Irish) Division.

It fell into German hands again in April 1918 before being regained by the Allies again on 28th September 1918.

Out of a total of 1,002 burials, there are 511 from the United Kingdom.

The cemetery is really a concentration cemetery, when after the Armistice, graves were brought in from isolated sites and small cemeteries.

Outside and adjacent to the cemetery is a Celtic Cross in memory of the 16th (Irish) Division.

Rfn T. R. Corkin, 186, 16th (Pioneer) Battalion, Royal Irish Rifles, 21st June 1917 - I F 4. He lived at Ballygargan. He was an uncle of the late Harold McCusker, Ulster Unionist MP for Upper Bann.

Kemmel Chateau Military Cemetery

Take Wytschaetestraat and continue onwards until you reach Kemmel. Travel along Reningelstraat and take the first road on the right Nieuwstraat, the cemetery is on the right hand side.

The cemetery was established on the north side of the chateau grounds in December 1914. It continued to be used by divisions fighting on the southern sectors of the Belgian front until March 1918, when after fierce fighting involving both Commonwealth and French forces, the village and cemetery fell into German hands in late April.

The cemetery was retaken later in the year, but in the interval, it was badly shelled and the old chateau destroyed.

Cpl R. Whiteside, 443, 16th Royal Irish Rifles (Pioneers), 18th June 1917 - O 2. Lived in the Carrickblacker Road. One of his sons later played for Glasgow Celtic.

Lt Col Guy du Maurier, 3rd Royal Fusiliers, 9th March 1916 - L 4. A brother of novelist Gerald du Maurier. Uncle of G. L. Davies who wrote "Peter Pan."

Pte Count Ove Krag-Juel-Vind-Frijs, 28th Canadian Infantry (Saskatchewan Regiment), 15th November 1915 - K 59. He was from Denmark. His gravestone is inscribed with the words of a Danish bed-time prayer.

2nd Lt Michael Wall, 6th Royal Irish Regiment, 7th June 1917. – X 73. He had attended the Christian brothers School in Dublin. His Commanding Officer was Major Willie Redmond.

Locre Hospice Cemetery & Isolated Grave Loker

Leaving Kemmel, take the N304 and when you reach the junction with N375 take left. On reaching the village of Loker take Kemmelbergweg. Take an immediate right turn into Godtschalckstraat. The cemetery is 900 metres on the right hand side of the road. There is a small 20 metres grass access path.

Loker was in Allied hands during the greater part of the war and field ambulances were stationed in the convent of St Antoine. The village changed hands several times between 25th April – 30th April 1918, when it was recaptured by the French.

The hospice or convent was the scene of severe fighting on 20th May, but it was not retaken until the first week in July.

The cemetery contains 244 Commonwealth graves.

Brigadier General R. Maclachlan DSO, formerly Rifle Brigade, Commanding 112th Infantry Brigade, 11th November 1917 - II C 9

Lt Col R. Chester-Master DSO and Bar, 13th King's Own Rifle Corps, 30th August 1917 - II C 8

Major William Hoey Kearney Redmond MP, Legion D'Honneur, 6th Royal Irish Regiment

Willie Redmond was born in Wexford and had been a Catholic Nationalist Member of Parliament for almost thirty four years representing Wexford, North Fermanagh and East Clare.

June 1917 the Battle of Messines was a text book success, in which the 36th (Ulster) Division and the 16th (Irish) Division fought side by side. At 3.10 hrs on 7th June the 1st Munsters in the second wave led the charge into Wytschaete where they linked up with the 9th Inniskillings to their south.

When those nineteen mines blew up on 7th June to signal the start of the Battle of Messines, Redmond's regiment had been close to the one which exploded at Macdelstede Farm.

Major Willie Redmond led his men of the 6th Royal Irish Regiment into battle at the age of 56 years. He was wounded twice. As he fell he cheered his men onwards into battle.

Carried from the battlefield by **John Meeke, a stretcher bearer in the 36th Division**, he was carried to the 36th 's Dressing Station beside Locre Hospice where he died, from shock, later the same day.

General Hickie managed to find a coffin, a rare thing on the battlefield for the burial on 8th June at 18.30 hrs. **Troops from the 10th Inniskillings, 35th Division and 2nd Royal Irish Regiment, 16th Division provided the Guard of Honour. Officers from both Divisions were present.**

His grave is outside the cemetery wall on the right hand side towards the rear of the cemetery.

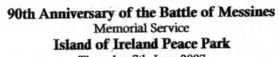

90th Anniversary of the Battle of Messines
Memorial Service
Island of Ireland Peace Park
Thursday 7th June 2007

Conducted by
Rev. Maynard Cathcart MA
Father Kevin Mullan
Rev. Canon John Mayes

in the presence of assembled guests

To the glory of God and in perpetual memory of all those from the Island of Ireland who made the supreme sacrifice in The Great War.

Dickebusch Old Military Cemetery
Dikkebus

From Loker take the N375 to Dikkebus. Dickebusch Old Military Cemetery is locates on a street called Neerplats. Turn left of the Dikkebusseweg into a small street called Kerkstraat and 200 metres along this street, just beyond the village church, take left into Neerplats.

The old military cemetery was used as a front line cemetery in January, February and March 1915. The cemetery contains 46 World War One burials.

There are also 10 burials from the Second World War, all dating from late May 1940 when the British Expeditionary Force withdrew ahead of the German advance.

There are five members of the Royal Irish Regiment and two members of the Royal Irish Fusiliers interred here.

The cemetery was designed by J R Truelove.

Pte David H. Cranston, 10997, 2nd Royal Irish Fusiliers, 13th February 1915 - A 9. He lived in Garvaghy Road and his parents lived in Parkmount.

Belgian Battery Corner Cemetery
Ieper

Continue on the N375 out of Dikkebus in the direction of Ieper. A couple of kilometres prior to Ieper there is a sharp bend to the left. Take Dikkbusseweg and turn right into Frezenbergstraat and 200 metres further on is Omloopstraat where the cemetery is situated.

The cemetery occupies a site at a road junction where three batteries of Belgian artillery were positioned in 1915.

The cemetery was begun by the 8th Division in June 1917 after the Battle of Messines and it was used until October 1918, largely from burials from a dressing station in a cottage nearby.

Almost half the graves are of casualties who belonged, or were attached, to artillery units.

There are now 573 First World War casualties buried or commemorated in this cemetery

The cemetery was designed by Sir Edward Lutyens.

Pte W. A. Allen, 2345, 2nd Australian Imperial Force, 27th October 1917 - II H 5. He lived in Carleton Street but had emigrated to Singleton, New South Wales where he enlisted. He had served for four years in the Royal Irish Fusiliers Militia.

Voormezeele Enclosure No. 3
Ieper

Return to the N375 to the direction from whence you came and when you reach Ruuschaartstraat, turn left into it. This will bring you to Voormezele. The cemetery is situated just after Voormezeele Drop.

There were originally four enclosures at Voormezeele, although there are now only three. These were originally regimental groups of graves, begun early during the war and gradually increased until both the cemetery and the village were captured by the Germans on 29th April 1918.

Enclosure No. 3, the largest of these burial grounds , was started by Princess Patricia's Light Infantry in February 1915. They buried their men in what is now Plot 3, the other Plots I -9 are the work of other units or pairs of units, and they also include a few burials from October 1918.

Plots 10-12 are of more general character, whilst Plots 13-16 were made after the Armistice.

The area was recaptured by Commonwealth forces in early September 1918.

There are 1498 UK graves, Canada 99, Australia 11, New Zealand 2, South Africa 1 and Germany 1.

Rfn James Gracey, 9969, 2nd Royal Irish Rifles, 15th April 1915 - XIV G 2. He lived in Florence Court. James was wounded on 13th April and evacuated to No. 10 Casualty Clearing Station at Hazebrouck where he died. His father W. J. Gracey served with Lord Robert's in the Afghanistan War of 1881. His brother Joseph served with 1st Royal Irish Fusiliers in the Great War.

Bedford House Cemetery
Ieper

From Voormezele take Sint –Elooisweg to reach the N365, where you take left in the direction of Ieper. The cemetery is on the main Ieper-Armentieres road on the right hand side. Access is easy and parking is provided.

Bedford House was the name given to Chateau Rosendal which stood in this area before being destroyed in the war. It was a country house set in a small wooded park with a moat.

It was used by Field Ambulances and also as a Headquarters for brigades and fighting units. Gradually small cemeteries covered the area and at the Armistice there were five enclosures

No 1 and No. 5 Enclosures were moved to other cemeteries. This left the remaining three enclosures. No. 2 was begun in December 1915 and used until October 1918 and enlarged by 437 graves after the Armistice.

No. 3 was started in February 1915 and used until December 1916. The largest No. 4 was used from June 1916 until February 1918. After the Armistice 3,324 burials were added. No. 6 was made in the 1930's from the concentration of burials from the surrounding battlefields.

Pte W. J. Campbell, 24952, 9th Royal Irish Fusiliers, 16th August 1917 - Enc. 4, Grave XIII F 9. He lived in Montague Street. He was killed during the Battle of Langemarck (Third Ypres.)

Pte James Benson, 55571, 19th Canadian Infantry (Central Ontario Regiment), 25th July 1916 - Enc.4, Grave G 2. James hailed from Derrykeevan Post Office. He enlisted in Toronto. He was on duty with his machine-gun section of his battalion, in the front line trenches when an enemy mine exploded. The dug-out he was in collapsed and his body was found crushed with the weight of fallen timbers. His brother John, was also killed in the war.

Route 7 - Ieper
(Ypres) and the West

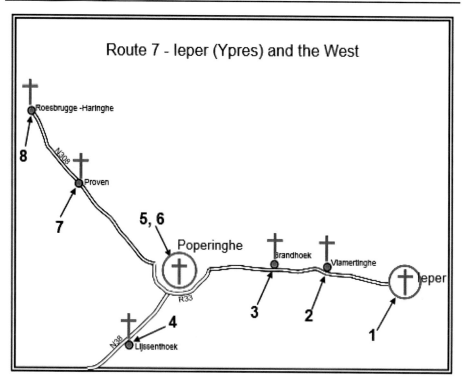

Route 7 - Ieper (Ypres) and the West

1.   Ieper (Ypres) - Cloth Hall/ St Martin's Cathedral/ St George's Memorial Church/Ramparts Cemetery/ Reservoir Cemetery/ Ypres Town Cemetery and Extension, Menin Gate

2.   Vlamertinghe Military Cemetery

3.   Brandhoek New Military Cemetery/ Brandhoek New Military Cemetery No. 3

4.   Lijssenthoek Military Cemetery, Poperinghe

5.   Nine Elms British Cemetery, Poperinghe

6.   Poperinghe - Talbot House/The Shooting Post, Stadhuis/Death Cell

7.   Mendinghem Military Cemetery, Proven

8.   Haringhe (Bandaghem) Military Cemetery, Haringhe

Route 7 - Ieper (Ypres) - and the West

The **Ypres Salient** even today still holds great historical interest for many British people. In compiling a route which is particularly relevant to the people of the island of Ireland I have had to be prescriptive , bearing in mind **there are over 170 Commonwealth War Grave Commission cemeteries** within a relatively small area.

Ieper(1), formerly Ypres,was completely rebuilt after the war. One can easily spend an entire day exploring Ieper.

The Cloth Hall in the Groete Markt has been rebuilt in its original style and houses the award winning In Flanders Fields Museum, a visit not to be missed.

St George's Church and St Martin's Cathedral are very close by.

There are three cemeteries within the town itself, all within walking distance, Ramparts Cemetery, Reservoir Cemetery and Ypres Town Cemetery and Extension.

Visit the **Last Post Ceremony which is held at the Menin Gate Memorial every evening at 20.00 hours** where you can literally join hundreds of pilgrims wishing to pay their respects to the fallen of the Ypres Salient.

From Ieper travel on the N308 in the direction of Vlamertinghe. **Vlamertinghe Military Cemetery (2)** is located in Hospitaalstraat which is second right after the village church.

Here you will find the grave of Pte John Girvan, 1st Royal Irish Fusiliers who came from Kernan.

Also buried here is Capt F. O. Grenfell VC, 9th Lancers and English war poet, 2nd Lt H. Parry, 17th King's Own Rifle Corps.

Continue on the N308 and you will shortly reach the hamlet of **Brandhoek** where you take left at the church, cross the dual carriageway and turn first right.

Brandhoek New Military Cemetery (3) was opened in 1917 due to the continued Allied Offensive. This is a much visited cemetery as it **contains the grave of Double VC winner, Captain Noel Chavasse.**

Alongside is **Brandhoek New Military Cemetery No.3 (3)**, where there is a strong Ulster connection. Buried in this cemetery is Capt T. G. Shillington, a member of a well known Portadown family and also that of Lt J. M. Stronge of Tynan Abbey, both members of the 8th Royal Irish Fusiliers.

Follow the **Poperinghe ring road R33 as far as Lenestraat**, take left and then first right. In 2 kilometres you will reach **Lijssenhoek Military Cemetery (4)**. There are over 9,900 burials here.

Here lies Pte George McFadden, 42nd Canadian Infantry (Quebec Regiment) who had lived at Castleisland House, Garvaghy Road. He had played for Portadown Football Club. Another grave is of Pte John Lynn, 1st Royal Inniskilling Fusiliers, Mousetown, Coalisland, one of four brothers to be killed in the Great War.

Many other Ulster and Irish casualties lie alongside Major F. H. Tubb VC, 7th Australian Infantry, Lt J. E. Raphael , an English Rugby International and Staff Nurse Nellie Spindler.

Return to the R33 ring road in the direction of Oost Capel. Take a left hand turn into Helleketelweg to reach **Nine Elms British Cemetery (5)**.

Sgt David Gallaher, 2nd New Zealand Expeditionary Force who hailed from Ramelton, County Donegal is buried here. After emigrating to New Zealand he went on to become a New Zealand All Black rugby international playing 36 times for his country, 27 of them as captain.

Poperinghe (6) was used to billet British troops during the war. From the town centre walk along **Gasthuistraat to No. 43 which is Toc "H" or Talbot House which was a soldiers club for all ranks.**

In the courtyard of the **Stadhuis (Town Hall)** you will find **the Shooting Post** where a number of British soldiers had been executed. Alongside is the **Death Cell** in which the condemned men spent their final hours.

Continue on the Poperinghe Ring road R33 until you join the N308 in the direction of Oost-Capel. You will soon reach the village of **Proven**, where in Roesbruggestraat you will find **Mendinghem Military Cemetery (7)**.

Trooper Samuel Robinson, 1st North Irish Horse , originally from Seagoe is buried here alongside Pioneer James Taylor, Royal Engineers from Jervis Street. whilst Lt Col B. Best-Dunkley VC, Commanding 2/5th Lancashire Fusiliers lies close by.

Travel on to Roesbrugge. Take second left into Haringhestraat and then second right into Naachttegaalstraat where 400 metres further along is **Haringhe (Bandaghem) Military Cemetery (8)**.

Buried here is 2nd Lt James Cullen MC, 1st Royal Irish Fusiliers who lived at Thomas Street.

During the war there were three Casualty Clearing Stations in this area, the troops naming them, Mendinghem, Dozinghem and Bandaghem. They were used by 36th (Ulster) Division.

This concludes a rather short route west of Ieper, to which you can now return, the fastest route being via Poperinghe.

The Buglers at the Last Post Ceremony at the Menin Gate.

Ieper - Ypres

During World War One Ypres was the centre of sustained battles between the German and Allied forces. The city was known by the soldiers as "Wipers."

Ypres occupied a strategic position as it stood in the path of Germany's Schlieffen Plan, to conquer Belgium and then France.

With the exception of a few days, Ypres remained in Allied hands during the Great War.

The town with its 14,080 inhabitants witnessed its destruction including the buildings such as the Cloth Hall and the Cathedral.

The Germans surrounded the city on three sides, bombarding it throughout the war. The Allies made costly advances into the Ypres Salient on the German lines.

During the First Battle of Ypres, 31st October 1914 to the 22nd November 1914, the Allies captured the town from the Germans.

In the Second Battle of Ypres, 22nd April 1915 – 25th May 1915, the Germans first used poison gas and captured high ground, east of the town.

The most costly in terms of human suffering was the Third Battle of Ypres, 21st July 1917 until 6th November 1917, which was also known as the Battle of Passchendaele. The Allied forces at a terrible cost of lives on both sides,

recaptured **Passchendaele Ridge. The town of Ypres, by then had been razed to the ground**.

Over these turbulent years the Ypres Salient saw over 500,000 men pay the ultimate sacrifice. The restoration of Ypres ensured the buildings were replaced in the same style as they had been prior to 1914.

The **Cloth Hall** today is home to the prestigious **In Flanders' Fields Museum,** which is dedicated to Ypres role in World War One. The Cloth Hall, was originally built in the 13th Century. The belfry that surrounds the hall has a 49 bell carillon. In 1999 the building was designated as a World Heritage Site by UNESCO.

The museum at the **Grote Markt 34,** is open almost every day of the year with the exceptions of Christmas Day, New Year's Day and the last three weeks in January. The museum is an essential visit to all those who visit what is now Ieper.

The Last Post Ceremony

At 20.30 hours on the 2nd September 1928, the first Last Post Ceremony was held with about 70 people present.

Despite criticism from some quarters the ceremony was re-started after the winter break on 1st May 1929 and since that date the Last Post has been played every evening under the Menin Gate with the sole exception of the period of the German occupation between May 1940 and September 1944.

The buglers nowadays are members of The Last Post Committee.

No one can failed to be moved by this nightly 20.00 hours ceremony, no matter how many times one may be present.

Very often particular visits by various groups, organisations or individuals add much to the occasion.

In July 2012 when I was fortunate to attend the ceremony on three separate occasions, I was privileged to be in the company of American Legionnaires with their Harley Davidson motorcycles, the Auckland Police Pipe Band, New Zealand and Eddie Mercyx, five times winner of the Tour de France, who laid a wreath in memory of all Olympians who were killed in the war. (See overleaf.)

Make a point of expressing your appreciation to the buglers at the close of the ceremony as they are very willing to participate with your photographic requests.

Please remember that despite who may be taking part in the ceremony, as you may at times be listening to solo singers or musicians, **it is imperative that there is no applause.**

The wreath laid at the Menin Gate by Eddie Mercyx in July 2012 in memory of all Olympians killed in the First World War.

St Martin's Cathedral

The Cathedral is situated behind the Cloth Hall and was originally built in 1221. After the war it was completely reconstructed with a higher spire. Above the south door is the Rose Window which is the British Army and Royal Air Force Memorial to King Albert.

In the garden to the north-east of the Cathedral is a Celtic Cross, a memorial to the men of the Royal Munster Regiment.

251

St George's Memorial Church

St George's Memorial Church is situated in Elverdinghestraat. It was built by Sir Reginald Blomfield in the years 1928/1929. This was an idea of Earl Haig's so pilgrims could worship when visiting the Salient.

Almost every item contained in the building is a memorial of some kind. The foundation stone was laid by Lord Plumer on 24th July 1927, following the Menin Gate Memorial Dedication Service.

Two years later the church was dedicated and opened by the Bishop of Fulham on 24th March 1929.

It is a memorial church for all who died in the two world wars.

On 29th June 2012 I happened to be present by sheer coincidence and attended a Dedication Service for St Clement Danes School, Chorleywood which was celebrating its 150th anniversary. Today's students paid tribute to 27 of their former pupils who had fallen during the course of the Great War. A very poignant service that will long be remembered by those present.

Ramparts Cemetery

This is the only British cemetery within the walls of the old city. The first burials were made by the French in 1914. It has only 198 graves.

The cemetery is particularly attractive with the view of the moat surrounding Ieper. The Lille Gate is next to the cemetery.

There is also walk to the cemetery from the Menin Gate dedicated to the late Rose Coombs MBE, whose book, "Before Endeavours Fade", revived interest in World War One when it was first published in 1976. An updated version was published again in 2006.

Pte C. Thompson 10302, 2nd Royal Irish Rifles, 28th May 1915 – B 24. A native of Newtownards.

Lt W. T. McCurry, Royal Army Medical Corps, 14th March 1915 – D 27. Shankill Road, Belfast.

Reservoir Cemetery

From 1914-1918 Ypres was in a salient occupied by Commonwealth forces. Then, there were only three cemeteries near the western gate of the town although now only one of them, Reservoir Cemetery still exists. It was once called Cemetery North of the Prison.

It was enlarged after the Armistice. In Plot V, Row AA lie 16 men of the Duke of Cornwall's Light Infantry. They were billeted in the vaults of the Cathedral and were all killed during shelling on 12th August 1915. Their bodies were recovered after the Armistice.

Brigadier-General F. A. Maxwell VC; CSI;DSO and Bar, Cmdg 27th Brigade, 9th (Scottish) Division

21st September 1917, - I A 31

His headstone with its VC inscription with the Stone of Remembrance and the Cross of Sacrifice in the background.

Town Cemetery and Extension
Ieper

The cemetery is 1 km east of the town centre on the Zonnebeekseweg, the N345 connecting Ieper and Menen. Simply walk through the Menin Gate and in about six minutes you will reach the cemetery on the left hand side.

From October 1914 until the summer of 1918, Ypres formed the centre of a Salient held by Commonwealth Forces. From April 1915 the town was bombarded and destroyed more completely than any other town of its size on the Western Front.

The Town Cemetery was used from October 1914 until May 1915 and once in 1918. There are 145 burials amongst the civilian graves.

The Extension on the east of the Town Cemetery was also begun in October 1914 and was used until April 1915 and twice in 1918. It was increased after the Armistice when 367 graves were brought in from cemeteries and isolated positions east and north of Ypres.

There are now 598 Commonwealth burials in the extension of which 137 are unidentified and there are special memorials to 16 servicemen known or believed to be buried amongst them. There are 43 Second World War burials of which 13 are unidentified.

The cemetery was designed by Sir Reginald Blomfield.

In Ypres Town Cemetery the British burials are widely scattered.

Prince Maurice V D of Battenberg KVCO, Mentioned in Despatches, 1st King's Royal Rifle Corps, 27th October 1914. -IB. He was a grandson of Queen Victoria and he was killed in action at Broodseinde Ridge. His nephew was Lord Mountbatten.

Ypres Town Cemetery Extension has both First and Second World War burials.

Lt Lord Charles Worsley, Bt (Charles Sackville Pelham), Royal Horse Guards, 30th October 1914. - II D 4. Son of the Earl of Yarborough. He was killed in action during the defence of Zandvoorde.

Capt Alfred S. Taylor, Royal Army Medical Corps, Attd. 10/11th Highland Light Infantry, 31st July 1917. - 111 B 21. He lived in Belfast and had played international rugby for Ireland.

2nd Lt J. H. Wilkie DCM, 1st Leinster Regiment, 9th April 1915 - I G I. A member of Wanderers Masonic Lodge No. 1604, London.

The Tourism Office is in **Groete Mart** has an excellent free, street plan of Ypres with all the aforementioned points of interest clearly marked and all within easy walking distance. Details of accommodation are available in the Tourist Office or these can be accessed on www.toerisme@ieper.be. Ieper (Ypres) is full of shops, hotels and restaurants and is now a lively bustling area. A pleasant few hours can be spent exploring within the town walls.

Menin Gate
Ypres – Ieper

The Menin Gate Memorial marks the starting point for one of the main roads out of the town that led Allied soldiers to the front line during World War One. **At that time no actual gate existed on the site.** It was indicated by the presence of two lions, one on each side of the roadway which cut through the walls. These lions are now in Canberra. Through this cutting, many thousands of men passed on their way to the Salient. A tag line at the time was, **"Tell the last man though to bolt the Menin gate".**

The British Memorial to the Missing or the Menin Gate was **inaugurated on 24th July 1927 by Field Marshal Plumer in the presence of King Albert**. Built by the British Government, it is a monument dedicated to the missing British and Commonwealth soldiers who were killed in the fierce battles around the Ypres Salient. **It bears the names of 54,896 men who died between 1914 and 15th August 1917 and have no known grave.**

it was designed by Sir Reginald Blomfield.

Every night since the 11th November 1929, (except during the German occupation of Ypres 20th May 1940 – 6th September 1944), the traffic is stopped from driving through the Menin Gate and The Last Post is sounded and wreaths are left by various organisations at 20.00 hrs.

There are many names of local people on the Menin Gate.

Panel 42 Royal Irish Fusiliers

L/Cpl A. Doherty 10674 2nd Btn, 24th February 1915 - Drumnahuncheon LOL 371 - Battlehill

Pte G. H. Adamson 8105 1st Btn, 25th April 1915 - Member of Parkmount Flute Band. Killed at St. Julien.

Pte J. G. Bell 7036, 10th June 1915. He hailed from Eglish

Pte J. Grimason 6234 2nd Btn, 13th May 1915 - Battle of Frezenburg - 2nd Ypres - Carleton Street

Pte W. H. Lappin 4745 7/8th Btn, 10th August 1917 - Obins Street

Pte W. Malcolmson 4142 1st Btn. 25th April 1915, Battle of St. Julian 22/25th April 1915 – Watson St.

Pte C. McKeown 11142 Portadown - Listed as missing. Accepted as having been killed in action at St. Julien on 25th April 1915.

Pte J. Mills 8527 1st Btn. 25th April 1915 - Mourneview Street

Pte. J. Quinn 9891 2nd Btn. 19th January 1915 - West Street

Pte W. Quinn 10348 2nd Btn. 14th March 1915 - Battle of St. Eloi 14/15th March - Battlehill

Pte W. Ross 11217 1st Btn. 15th September 1916 - Atkinson's Avenue

Pte C. Tedford 7354 1st Btn. 25th April 1915 - Irwin Street - Killed at St. Julien.

Pte S. J. Woods 11355 25th April 1915 - Portadown

Panel 5 Queen's Own Hussars

Pte J. Warnock 2268 4th Btn., 31st October 1914 - Park Road

Panel 11 Irish Guards

L/Cpl W. J. Jamison 3105 1st Btn 6/11/14 Killed at Zillebeke - Jervis Street

Panel 30/32 Canadian Mounted Rifles

Pte A. Porter 7825 1st Btn., 9 Saskatchewan Regt. 2nd June 1916 - Union Street. Enlisted in Toronto.

Panels 36 - 38 Durham Light Infantry

Pte Isaac Gilpin 20795, 2nd Btn, 9th August 1915. - Lived at Florence Court.

Panel 40 Royal Irish Rifles

Sgt Major James Campbell 4842, 7th Btn, 9th August 1917. He lived in Thomas Street and had served in India and Africa.

Rfn William Hall 5545, 2nd Btn, 20th July 1915. He played for Linfield Football Club.

Panel 3 Life Guards

Capt A. E. B. O'Neill, 6th November 1914. MP for Mid-Antrim. The first British MP to die in the First World War. On the 100th anniversary of his death, on the 6th November 2014, a memorial note was printed the House of Commons Order Paper to remember his death at Zillebeke Ridge.

Panel 3 Irish Guards

Brigadier General Charles Fitzclarence VC, mentioned in despatches, 1st Guards Brigade and Irish Guards, 12th November 1914. On 31st October 1914 he directed a counter-attack of 2nd Worcesters at Polygon Wood, which resulted in the retaking of Gheluvelt. (First Ypres.) He was killed in action at this time. **Sir John French declared, "It was the most critical moment in the whole of this great battle."** He won his Victoria Cross in 1899 during the siege of Mafeking. **He is the highest ranking officer commemorated on the Menin Gate Memorial to the Missing.**

Panel 11 Scots Guards

Pte P. J. Kerr 8778, Scots Guards, 11th November 1914, Lived in Carleton Street.

Panel 44 - 46

Capt Basil MacLear, 2nd Btn, 24th May 1915. He was an Irish rugby international. His brother Lt Col Percy MacLear was also killed in the Great War.

Panels 22 and 34 Gloucester Regiment

Pte T. W. King 20260, 1/5th Btn, 7th August 1917. Played 22 times for Linfield Football Club.

2nd Lt Robert Kelly Pollin 4th Royal Irish Rifles 31st July 1917 (20) Pier 40 Menin Gate

An old memorial stone found lying in the Annalong River in 2010 and bearing the name of a First World War soldier, 2nd Lt Robert Kelly Pollin led to a two part BBC N. Ireland documentary, "The Soldier and the Stone."

2nd Lt Collen had been killed during the Battle of Passchendaele on 31st July 1917 and like so many others his body had never been recovered.

The documentary traced Robert's roots to a Belfast solicitor's office where he himself had trained as a solicitor prior to enlisting.

It is surmised that the memorial stone had been commissioned by Robert's father but there was still no explanation of how or why it had ended up in the river at Annalong.

Fittingly, the memorial stone now rests in the Passchendaele 1917 Memorial Museum in Zonnebeke, Belgium situated close to the site of the battle.

Robert was the son of James M. And Martha Pollin, "Westhoek", Taunton Avenue, Belfast.

His name is commemorated on Panel 40 on the Menin Gate Memorial in Ypres.

Lt Col Edgar Mobbs DSO

7th Northamptonshire Regiment

31st July 1917

Panel 43/45

Edgar was an English rugby international who played for and captained Northampton. He played for the East Midlands and the Barbarians before being awarded an England cap in 1909. In that year he captained his country against the touring Australians.

At the outbreak of the First World War he personally raised a company of 250 sportsmen, known as Hobb's Own.

He was killed on 31st July at Zillebeke during the Third Battle of Ypres whilst attacking a German machine-gun post.

In 1921 the first Mobb's Memorial Match was held between the East Midlands and the Barbarians at Franklin's Garden and has continued ever since.

Today there stands a memorial to him in Northampton raised by subscriptions from admirers the world over to the memory of a great and gallant soldier and sportsman.

Vlamertinghe Military Cemetery

Leave Ieper via N308 towards Vlamertinghe. The cemetery is located in Hospitaalstraat, second right after the village church.

The cemetery was started by French troops in 1914. It was then used by field ambulances and fighting units until June 1917, when the land adjoining the cemetery was required for a military railway station. The cemetery is remarkable for the care with which men of the same unit were buried side by side.

The wrought iron gates were presented by the family of the late Lord Redesdale, whose son, Major Mitford, is buried therein.

Pte John Girvan, 8429, 1st Royal Irish Fusiliers, 15/16th September 1916 - IV D 5. He lived in Kernan.

Captain F. O. Grenfell VC, 9th Lancers (Queen's Royals), 24th May 1915 - II B 14. He was killed at Hooge, when 208 out of 350 Lancers, in the line that day, perished. His epitaph reads, "I die happy, tell the men I love my Squadron."

2nd Lt H Parry, 17th King's Own Rifle Corps,6th May 1917 - VI L 12. A war poet.

Major the Hon C. B. Ogilvie Freeman-Mitford, DSO, 10th (Prince of Wales Own Royal Huzzars), - I E 8.

Brandhoek New Military Cemetery Ieper

Pass through the village of Vlamertinge into the hamlet of Brandhoek. After the church, take left into Grote Branderstraat which is **reached by crossing the dual carriageway**. Then take first right into Zevekotestraat. Easy parking is available.

Brandhoek was considered relatively safe being out of range of the German artillery. As a result it became a centre for supplies, hospitals and burial grounds. When the nearby Military Cemetery became full, the New Military Cemetery was opened. A short time later a third cemetery was to be required. This cemetery is the last resting place of Double Victoria Cross winner Captain Noel Chavasse. As a result the cemetery is one of the most visited in the area.

Double V C winner

The reason why this is one of the most visited cemeteries in Belgium is that Double VC winner Captain Noel Chavasse MC; DSO; VC and Bar: is buried In grave 3 B 15.

A member of the **Royal Army Medical Corps and the 1st/10th The King's (Liverpool) Regiment** was the son of the Right Rev. The Lord Bishop of Liverpool.

His headstone has two Victoria Crosses inscribed thereon. He won his Military Cross for action at **Hooge, Belgium in 1915**. His first Victoria Cross was awarded for his actions in **Guillemont on 9th August 1916** for tending to the wounded, all day in the open under heavy fire. Although injured he went out at night to bring back more injured. He also collected identity discs off the dead and buried fallen officers.

He repeated these brave actions at **Wieltje** during the **Third Battle of Ypres** bringing in casualties between **31st July and 2nd August 1917**.

Wounded several times he eventually succumbed to his injuries in Brandhoek Military Hospital on 4th August 1917.

He is one of only three men to have won the Victoria Cross twice.

On 29th August 1997 a plaque was unveiled outside the church to commemorate Capt Chavasse in the presence of a contingent from the Liverpool Scottish Territorials. The plaque was initiated and funded by the commune of Brandhoek.

Pte. J. Colhoun 15417 10th Royal Inniskilling Fusiliers 10/8/17, V C 13 – Londonderry

Brandhoek New Military Cemetery No. 3

Capt T. G. Shillington, 9th Royal Irish Fusiliers 18th August 1917, II E 31 - A member of the noted Shillington family of "Ardeevin", Portadown, who had strong connections with the Methodist church.

In November 1915 he commanded a night patrol of thirty men. They encountered a German patrol in No Man's Land and a firefight ensued. He had been wounded in action at the Somme.

He was wounded again on 16th August during the Battle of Langemarck and died two days later at No. 3 Australian Casualty Clearing Station.

Lt J. M. Stronge, 9th Royal Irish Fusiliers, 16/8/17, II F 22 - Tynan Abbey, Co. Armagh - A member of **Caledon Masonic Lodge No. 210**.

Sgt M. Curley 7261, 6th Connaught Rangers, 3/8/17, II C 2 - He had several spells in the army with 2nd Connaught Rangers and had fought in the battles of Mons, Marne, Aisne and the First Battle of Ypres. **He had been instrumental in forming the Midlands Volunteer Force, a nationalist organisation dedicated to the defence of Home Rule. In fact the Midlands Volunteer Force pre-dated the formation of the Irish Volunteers**. In late 1914 he saw action in Mesopotamia. In 1917, again back in the army, this time with the 6th Connaught Rangers he took part in the **Battle of Messines Ridge**. During the Third Battle of Ypres he was fatally wounded and died at the 32nd Casualty Clearing Station at Brandhoek.

Lijssenthoek Military Cemetery Poperinghe

Travel along the R33 Poperinghe Ring Road. Continue to the left hand junction with the N38 Frans-Vlaanderenweg, 800 metres along take a left into Lenestraat. Then right into Boeschheepseweg and two km along is Lijssenthoek Military Cemetery.

During the First World War, the village of Lijssenthoek was situated on the main communication line between the Allied military bases in the rear and the Ypres battlefields. Close to the Front, but out of range of most German field artillery, it became a natural place to establish casualty clearing stations.

The cemetery was first used by the French 15th Hopital D'Evacuation and in June 1915, it began to be used by casualty clearing stations of the Commonwealth forces. From April to August 1918, the casualty clearing stations fell back before the German advance and field ambulances took their places.

The cemetery contains 9,901 Commonwealth burials of the First World War and 883 war graves of other nationalities, mostly French and German.

It is the second largest Commonwealth cemetery in Belgium.

The cemetery was designed by Sir Reginald Blomfield.

Pte George McFadden, 419113, 42nd Canadian Infantry (Quebec Regiment), 27th March 1916 V B 26. He was born in Castleisland House, Garvaghy Road. He played for Portadown Football where his brother William was goalkeeper.

He was living in Hamilton, Ontario, when war was declared. He was part of a section sent out on patrol on the night of 22nd - 23rd March. He received a gunshot to his upper arm, suffering a compound fracture as a result. Although suffering from shock, he remained conscious. He was treated at No. I Canadian Field Ambulance where his condition worsened and he passed away.

265

Captain F. H. Tubb VC, 7th Australian Infantry, 27th September 1917 - XIX C 5. He won his Victoria Cross in Gallipoli for displaying exceptional bravery in repelling a Turkish advance at Lone Pine on 9th August 1915. He was killed leading a company in action at Polygon Wood.

Staff Nurse Nellie Spindler, Queen Alexandra's Imperial Nursing Service, 21st August 1917. - XVI A 3. Nellie worked in the Casualty Clearing Stations. She was working in the 44th Casualty Clearing Station near Brandhoek, when it was shelled and she was critically wounded. She lost consciousness and died twenty minutes later. Now she lies in Lijssenthoek amongst 10,000 men.

Pte John Lynn, 4471, 1st Royal Inniskilling Fusiliers, 9th August 1916. - VII D 32A. He came from Mousetown, Coalisland. **He was one of four brothers killed in the war.** Sgt W. E. Lynn is buried in Auchonvillers Military Cemetery, Somme, Driver R. Lynn in Hop Store Cemetery, Belgium and Sgt J. Lynn in Haifa War Cemetery, Israel.

Lt John E. Raphael, 18th King's Own Rifle corps, 11th June 1917 - XIII A 30.

He was a Belgian born English sportsman who was capped nine times for England at Rugby Union and played First Class Cricket for Surrey.

He won his first cap against Wales in 1902. He scored a try against Scotland in 1906.

In 1910 he captained the British Lions in a tour to Argentina.

Raphael who was Jewish was a specialist batsman and most of his appearances at first class level were for either Surrey or Oxford University. He also played first class matches for Marylebone Cricket Club, Gentlemen of England, London County and an England XI.

Four of his five centuries were for Oxford University, his best career score was 201 against Yorkshire. His only century for Surrey was in the 1904 County Championship against Worcestershire scoring 111 runs and he captained his County.

In 77 first class matches he notched 3,717 runs and took 36 catches. He died of wounds at Remy, Belgium.

There are five members of the Army Chaplain's Department buried in this cemetery.

Nine Elms British Cemetery Poperinghe

Travel left on the Poperinghe Ring Road R33 and join the N308 in the direction of Oost-Capel, 2.5 km further on turn left into Helleketelweg and Nine Elms British Cemetery is a further 700 metres on the left.

It was first used in late September 1917 for burials from 3rd Australian and 44th Casualty Clearing Stations. It was further used again during the German Offensive in Flanders from March to October 1918.

Sgt David Gallaher 32513, 2nd Auckland Regiment, New Zealand Expeditionary Force, 4th October 1917 - III D 8.

Dave Gallaher was born in Ramelton, County Donegal. The family moved in 1878 to New Zealand, moving from Katikati to Auckland in the 1890's.

He began his rugby career as a hooker. He played 26 representative matches for Auckland.

267

Dave became All Black No. 97 when he made his debut on 11th July 1903 against Wellington Province. He made his debut against Australia on 15th August 1903 and his last Test was as Captain of the "Originals" on New Year's Day against France in Paris.

He played six Tests, four as Captain and a total of 36 All Black matches, 27 as Captain. The only Test Match that he lost was against Wales.

In January he joined up to serve in the Boer War. In South Africa, he saw service in the Transvaal, Orange Free State and the Cape Colony.

Following the death of his younger brother in France, Dave , a married man with a family signed up on 25th July. He was in action during the Battle of Messines.

On 4th October his battalion was in action at St Juliaan and Langemarck. They were part of a second wave continuing the attack behind the advancing artillery barrage as far as Ravebeek.

He was wounded in the head and evacuated to an Australian Advanced Dressing Station on Abraham Heights, some 700 metres from where the New Zealand Memorial now stands at Graventafel. He was transferred to the 3rd Australian Casualty Clearing Station near Poperinghe but died of his wounds later that day.

Of the nine Gallaher brothers, six had joined up for service, and three, Dave, Henry and Douglas lost their lives.

Dave was one of 23 All Blacks who died in the Great War.

Poperinghe

Poperingo ic a town 10 km to the west of Ieper. During the war it was used to billet British troops and was a safe area for British hospitals.

Toc "H" - Talbot House

The charity Toc "H" was formed in Poperinge. On 11th December 1915 the house at No.43 Gasthuisstraat, welcomed British soldiers to a new club. It is found on the street next to the Cafe de la Paix. Above No. 43 is a sign, "Everyman's Club".

An Army chaplain, Rev Philip (Tubby) Clayton saw it as a place where British soldiers, regardless of rank, could meet to relax. A notice was hung by the front door, bearing a message, "All rank abandon, ye all who enter here."

The house was named Talbot House in memory of Lt G. W. L. Talbot, 7th Rifle Brigade who was killed at Hooge on 30th July 1915. He was the brother of Padre Neville Talbot. He is buried in Sanctuary Wood British Military Cemetery in Zillebeke.

The Shooting Post - Stadhuis (Town Hall)

In the courtyard between 1916 and 1918 a number of British soldiers were executed. Most of them had been sentenced to death as deserters.

How many were killed is a mystery although records show at least eight deaths. Other sources claim it could have been double that.

The French expression, "pour encourager les autres", was the common justification for confirming the execution of the men who had been sentenced to death by courts-martial.

Death Cell

In early 1997, two of the four cells in which condemned men spent their final hours were restored to the state they had been during the First World War.

The cell, with two windows giving a View of the courtyard contains the work, "Shot at dawn" created by Paul Reniere, a local artist.

Mendinghem Military Cemetery Proven

From Nine Elms Military Cemetery rejoin the N308 towards Oost-Capel and 6.6 km further you will reach the village of Proven. Menginghem Military Cemetery is on the left hand side of the road, in Roesbruggestraat. The cemetery is accessed by a 200 metre gravel track, suitable for vehicles.

Mendinghem is one of a trio of cemeteries given names by the troops to recognise the work of the Casualty Clearing Stations. The other two, are Bandaghem and Dozinghem. In July 1916 the 46th Casualty Clearing Station was opened at Proven and this site was chosen. The first burials were in August 1916. In July 1917, four further clearing stations arrived in readiness for the forthcoming German Spring Offensive and three of them, 46th, 12th and 64th stayed until 1918.

Pioneer James Taylor, 282271, Royal Engineers, Attd 4th Brigade, Royal Garrison Artillery, 25th April 1918 - X C 17. He came from Jervis Street. He died of wounds at No. 64 Casualty Clearing Station.

Trooper Samuel Robinson, 850, 1st North Irish Horse, 9th August 1917 - IV B 23. Lived at Seagoe.

Lt Col Bertram Best-Dunkley VC, Commanding 2/5th Lancashire Fusiliers, 5th August 1917 - D I

Haringhe (Bandaghem) Military Cemetery Haringhe

Continue on the N308 to the village of Roesbrugge , take the second left into Haringhestraat and after 2 kilometres you will reach Haringhe. Take the second right in the village into Naachtegallstraat and the cemetery is 400 metres further on.

During the war there were three Casualty Clearing Stations in the area, Bandaghem, Mendinghem and Dozinghem. Haringhe (Bandaghem) was used by 62nd and 63rd Casualty Clearing Stations from July 1917 who used it continuously until October 1918. It was also used by 36th Casualty Clearing Station in 1918.

2 Lt James Cullen MC, 1st Royal Irish Fusiliers, 3rd October 1918 - III A 8. Lived at Thomas Street. He was wounded in action on two occasions and rose to the rank of Company Sergeant Major. Late in 1917 he gained his Commission. **He was awarded the Military Cross in 1918, "for most conspicuous gallantry and a devotion to duty, while in command of a platoon during an enemy attack."**

Albert Medal

Sapper J. C. Farren, Sapper G. E. Johnson and Company Sergeant Major A. H. Furlonger, 19th, 29th and 21st Light Railway Operating Company Royal Engineers 30th April 1918 Graves III D 31 - III D 33

They were manning an ammunition train as it arrived at a refuelling point. They had just uncoupled the engine when the second truck burst into flames. Two trucks were drawn clear of the ammunition dump but the ammunition in the burning truck exploded, completely wrecking the engine and both trucks. Had it not been for the courageous action of those men, the whole dump would have been destroyed and many lives lost.

The rare Albert Medal (less than 600 awarded) was instituted by a Royal Warrant, dated 7th March 1866, for acts of gallantry at sea. In 1877, it was extended to the land. The criteria is that, "the recipients risk of death has to be greater than his chance for survival."

9

Route 8 - Ieper (Ypres) North and East

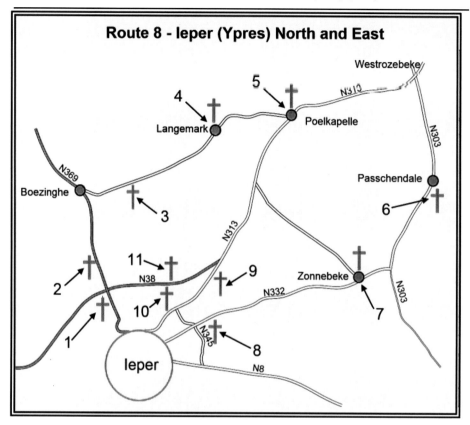

Route 8 - Ieper (Ypres) North and East

1. Duhallow ADS Cemetery
2. Essex Farm Cemetery
3. Artillery Wood Cemetery
4. Langemark German Cemetery
5. Poelkapelle British Cemetery
6. Tyne Cot Cemetery
7. Dochy Farm New British Cemetery
8. Potijze Chateau Wood Cemetery
9. Oxford Road Cemetery
10. White House Cemetery
11. New Irish Farm Cemetery

Route 8 Ieper (Ypres) - North and East

This route will take you to the killing fields of Passchendaele where in the Battle of Third Ypres 1917, thousands of men and animals perished in the mud of Flanders. You will visit Tyne Cot in Passendale which is the largest Commonwealth cemetery in the world.

Drive out of Ieper using the N369 in the direction of Boezinge via Diksmuidseweg and you will soon reach **Duhallow ADS Cemetery (1)**. It is named after a Southern Irish hunt.

Here you will find the grave of **Sapper D. Morton, 150th Coy, Royal Engineers who lived in Thomas Street.**

Keep on this road and just after you drive under the motorway bridge, you will reach **Essex Farm Cemetery (2)**, on your right.

It was here where Lt Col John McCrae, Canadian Royal Medical Corps penned his famous poem, "In Flanders' Fields".

You are able to access restored bunkers to the left of the cemetery. In the cemetery are the graves of **Pte T. Barratt VC, 7th South Staffs Regiment, Lt C. R. le Blanc Smith, 8th Rifle Brigade, a distinguished rower and Pte V. Strudwick also 8th Rifle Brigade who died at sixteen years of age.**

Keep on the N369 and as you approach Boezinge, take right into Bruggestraat. Go over the bridge and into Molenstraat and second right into Poezelstraat where you will arrive at **Artillery Wood Cemetery (3)**.

The renowned Irish poet, Pte Francis Ledwidge, 5th Royal Inniskilling Fusiliers is buried here as is another bard, Pte E H Evans, known as Hedd Wyn, Royal Welch Fusiliers, who had won six Bardic chairs.

Along the roadside is an Irish tricolour and plinth marking the spot where Ledwidge fell.

A matter of metres away is **Carrefour des Roses, a memorial to both French and Algerian Divisions who suffered the first use of poison gas in a German attack on 22nd April 1915.**

Now follow the N313 in the direction of Langemark. Follow the signs for **Deutsche Soldaten Friedhof** which is **Langemark German Cemetery (4)**, which is located north of the village on the road to Houstuist. **It is the only German cemetery in the Salient proper and contains 44,492 burials. The Kameraden Grab (Comrades Grave) contains the remains of the unidentified dead.**

Two British soldiers are buried here and are commemorated by means of a private plaque.

Take the N313 to nearby Poelkapelle, where in the village square is the **Guynemer Memorial**, in memory of the great French flying ace.

Take the Brugseweg out of the village and you will soon reach **Poelkapelle British Cemetery (5).** **This is another well visited site as 14 years old Pte John Condon, Royal Irish Regiment lies here. He is believed to be the youngest soldier killed in the First World War and is now immortalised in a folk song.**

Another interesting grave is that of **Lt H. G. Langton, 4ᵗʰ London Regiment, which has a musical inscription on the headstone, the only one of its type on the Western Front.**

From Poelkapelle head to Passendale. One way is to follow the N313 to Westrozebeke and join the N303 to Passendale. Three hundred metres off the Beselare to Passendale road is **Tyne Cot Cemetery (6). Formerly Passchendaele, Tyne Cot is the largest Commonwealth cemetery in the world.**

It contains 11,873 graves, whilst etched on the walls surrounding the cemetery are the names of 35,000 names of men with no known grave.

The Northamptonshire Fusiliers saw a resemblance to Tyneside cottages, in the German pillboxes situated here, hence the name, Tyne Cot.

On Panel 70 is the name of L/Cpl E. Seaman VC, 2ⁿᵈ Royal Inniskilling Fusiliers. Many local men from different regiments are commemorated on the walls, notably 9ᵗʰ Royal Irish Fusiliers.

Panel 160 bears the name of Rev Fr W. J. Doyle MC of the Royal Dublin Fusiliers.

Now take the N303 towards Zonnebeke and on the N332 out of the village is **Dochy Farm New British Cemetery (7). Here you will find the grave of Sgt Jimmy Spiers, 7ᵗʰ Queen's Own Cameron Highlanders, who scored the only goal of the game in the 1911 F A cup Final for Bradford against Newcastle United. He had also played for Glasgow Rangers.**

Take the N32 to Potijze and then the N345 on to Potijzestraat. Potijze Chateau Wood Cemetery is one of four cemeteries almost together. Walk along a small path between the local houses and left past Potijze Chateau and Lawn Cemetery, towards the wood.

Potijze Chateau Wood Cemetery (8) contains the graves of 19 men of the 1ˢᵗ Royal Inniskilling Fusiliers, killed by a gas attack on 8ᵗʰ August 1916, one

being Sgt Millar Cole of Castle Avenue. There are also 46 officers and men of 2nd Hampshire Regiment buried here.

Now head for the village of St Jan. On the N313 between St Julian and St Jan is **Oxford Road Cemetery (9). Here lies Capt C. Robertson VC of the Tank Regiment, as does Lt Colin Blythe, King's Own Light Infantry who played 19 Test matches for England and participated in 439 first class cricket matches.**

On the outskirts of St Jan on the N313 is **White House Cemetery (10). Within its confines is the grave of Pte Robert Morrow VC, 1st Royal Inniskilling Fusiliers from Newmills, outside Dungannon.** A local pub, the VC Inn was named in his memory, but sadly closed in recent years.

Now look for Zwaanhofweg just outside St Jan and follow this country road to the crossroads where you will reach **New Irish Farm Cemetery (11).**

Here is the grave of L/Cpl W. J. Benson, 14th Royal Irish Rifles who lived in Drumcree.

Another grave is that of Lt C. L. C. Bowes-Lyon, The Black Watch, a nephew of the late HRH, The Queen Mother.

Return to Ieper to begin the final journey on the Western Front.

Tribute from the Masonic Order to the Fallen.

Duhallow ADS Cemetery
Ieper

The cemetery is on the N369, the main Ieper to Boezinge road.

Duhallow Advanced Dressing Station Cemetery is believed to have been named after a Southern Irish Hunt. It was a medical post close to Ypres, and the cemetery was started in July 1917 on the first day of the Third Battle of Ypres. It was used continuously until the Armistice,

The cemetery contains the graves of many engineers and artillerymen and has also the graves of 41 men of the 13th Labour Corps, who were killed when a German aircraft dropped a bomb on an ammunition truck in January 1918. These graves are in Plot 2.

The cemetery was located next to a canal and the 11th, 36th and 44th Casualty Clearing Stations were posted here in October and November 1918.

The cemetery contains special memorials to ten soldiers buried in Malakoff Farm Cemetery and twenty nine buried in Fusilier Wood Cemetery whose graves have been destroyed.

The cemetery was enlarged after the Armistice when graves were moved here from other small cemeteries and isolated sites in the area.

Sapper David Morton 64389, 150th Coy Royal Engineers, 15th October 1918 - IV E 2. He lived in Thomas Street and came home from Canada to enlist after the outbreak of war. He was seriously wounded in October 1916 and spent a few months in hospital. He was again wounded in October 1918 and moved to No. 44 Casualty Clearing Station where he died later the same day.

Pte R. Templeton 16138, 9th Royal Irish Fusiliers Attached 108th Trench Mortar Battery, 25th October 1918 - IV I 31. He lived in Ednaferkin, Ballybay, County Monaghan and was related to Alderman Woolsey Smith and Alderman Robert Smith of the former Craigavon Borough Council.

Essex Farm Cemetery
Boezinghe

Boezinge is a village north of Ieper on the N369.

The land south of Essex Farm was used as a Dressing Station Cemetery from April 1915 to August 1917. The dead of the divisions who occupied this sector are buried here. It was designed by Sir Reginald Blomfield.

Total: 1,199

It was in Essex Farm Cemetery that Lt Col John McCrae of the Canadian Army Medical Corps penned his immortal poem, "In Flanders Fields" and an Albertina marker was unveiled to commemorate this.

The 49th (West Riding) Division Memorial is immediately behind the cemetery on the canal bank.

During excavation here in October 2001, **a narrow gauge railway was uncovered** which would have been used to transport supplies.

Alongside the cemetery are concrete structures used by the Advanced Dressing Station during the war. **These bunkers have been restored and are now accessible.** North of the bunkers **two dugouts** can be seen.

Pte T. Barratt VC 17114, 7th South Staffs Regt, 27th July 1917, 1 Z 8 - he killed two snipers and helped a patrol return safely from No Man's Land. Later the same day he was killed by a shell.

Lt C. R. Le Blanc-Smith, 8th Rifle Brigade, 27the November 1915, 1 R 9 - Rowed in 1910, 1911, 1912 Boat Race. President of Cambridge University Boat Club 1913.

Lt F. L. Pusch DSO, 15th Irish Guards, 27th June 1916, 1 A 1.

Rfn V. J. Strudwick 5750, 8th Rifle Brigade, 14th January 1916, 1 U 8 - Died aged 15 years, one of the youngest casualties of the war.

Artillery Wood Cemetery
Boezinghe

Boezinge is on the Ieper to Diksmuide road the N369. Take right at the crossroads at Boezinge, to the east side of the village. Drive along and take second right into Brugstraat. Go over the bridge and take second right into Poezelstraat.

Until July 1917 Boesinge, now Boezinge, directly faced the German front line across the Yser Canal. After the Battle of Pilkem Ridge, late July, the Germans were pushed back and Artillery Wood was taken by the Guards Division. The Guards found an almost deserted frontline German trench.

The Royal Engineers had cut through the canal banks to lay bridges over the canal for the attack on 31st July 1917. The Germans thinking that tunnelling had been undertaken and fearful of underground explosions had moved their men back to the second line of defence.

They began the cemetery which was enlarged following the Armistice. There are 1,307 casualties buried or commemorated here.

Two hundred metres south of the cemetery is the memorial ,"Carrefour des Roses", in memory of the 87th French Territorial Infantry known as Les Peperes or Grandfathers and the 45th Infantry Division known as Les Joyeux who had defended this area in the first gas attack on 22nd April 1915.

Pte Francis Ledwidge 16138 5th Royal Inniskilling Fusiliers 31st July 1917 II B 5

An Irish tricolour marks the spot where Pte Ledwidge, an Irish nationalist and poet fell on 31st July 1917, on the first day of the Third Battle of Ypres. A memorial stone was unveiled in 1998.

Ledwidge was born in Slane, County Meath. He joined the Irish Volunteers in Spring 1914. In October of that year he joined the 5th Royal Inniskilling Fusiliers.

He served in Gallipoli and Salonika before returning to the Western Front in December 1916 with the 1st Battalion. He was hit by a shell whilst laying duckboards over the muddy fields of Pilkem Ridge and was killed instantly.

He wrote his verses throughout his service in the most appalling conditions and his anthology, "Songs of the field," was published in 1915 to great critical acclaim. In his poem, "Soliloquy", he wrote the lines, "And now I'm drinking wine in France, the helpless child of circumstance, tomorrow will be loud with war, how will I be accounted for?"

He is commemorated in the folk song, "The Blackbird of Slane."

Pte E. H. Evans – (Bardic pseudonym – Hedd Wyn) - 15th (The London Welch) Royal Welch Fusiliers, 31st July 1917, II F 11

Hedd won six Bardic Chairs before he enlisted. He was part of the 38th (Welch) Division chosen to lead the attack on Pilkem Ridge and Langemarck.

The 15th Royal Welch Fusiliers lost every officer in the attack on 30th July but they took 500 prisoners. Hedd was wounded in the chest by shrapnel from a shell. He is known as, "The Black Bard."

Guardsman R. H. Pike, 24462, 2nd Grenadier Guards, 6th July 1917 – VI D 18. Captain of Callingwood Cricket Club, Cornwall.

Carrefour des Roses

Just along from the Ledwidge memorial at the junction of the Boezinghe and Langemark road is the **Carrefour des Roses**, a memorial to the **French 87eme Division d'Infanterie Territoriale and the 45eme Division d'Infanterie Algerienne.**

The memorial takes the form of a calvary and dolmen.

A map shows the stand made by the two Divisions in the German gas attack on 22nd April 1915. **This was the first use of poison gas on the Western Front.**

Langemark German Military Cemetery Langemark

The cemetery is situated to the north of Langemark village in the direction of Houthuist. It is 6 km NE of Ypres. There are four German cemeteries in Flanders and 13 World War 1 and World War 2 in Belgium.

The cemetery began with a small group of German graves here in 1915.

On 10th July 1932 the cemetery was renamed as German Military Cemetery 123. During the 1930's 10,000 soldiers were brought here from 18 German burial sites around the Langemark region. The oak trees were planted as they are the national tree of Germany.

In the late 1950's the cemetery underwent major redevelopment. Basalt lava crosses were placed in the ground. **The Kameraden Grab (Comrades Grave) was made for the unidentified dead.**

The lifesize bronze statue of four mourning soldiers by Munich sculptor Prof. Emil Kreiger was placed at the upper end of it. They solemnly watch over the many thousands of German dead.

The names of those known to be dead but not identified are carved onto oak panelling at the entrance building.

The total number of soldiers buried or commemorated stands at 44,234.

In recent years research by the Volksbund Deutche Kreigsgraberfurserge (VDK) has identified 16,940 of the previous 24,000 unknown soldiers and since 1984 their names have been inscribed on granite blocks by the communal grave.

There is a private plaque indicating that two British soldiers are buried here:

Pte A. Carlill 31006, Loyal North Lancs Regt, 4th November 1918

Pte L. H. Lockley S/43486, Seaforth Highlanders, 30th October 1918

Poelkapelle Village

In the village square is the Guynemer Memorial, commemorating **Capitaine Georges Guynemer, the** great French air ace who was killed on 11th September 1917 during a combat with an Aviatik.

The flying stork, the emblem of his Squadron, Escradille 3, flies in the direction of his crash.

Guynemer became influential enough to affect French fighter aircraft design.

He was the first French fighter ace to attain 50 victories.

He failed to return from a combat mission on 11th September 1917. Neither the wreckage of his aeroplane, his body or his personal effects were ever found.

The Germans announced he had been shot down by Lt Kurt Wissemann of Justa 3, who in turn, was killed in action 17 days later.

The monument was unveiled in 1923.

Poelcapelle British Cemetery
Poelkapelle

When you reach the village of Poelcapelle, follow the Brugesweg and the cemetery is just beyond the village.

Poelcapelle, now Poelkapelle, was taken by the Germans from the French on 20th October 1914, entered by 11th Division on 4th October 1917, evacuated by Commonwealth forces in April 1918 and retaken by the Belgians on 28th September 1918.

The cemetery was made after the Armistice when graves were brought in from surrounding battlefields and smaller cemeteries. The great majority of graves date from the last five months of 1917. There are 7,478 Commonwealth burials of which 6,321 are unidentified.

Pte John Condon 6322, Royal Irish Regiment, 24th May 1915 - LVI F 8. Aged 14 years, he is believed to have been the youngest casualty of the war . His home was in Waterford. This is one of the most visited graves in the Salient.

Lt H. G. Langton, 4th London Regiment, 26th October 1917, Sp Mem 3. This gravestone is unusual because of its musical inscription, believed to be the only one on the Western Front.

Tyne Cot Cemetery
Passendale

Tyne Cot Cemetery at Passendale, **formerly Passchendaele, is the largest Commonwealth cemetery in the world.**

Two mourning angels kneel on top of the dome covered pavilions at either end of the memorial wall, which in its sickle form echoes the shape of the Salient itself. It was designed by Sir Richard Baker.

In all 11,874 graves are registered, of which 70% are unidentified. Three unknown South African soldiers who died in 1917 were re-interred during a ceremony on 9th July 2013. Their remains had been found near a brick factory in Zonnebeke at the end of 2011. It was believed that the soldiers were never formally buried but that their graves were covered during battle by mortar or artillery fire, based on objects recovered. The soldiers had formed part of the 4th Regiment South African Infantry.

On the walls at the rear of the cemetery are the names of almost 35,000 soldiers who have no known grave and who died from August 1917 to the end of the war. There are 33,700 names from the UK and the New Zealand Memorial records 1,176.

Capt C. S. Jeffries VC, 34th Australian Infantry, 12th August 1917, XL E 1 – He led the attack on the blockhouse that now forms the base of the Cross of Sacrifice, capturing four machine guns and 35 prisoners. He then continued with a sergeant and ten men to the pillbox on the south-east corner in front

of which he was killed. His epitaph reads, " On fames eternal camping ground, their silent tents are spread."

"Comrades in Death"

The Northumberland Fusiliers saw a resemblance to Tyneside cottages in the German pillboxes silhouetted on the horizon which led them to calling them Tyne cottages and hence the name of the cemetery, Tyne Cot.

Aerial views of the cemetery show a remarkable resemblance to a great church or cathedral , the serried ranks of headstones in the first section resemble rows of pews, the choir stalls are to each side of the cross and the Stone of Remembrance represents the altar.

Two mourning angels kneel on top of the dome – covered pavilions at either end of the memorial wall which, in its sickle shape, echoes the form of the Salient itself.

The pavilions were built over two German blockhouses. Two other German blockhouses are also noticeable.

It is inevitable when travelling on Western Front tours you will meet others who are keen on what your particular interest may be. On one of my trips with Battlefield Tours, Birmingham, I met a pleasant traveller called Peter Butterworth, who very kindly pointed out the spot in the cemetery where the above poignant photograph could be taken.

Peter's forte was writing poetry about the First World War and I have been fortunate to receive his poems on a number of occasions.

Battle of Langemarck (Part of the Third Battle of Ypres)
16th – 18th August 1917

During the Battle of Langemarck, part of the Third Battle of Ypres, Field -Marshal Haig committed six divisions of the British Fifth Army, including both the 36th (Ulster) Division and the 16th (Irish) Division.

From the 16th August until 18th August, the 36th (Ulster) Division lost 74 officers and 1,940 other ranks, killed, wounded or missing. Casualties for the 9th Royal Irish Fusiliers totalled, 35 killed in action, 323 wounded , 12 suffering from shellshock and 83 missing.

The 16th (Irish) Division lost 125 officers and 2,042 other ranks .

These battles raged until 10th November.

L/Cpl Ernest Seaman VC: MM Army Service Corps Royal Inniskilling Fusiliers 29th September 1918 Panel 70

He was born near Norwich. He was originally a baker in the Army Service Corps. It was not until late in the war he was allowed to join a front-line unit.

On 29th September 1918 at Terhand, Belgium, he went forward with his Lewis gun under heavy fire, engaged the position that was holding up his company and single-handedly captured two machine-guns and 12 prisoners, killing two officers and one man. Later in the day he engaged another enemy machine-gun post capturing the gun under heavy fire. He was killed immediately afterwards.

There are numerous soldiers from the Portadown area named on the walls surrounding Tyne Cot Cemetery. Only a few of them have individual graves.

Many of them fell during the Third Battle of Ypres 31st July – 10th November 1917 and especially in the Battle of Langemarck 16th – 18th August 1917.

The exceptionally wet August weather turned parts of the Ypres battlefield into a quagmire.

Royal Irish Fusiliers Panel 140 – 141

Capt T. E. C. Crosbie MC and Bar, 9ᵗʰ Btn, 15ᵗʰ April 1918. He lived at Ballinteggart. He was educated at Lurgan College and Queen's University, Belfast. He was awarded his Military Cross for a raid at Havrincourt on 3ʳᵈ November 1917 and awarded a Bar at St Quentin on 21ˢᵗ March 1918. He was wounded at Regent Street Dugouts, north of Wulverghem.

2ⁿᵈ Lt H. E. Cowdy, 9ᵗʰ Btn, 16ᵗʰ August 1917 . He lived at Carrickblacker Road His family business was Messrs William Cowdy and Sons, handkerchief makers.

Cpl J. Balmer 13986, 9ᵗʰ Btn, 16ᵗʰ August 1917. Came from Mullavilly. He worked as a linen weaver.

Pte J. Allen 24847, 9ᵗʰ Btn, 16ᵗʰ August 1917. Scotch Street.

Pte P. Bennett 3920, 7/8ᵗʰ Btn, 16ᵗʰ August 1917. - Curran Street.

Pte J. Clulow 26914, 9ᵗʰ Btn, 16ᵗʰ August 1917. Montague Street. His son Sgt J E Clulow was killed on 4ᵗʰ August 1944 at Antello in Italy.

Pte E. Cranston 21673, 7/8ᵗʰ Btn, 17ᵗʰ August 1917 - Derrycrew

Pte E. Jones 14363, 9ᵗʰ Btn, 16ᵗʰ August 1917. South Street. A stretcher bearer who was shot in the back whilst carrying wounded back from the line. He had four brothers who served in the war.

Pte J. Magee 14459, 9ᵗʰ Btn, 16ᵗʰ August 1917. – Laurelvale

Pte H. Mortimer 24909, 9ᵗʰ Btn, 16ᵗʰ August 1917. He lived at West Street. Originally joined North Irish Horse in 1916 and transferred to Princess Patricia's (Royal Irish Fusiliers) in October 1916, before being posted to the 9ᵗʰ Btn.

Pte A. McCann 22780, 9ᵗʰ Btn, , 16ᵗʰ August 1917 - Atkinson's Avenue. He worked as a mechanic.

Pte A. McMullan 14569, 9ᵗʰ Btn, 16ᵗʰ August 1917. Park Road. A member of Edenderry Pipe Band

Pte J. Murray 5481, 1ˢᵗ Btn, 11ᵗʰ April 1918 - Woodhouse Street

Pte W. R. Stevenson 16474, 9ᵗʰ Btn, 16ᵗʰ August 1917 - Coronation Street

Pte A. Wilkinson 24910, 9ᵗʰ Btn, 16ᵗʰ August 1917 - Derrymacfall

Royal Irish Rifles Panels 138 - 140

Rfn J. Cassells 17421 14th Btn, 16th August 1917 - Tandragee

Rfn P. Murray 2980 (Served as P. Berney) 1st Btn, 16th August 1917 - Tandragee

Rfn W. J. Teggart 2307 15th Btn, 20th August 1918 - Burnbrae Avenue

Queen's Own Cameron Highlanders Panels 136 138

L/Cpl W. J. Redmond S/40807 5th Btn. 16th April 1918 - Curran Street,

Royal Dublin Fusiliers Panels 144 - 145

2nd Lt W. L. Reavie 3rd Btn. 16th August 1917 - Hanover Street,

South Staffordshire Regiment Panels 90 - 92

Pte J. Williams 40894 1st Btn. 26th October 1917 - Montague Street

There are four Portadown servicemen who are interred in Tyne Cot Cemetery.

L/Cpl A. Magowan MM, 18058, 16th August 1917, 9th Royal Irish Fusiliers - VIII D 13. Parkmount Terrace. He was awarded the Military Medal for action at Spanbroekmolen. He was a Lewis gunner.

Pte J. Quinn, 14625, 9th Royal Irish Fusiliers, 16th August 1917 - VI D 2. Wounded at Hamel on 1st July 1916.

Pte W. J. McGaffin, 24734, 16th August 1917, 9th Royal Irish Fusiliers - VI H 24 - Knocknamuckley

Pte Robert Gilmour 278417, 2nd Argyll and Sutherland Highlanders, 17th March 1918 - I I 2 - Timakeel

Two brothers lie side by side at Tyne Cot. They are Pte Creighton Wellington Hatt, 733115, 8th November 1917 - II E 10 and Pte F. Hatt, 734291, 6th November 1917 - II E II. They both served with 25th Btn Canadian Infantry (Nova Scotia Regiment.)

Pte William John McGaffin 24734 9th Royal Irish Fusiliers 16th August 1917 VI H 24

Pupils from Bocombra Primary School, Portadown interviewed his aunt, Mrs Mary Boyce of Bleary prior to their educational trip to Belgium. They learned that due to the fact William had previously been employed on a relative's farm in Scotland, he was conscripted and taken out of a field near his home in County Armagh, telling his mother at the time he did not want to join up.

William later made one journey home, wearing his uniform of the 9th Royal Irish Fusiliers. He walked from Lurgan Railway Station to his home in Bleary, some distance away.

The neighbours held a huge party to welcome him, but sadly it was to be the last journey he was to make to his homestead as he was killed in action at Passchendaele on 16th August 1917.

The young pupils from Bocombra Primary School laid a wreath on his grave and held a short service at Tyne Cot Cemetery. William lies alongside some of his comrades but a greater number has their name recorded on the walls of Tyne Cot Cemetery Memorial as they have no known grave.

William's name is recorded on the War Memorial Tablet in Newmills Presbyterian Church, close to his home. He had been a member of the Loyal Orders.

Rev Fr William J. Doyle MC Attd: 8th Royal Dublin Fusiliers 17th August 1917 Panel 160

Born in Dalkey, County Dublin, he was ordained in 1907. He was a well known and much loved preacher in both England and Ireland.

In November 1915 he became a Chaplain to the Forces.

He was at a heavy gas attack at the Loos Salient in April 1916. He was prominent at the front line at Frezenberg Ridge in the Third Battle of Ypres. His Military Cross was awarded for bravery at the Somme in 1916.

William was killed in action at Passchendaele. It was rumoured that he was recommended for a Victoria Cross but some historians say, rightly or wrongly, that his Clerical Superiors turned him down for this award.

William's name is recorded on Panel 160 on the wall of the Tyne Cot Memorial alongside other Chaplains who had made the supreme sacrifice:

Rev Fr Stephen Clarke, Attd: 7th Lancashire Fusiliers, 4th October 1917. Killed at Passchendaele.

Rev William I. S. Dallas, Attd: 5th Queen's Own (Liverpool Regiment), 20th July 1917

Rev John W. A. Eyre-Powell, Attd: 27th Labour Corps, 16th April 1918

Rev Wilfrid J. Harding MC, Attd: Drake Battalion, Royal Naval Division, 31st October 1917. Killed at Passchendaele.

Dochy Farm New British Cemetery Zonnebeke

The cemetery is on the N332. When you reach Zonnebeke turn into Langesmarkstraat and the cemetery is 1.5 km along this road.

Dochy Farm, which had become a German strongpoint, was taken by the 4th New Zealand Brigade on 4th October 1917, in the Battle of Broodseinde. The cemetery was made after the Armistice when isolated graves were brought in from the battlefields of Boesinghe, St. Julien, Frezenberg and Passchendaele.

Buried here are 8 Royal Irish Fusiliers, two of whom are from Lurgan, 7 Royal Inniskilling Fusiliers, 2 Royal Dublin Fusiliers and one member of the Royal Irish Rifles.

Sgt Jimmy Spiers MM S/18170

7th Queen's Own Cameron Highlanders

20th August 1917

VI E 15

Jimmy played football for Glasgow Rangers (53 appearances, 24 goals) and Clyde (14 matches and 7 goals) before moving to Bradford City (86 games and 29 goals.)

He became Captain of Bradford and scored the only goal of the game in the 1911 F A Cup Final against Newcastle United. He later transferred to Leeds United for £1,400. (73 appearances and 32 goals.)

He won one international cap for Scotland in a 2-1 victory against Wales. Killed at Passchendaele.

Potijze Chateau Wood Cemetery Potijze

From Zonnebeke take the N332 to Potijze In the village turn on to the N345 Potijzestraat and 400 metres further on you will find four Potijze cemeteries linked to one another.

Walk along a small path between local houses and left past Potijze Chateau and Lawn Cemetery towards the wood.

Potijze Chateau Wood Cemetery was used from April 1915 to June 1917 and three times in 1918.

Potijze was within Allied lines during practically the whole of the First World War and although subject to incessant shellfire, Potijze Chateau contained an Advanced Dressing Station.

Among those buried in the cemetery are 46 officers and men of 2nd Hampshire Regiment in Row A, and 19 of the 1st Royal Inniskilling Fusiliers in Rows E and F who died in a gas attack in August 1916.

Sgt Millar Cole, 7422, 1st Royal Inniskilling Fusiliers, 8th August 1916 - F 1 - Castle Avenue

Pte J. Devlin, 29009, 1st Royal Inniskilling Fusiliers, 9th August 1916 - F 3. He lived in Abington, Massachussetts.

Oxford Road Cemetery
St Jan

The cemetery is found on the N313 between St Jan and St Julian. It is named after a road running behind the support trenches. The original cemetery makes up Plot 1 and was used by fighting units from August 1917 until April 1918. In October 1917 another cemetery known as Oxford Road No. 2 started close by but this now forms Plot 5 of the present cemetery. Other burials were carried out after the Armistice following battlefield clearances.

Lt Colin Blythe 49296 King's Own Yorkshire Light Infantry 8th July 1917 I L 2

Colin, sometimes known as Charlie as a Kent and England left hand spinner who is regarded as one of the finest bowlers of the period 1900-1914 sometimes referred to as the "Golden Age" of cricket.

He played for Kent in 1899 and took a wicket with his very first ball in first class cricket. In 1902 and 1903 he became one of the leading wicket takers in county cricket. **He was Wisden Cricketer of the Year in 1904. He won the County Championship with Kent.**

In 1907 he took 25 wickets in three Tests against South Africa, including 15 for 99 in the Second Test at Headingly. His 17 for 48 (10 for 30 and 7 for 48) against Northamptonshire on 1st June 1907 still stands as the best bowling analysis in the County Championship.

He played 19 Tests for England and 439 first class matches. He took 100 Test wickets and 2,503 first class. He was a talented violinist but also suffered from epilepsy. Despite his problem he still enlisted in 1914.

White House Cemetery
St Jan

Drive out of the village of St Jan on the N313 on Brugeseweg, close to Jan Yperman Hospital.

"The White House", was on the Ypres road between St Jean and the bridge over the Bellawaerdebeek. The cemetery was started in March 1915 and used until April 1918, by fighting units holding this part of the line. At the time of the Armistice, the cemetery consisted mainly of Plots 1 and 2, but the cemetery was then enlarged by the concentration of burials from surrounding battlefields and other small cemeteries.

Pte Robert Morrow VC, 10531, 1st Royal Irish Fusiliers, 26th April 1915 - IV A 44

He came from Newmills, outside Dungannon. On 12th April 1915, the 1st Royal Irish Fusiliers were attacked by the enemy below Messines Ridge. **On six occasions he returned to the battlefield to rescue wounded** comrades. On 25th April during the Battle of St Julian, his battalion had to withdraw due to a German counter-attack. Again he went out into No **Man's Land to rescue his colleagues**. However on this occasion , he was badly wounded and died next day of his wounds.

He was awarded a posthumous Victoria Cross, whilst the Czar of Russia bestowed him with the Russian Cross of St George.

His mother presented his medals to his regiment. In Newmills the locals Constructed a memorial in his memory and the local pub, now sadly closed, was **named the VC Inn.**

301

New Irish Farm Cemetery
St Jan

Go out of St Jan and when you reach Zwaanhofweg, turn into this small country road and follow it to the crossroads, where you will find the cemetery.

It is named after a farm which stood nearby. The cemetery was begun in August 1917 and continued in use until November of that year. It was then further used in April and May of 1918.

After the Armistice the cemetery contained just 73 burials in three irregular rows. These can now be found as part of Plot 1.

Its location then made it an ideal cemetery to be enlarged and 4,500 graves were brought in from the surrounding battlefields and small isolated cemeteries.

L/Cpl W. J. Benson, 14084, 10th Royal Irish Rifles, 6th August 1917 - XVIII D 1 - Drumcree

Lt C. L. C. Bowes-Lyon, The Black Watch, 23rd October 1914 - XXX D 11. He was killed in action at Pilckem. He was the nephew of the late HRH Queen Mother.

10

Route 9 - Towards the coast - Beauvais Airport

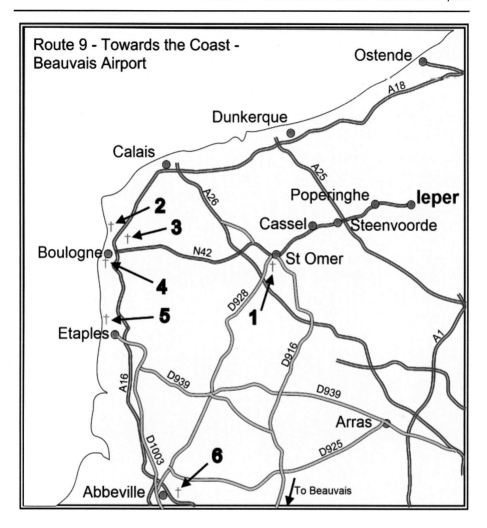

1. Longuenesse (St Omer) Souvenir Cemetery

2. Terlincthun Brirish Cemetery, Wimille

3. Wimereux Communal Cemetery

4. Boulogne Eastern Cemetery

5. Etaples Military Cemetery

6. Abbeville Communal Cemetery Extension

Route 9 - Towards the Coast - Airport to Beauvais

A sedate trip from **Ieper via St Omer** to the coast, opposite the Straits of Dover and the English Channel and then on to the motorway to the airports at Beauvais or Charles de Gaulle, Paris will prove a pleasant finale of your tour of the battlefields.

From Ieper, take the A38 passing **Poperinghe** on to **Steenvoorde**. Take the D948 to Cassel and then the D933 to St Omer, exiting the **N43 to Longuenesse**.

Longuenesse (St Omer) Souvenir Cemetery (1) is on the D928 to Wizernes (Abbeyville). St Omer was the General Headquarters of the British Expeditionary Force from October 1914 until March 1916.

The cemetery was used extensively by the hospitals and Casualty Clearing Stations and is **the final resting place of well known Portadown soccer player, Pte A. Hayes, 2nd (Garrison) Battalion, Royal Irish Regiment.**

Take the **N42** in the **direction of Boulogne** where the next stop is on the outskirts of **Wimille at Terlincthun British Cemetery (2)**.

Begun in June 1918 as a result of the cemeteries at Boulogne and Wimereux being exhausted. The cemetery also contains the remains of 46 Royal Air Force personnel who were killed in September 1918.

Now head for the **A16** in the direction of **Calais , exiting at Junction 33 on the D242 for Wimereux Communal Cemetery (3)** which is well signposted. In 1919, Wimereux became the General Headquarters of the British Army.

The most notable grave is that of Lt Col John McCrae, Canadian Army Medical Corps, author of the poem, "In Flanders Fields".

Two Portadown soldiers are buried in the cemetery, **Pte J. Matthews, 25th Australian Infantry from James Street and Pte W. Rea, 73rd Canadian Infantry from Balteagh. There are two nurses Sister Myrtle Wilson and Sister Christina Wilson both of Queen Alexandra's Imperial Military Nursing Service.**

You can also find the last resting place of the **first Icelander** to make the supreme sacrifice.

My wife's family has a relatives' grave here, **Pte F. W. Beaumont, Northumberland Fusiliers (20th Tyneside Scottish).**

Travelling towards **Boulogne** follow the signs for the city centre on the **RN42** and after a short distance, take left into the **Rue de Dringhen** which divides the civil cemetery into two. In this **Boulogne Eastern Cemetery (4) lie five men from the Portadown district.**

Sgt W. Hughes, 9th Royal Inniskilling Fusiliers from Mandeville Street; L/Cpl G. Hughes, 7th Royal Irish Rifles , Henry Street; Pte F. Greenaway, 1st Royal Irish Fusiliers, John Street; Pte Francis Gillespie, Royal Irish Regiment, transferred to 191st Coy Labour Corps, who lived in Railway (Watson) Street and Pte J. J. Cox, Irish Guards from Corcrain.

Pte Robert Craig, 5th South Wales Borderers had played for Glasgow Celtic.

Etaples is reached 27 km from Boulogne and **Etaples Military Cemetery (5)** is north of the town on the Boulogne road, overlooking the sea.

There are five Portadown servicemen interred in this cemetery, three of whom had previously emigrated. **Pte R. H. Cooper, 1st Australian Infantry, Atkinson's Avenue; Pte T. Flannigan, Canadian Army Medical Corps and Cpl A. Brownlee, 1st Royal Irish Fusiliers who had lived in Carleton Street. Pte R. Duke, 4th Canadian Mounted Rifles, formerly of Kilmore and Pte F. O. Wilson, 9th Royal Irish Fusiliers of Baltylum. Buried here also is Major R. O. Schwarz MC, a renowned cricketer and rugby international.**

Major D. C. Reynolds VC, a member of Kitchener Masonic Lodge is also buried here.

Abbeville is on the main N1 road from Paris to Boulogne. The two cemeteries **Abbeville Communal and Extension (6)** are on the left hand side leaving the town on the Drucat Road.

Here lies **Pte T. Kilpatrick, 14379, 9th Royal Irish Fusiliers who lived in Mount Pleasant, Seagoe.**

Also here is the grave of **L/Cpl L. J. Keyworth VC, 1/24ᵗʰ London Regiment.**

In the **Communal Cemetery Extension** lie the graves of two interesting civilians. **Emily Pickford, a member of the Lena Ashwell Concert Party and Fred Taylor, a baritone unable to serve due to a disability, who entertained the troops.**

The A16 motorway allows you a speedy travel via Abbeyville and Amiens and unto your choice of airport at Beauvais or Paris.

Longuenesse (St Omer) Souvenir Cemetery St. Omer

Leave Ieper on the N38, and travel through Poperinghe to Steenvoorde. Travel through Cassel and take the D933 to Arques to St Omer. The cemetery is about 3 km from St Omer on the Wizernes (Abbeville) D928 at its junction with the Rue des Bruyeres. There is a large car park at the rear of the cemetery.

St Omer was the General Headquarters of the British Expeditionary Force from October 1914 to March 1916. Lord Roberts died there in November 1914. The town was a considerable hospital centre with the 4ᵗʰ, 10ᵗʰ, 7ᵗʰ Canadian, 9ᵗʰ Canadian and New Zealand Stationary Hospitals, the 7ᵗʰ, 58ᵗʰ (Scottish) and 59ᵗʰ (Northern) General Hospitals, and the 1ˢᵗ and 2ⁿᵈ Australian Casualty Clearing Stations all stationed there at some time during the war.

St Omer suffered air raids in November 1917 and May 1918 with serious loss of life.

Pte A. Hayes, 714, 2ⁿᵈ (Garrison) Regiment, Royal Irish Regiment, 31ˢᵗ July 1918 - V D 18. He lived at Scotch Street and was a well known footballer. Two of his brothers were also killed in the war.

L/Cpl C. R. Noble VC, 3697, 2ⁿᵈ Rifle Brigade, 13ᵗʰ March 1915 - 1 A 57. He and his men found the wire intact in the section of German trenches at Neuve Chapelle, which they were ordered to take. Noble and his colleague Sgt Major Daniels began to cut through the wire despite machine gun and rifle fire. They succeeded and his men advanced. He died from wounds sustained. Daniels survived and was also awarded the Victoria Cross.

Terlincthun British Cemetery
Wimille

Wimille is situated on the northern outskirts of Boulogne. The entrance to the cemetery is in St Martin's Road which is the road on the left immediately after the cemetery.

The first rest camps for the Commonwealth forces were established near Terlincthun in August 1914 and during the whole of the Great War, Boulogne and Wimereux housed numerous hospitals and medical establishments. The cemetery was begun in June 1918 when spaces were exhausted in cemeteries at Boulogne and Wimereux.

It was used mainly for burials from base hospitals but Plot IV Row C contains the graves of 46 Air Force personnel killed at Marquise in September 1918 following a bombing raid by German aircraft.

In July 1920 the cemetery contained more than 3,000 burials but for many years it remained an "open" cemetery and graves continued to be brought in from isolated sites and other burial grounds throughout France where maintenance could not be assured.

The cemetery sustained significant damage both from the shelling in 1940 and under German occupation.

There is a communal grave just inside the entrance to the cemetery which commemorates 51 soldiers whose remains were found in 1982.

Major H. St A. Wake MVO, 8th Gurkha Rifles, 30th October 1914 - VII A 8

Lt H. Banks MC, 102nd Canadian Infantry (Central Ontario Regiment), 17th October 1918 - V F 36

Wimereux Communal Cemetery

Wimereux is a small town 5 km from Boulogne. Take the A16 in the direction of Calais and exit Junction 33. Take the D242 in the direction of Wimereux for approximately 2 km.

Take the first left immediately after the roundabout and the cemetery is well signposted and is found on the left hand side of the road 200 m along.

The Commonwealth War Graves are found at the rear of the Communal Cemetery.

Wimereux was the Headquarters of Queen Mary's Army Auxiliary Corps during World War One and in 1919 it became the General Headquarters of the British Army.

From October 1914 onwards Boulogne and Wimereux formed important hospital centres and until June 1918 the medical units at Wimereux used the communal cemetery for burials. By June 1918 this half of the cemetery was filled and subsequent burials from the hospitals at Wimereux were made in the new cemetery at Terlincthun.

Because of the sandy nature of the soil, the headstones lie flat against the graves. Many of the headstones have been badly weathered by wind and rain, this close to the sea.

There is an interesting collection of burials here, the most notable being that of Lt Col John McCrae, Canadian Army Medical Corps 28th January 1918 4 H 3, author of the poem "In Flanders' Fields", written in May 1915. There is a blue Plaque for Lt Col McCrae erected by the Ontario Heritage Foundation at the cemetery entrance.

Lt Col John McCrae

Canadian Army Medical Corps

28th January 1918

IV H 3

The famous poem was written when he was close to Essex Farm Cemetery, near Ypres. In November 1985 an Albertina Marker was unveiled to record this fact.

The Albertina Marker is one of a series of 25 diamond shaped stone markers unveiled at various points along the Belgian front in 1984, being 50 years after the death of King Albert and 70 years after the outbreak of war.

Pte J Matthews, 3973, 25th Australian Infantry, 21st June 1916 - 1 N 10A. James Street.

Pte W. Rea, 163913, 73rd Canadian Infantry, 16th April 1917 - II H 9A - Balteagh.

Sister Myrtle Wilson, Queen Alexandra's Imperial Military Nursing Service, 23rd December 1915 - III M 1 - Born Queensland.

Sister Christina Wilson, Queen Alexandra's Imperial Military Nursing Service, 1st March 1916 - III L 4 - Glasgow.

Bugler Rangiwinui Hiroti, 16/379, 1st New Zealand Maori (Pioneer) Btn, 5th June 1916 - 1 N 3A.

Pte Magdal Hermanson, 54, 8th Canadian Infantry (Manitoba Regiment), 3rd May 1915, - 1 F 23 - "He was the first Icelander to give his life for Canada. I thank you. My son."

Pte F. W. Beaumont, Mentioned in Despatches, 30200, Northumberland Fusiliers (20th Tyneside Scottish), 27th October - VI E 31A. Relative of Lesley Harkness, Breagh Lodge, Portadown.

Mrs Lesley Harkness of Portadown places a cross on the grave of her relative Pte F. W. Beaumont.

Boulogne Eastern Cemetery

This cemetery is in a large civil cemetery split into two by the Rue de Dringhem. It can be reached by approaching Boulogne from the RN42 from the direction of St. Omer. Relatively well signposted the Rue de Dringhem is on the left towards the centre of town.

Boulogne was one of three base ports most extensively used by Commonwealth armies of the Western Front throughout World War One. It was closed and cleared on 27th August 1918 when the Allied Forces were forced to fall back ahead of the German advance, but it was opened again in October until the end of the war.

Boulogne and Wimereux formed one of the chief hospital areas. Until 1918 the dead from hospitals at Boulogne itself were buried in Cimetiere de l'Est.

In the Spring of 1918, space was running short in spite of repeated extensions and the site of the new cemetery at Terlincthun was chosen.

Sgt W. Hughes, 14321, 9th Royal Inniskilling Fusiliers, 11th July 1916 - VIII D 104. Mandeville Street. He was wounded at Hamel on 1st July and died later of his wounds.

313

L/Cpl G. Hughes, 1203, 7th Royal Irish Rifles, 24th March 1917 - VIII A 180. Henry Street.

Pte F. Greenaway, 6119,1st Royal Irish Fusiliers, 28th April 1918 - VIII B 4. John Street. Died of wounds received at St Julian, in No. 13 General Hospital.

Pte Francis Gillespie, 16496, Royal Irish Regiment, 174930, 191st Coy Labour Corps, died of illness 17th November 1917 - VIII 1 115. Lived at Railway (Watson) Street.

Pte J. J. Cox, 1792, Irish Guards, 28th October 1914 - III A 20. Corcrain.

Pte Robert Craig, 30450, 5th South Wales Borderers, 19th April 1918- IX A 3. Pte Craig was the final **Glasgow Celtic** player to be killed in the war. He played from 1906 until 1909. He was a full back and made 13 appearances. He died of his wounds five days after being hit when the enemy recaptured Messines in Belgium.

Capt F. W. Campbell VC, 1st Canadian Infantry (West Ontario Regiment), 19th June 1915 - II A 24.

The plot and monument above commemorates Portuguese soldiers who made the supreme sacrifice.

Etaples Military Cemetery

The military cemetery is north of the town on the Boulogne road. During the First World War the area around Etaples was the scene of immense concentration of Commonwealth reinforcement camps and hospitals. It was remote from attack, except by aircraft and accessible by railway from both the northern and southern battlefields.

In 1917, 100,000 troops were camped amongst the sand dunes and the hospitals which included one General, one Stationary, four Red Cross and a convalescent depot, could deal with 22,000 wounded or sick.

In September 1917, ten months after the Armistice, three hospitals and the QMAAC convalescent depot remained.

Pte R. H. Cooper, 3549, 1st Australian Infantry, 28th August 1916 - X A 12A - Atkinson's Avenue. There was much argument about how he died. After an Adjutant General Court in March 1917 he was deemed to be feloniously killed (manslaughter) at Etaples.

Cpl A. Brownlee, 6370, Royal Irish Fusiliers, 23rd April 1918 - XXVIV L 3A. Carleton Street.

Pte T. Flannigan, 34462, Canadian Army Medical Corps, 19th May 1918 - LXVI D 2 – Hanover Street.

Pte R. Duke 159516, 4th Canadian Mounted Rifles, 23rd February 1917, XXI H 3 - Ballywilly, Kilmore.

Pte F. O. Wilson 17657, 9th Royal Irish Fusiliers, 19th August 1917, XXII Q 21A - Baltylum.

Major D. Reynolds VC, 83rd Bde, Royal Field Artillery, 23rd February 1916 - I A 20. A member of Kitchener Masonic Lodge No.2998 Simla (now Janpath, New Delhi, India).

Major O. R. Schwarz MC, 6th Own King's Rifle Corps, 18th November 1918 - XLV A 4. He was a renowned cricketer and a rugby international.

Reggie was born in London and was a South African cricketer and international rugby footballer.

He won three caps for England at rugby, against Scotland 1899; Wales and Ireland in 1901.

Reggie played a handful of games for Middlesex in 1901 and 1902 before emigrating to South Africa and joining Transvaal.

In 1904 he returned to England with the South African Cricket Team. He had learned how to bowl the googly. In 1904 and 1907 he topped the bowling averages.

He was named Wisden Cricketer of the Year in 1908.

In all he took 398 wickets at an average of 17.58 runs per wicket and in Tests he took 55 wickets at an average of 22.6 runs per wicket.

He actually survived the war but died during a Spanish Flu epidemic just seven days after the Armistice had been signed.

He played in 20 Tests and 125 First Class matches.

Abbeville Communal Cemetery Extension

Abbeville is on the main N1 road from Paris to Boulogne. The two cemeteries Communal and Extension are on the left hand side of the road leaving the town on the Drucat road.

For most of World War One, Abbeville was the HQ for Commonwealth communication and the No.3 BRCS, No. 5 and No. 2 Stationary Hospitals were stationed there from 1914 until 1920.

During the Second World War, the Germans took Abbeville at the end of May 1940 but it was re-taken by Canadian and Polish units on 4th September 1944.

There are 774 Commonwealth burials in the Communal Cemetery from the First World War and 30 burials from the Second World War. The Extension contains 1754 First World War burials and a further 348 from the Second.

Both cemeteries were designed by Sir Reginald Blomfield.

In the Abbeville Communal Cemetery rests one member of the Royal Irish Fusiliers.

Pte T. Kilpatrick, 14379, 9th Royal Irish Fusiliers, 11/7/16, (20), V E 13 – Mount Pleasant, Seagoe, Portadown.

Thomas was wounded at Hamel between 25th - 27th June 1916 as a result of enemy returning fire after shelling by the British artillery. He was taken to No. 2 Stationary Hospital. His parents received many condolence letters including those from six hospital chaplains and nurses, Major T J Atkinson, (D) Coy Commander who was later killed on 1st July 1916 and from Lt Geoffrey ST. G. Cather VC.

Thomas had two brothers who had served in the Great War.

Lance Corporal L. J. Keyworth VC, 1st/24th London Regiment, 19/10/15, 111 C 2, Medal of St George (2nd Class) of Russia.

Awarded for conspicuous bravery at Givenchy on the night of 25th/26th May 1915. An assault on a German position resulted in 58/75 casualties. He stood exposed for two hours on top of the enemy's parapet and threw up to 150 bombs into the German trenches.

In the **Communal Cemetery Extension** lie the graves of two interesting civilians.

Lena Ashwell was a well known actress and theatre manageress who from 1915 brought companies of actors to perform for the troops. Though the war ended in 1918 there were still many soldiers stationed in France.

Several members of her troupe were returning from a show near Beauvais after performing at Guoy l'Hopital on 7th February 1919.

Close to the SNCF railway station along the banks of the River Somme, their car skidded on the towpath into the river. The driver and a passenger were saved but two members of the company drowned.

Emily Pickford, Lena Ashwell Concert Party, 7/2/19, Musician, VG 23

Fred Taylor, Baritone, Unable to serve due to a disability, VG 24

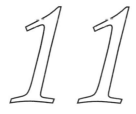

Postscript

Postscript

The battlefields of World War 1, almost a century after the conflict had ended, still unearths the fallen.

On 21st July 2013, a troop of 21 German soldiers found entombed in a preserved World War One shelter were given full military burials after French archaeologists had earlier in the year stumbled across a mass grave at Carspach, in Alsace, during excavation work for a road building project. All the dead were identified by documents found in the shelter. A number of the soldiers were discovered sitting upright on a bench, one was lying on his bed and another in a foetal position having been thrown down a flight of stairs.

The men had been part of a group of thirty four from 6th Company, 94th Reserve Infantry Regiment, buried in the blast.

Thirteen bodies had been dragged free following the attack by French forces on 18th March 1918, but the remaining bodies had to be left.

They were buried with full military honours at the nearby Illfurth German War Cemetery.

On 23rd April 2013, the remains of Lt John Pritchard and Pte Christopher Elphick of the Honorable Artillery Company were buried with full military honours in the H.A.C. Cemetery at Ecoust-St Mein.

Their remains had been discovered by a French farmer in 2009 when clearing his field. The men had been killed on 15th May 1917 during an enemy attack at Bullecourt, near Arras.

Lt Pritchard had been identified by his identity bracelet and Pte Elphick by his signet ring.

Two further set of remains, which could not be identified were re-interred at the same time as, "HAC soldiers known unto God".

On 16th April 2015, 6 British unknown soldiers were re-buried in Prowse Point Cemetery, Ploegsteert in Belgium. Two were from the Lancashire Fusiliers, two from the King's Own Lancaster Regiment and two unidentified.

it is estimated that 165,000 Commonwealth soldiers are still unaccounted for on the Western Front.

This area attracts countless visitors from many parts of the world on an annual basis, almost a century on, after the First World War began. The battlefields continue to unearth their war dead and each one will be re-interred where the brave will live forever.

RAH May 2015

Remembrance Sunday

In the United Kingdom and many other places, Remembrance Sunday is observed annually on the **second Sunday in November,** which is the Sunday nearest to Armistice Day, the Armistice being signed on 11th November 1918. Thus, this particular day commemorates British and Commonwealth military and civilian personnel who died in both World Wars and other conflicts.

Throughout the length of Great Britain and Northern Ireland and beyond, Remembrance Sunday is marked by ceremonies in most cities, towns and villages. Wreaths of poppies are laid on these memorials and a Two Minute Silence ensues.

The largest ceremony is held at the Cenotaph, Whitehall, London (above), which was designed by Sir Edward Lutyens. It was he who influenced the designs of many other war memorials found throughout the Western Front and in other Commonwealth nations.

In London, the tributes are led by HRH Her Majesty the Queen, other members of the Royal Family, the leaders of the main political parties, Commonwealth High Commissioners ,other dignitaries and members of the Armed Forces.

The Two Minute Silence, referred to earlier, is held at 11.00 am, and represents the eleventh hour of the eleventh day of the eleventh month in 1918 when the guns of Europe fell silent to end the First World War.

The ceremony has been televised since 1946.

In Northern Ireland, until fairly recently, Remembrance Sunday has tended to be associated with the Unionist community. The majority of Nationalists and Republicans tend not to take part in commemorating British soldiers.

Times are slowly changing in the island of Ireland. On Remembrance Sunday 2012, the Irish Prime Minister, the Taoiseach, Enda Kenny, laid a laurel wreath at Enniskillen whilst his Deputy, the Tanaiste, attended the ceremony at Belfast City Hall.

On 31st July 2014 the President of Ireland, Michael D Higgins joined the Duke of Kent and Northern Ireland Secretary of State, Theresa Villiers, to dedicate a Cross of Sacrifice at Glasnevin Cemetery, Dublin to commemorate the 100th anniversary of the outbreak of war.

President Higgins said, "We cannot give back their lives to the dead, nor whole bodies to those who were wounded, or repair the grief, undo the disrespect that was sometimes shown to those who fought or their families. But we honour them all now, even if at a distance, and we do not ask, nor would it be appropriate to interrogate their reasons for enlisting. To all of them in their silence, we offer our own silence, without judgment and with respect for their ideals as they knew them and for the humanity they expressed towards each other. We offer our sorrow too that they and their families were not given the compassion and the understanding over the decades that they should have received."

Throughout many venues on the Western Front, Remembrance Sunday is observed with large crowds attending the Somme Memorial to the Missing at Thiepval and also at the Menin Gate, Ieper.

If this book has emphasised to you, the ultimate sacrifice made by so many to ensure your freedom then I would implore you to support the Royal British Legion's Annual Poppy Appeal and I urge you to pay your respects to the fallen in all conflicts by attending the Remembrance Sunday Public Service at your local war memorial.

Major (Retd) P Hodgson, President, Portadown Royal British Legion and bugler Mark Mullen, St Mark's Band at the Cenotaph on Armistice Day, 11th November 2014.

Lest We Forget

The Author

<u>Ronnie Harkness</u>

Born in Cookstown County Tyrone, he later moved to Portadown where for thirty years he was employed in the field of education, twenty four of them as a Primary School Principal in three different schools in the area.

His interest in the Great War stemmed from a school visit to Belgium when his group of young students visited Tyne Cot Cemetery at Passendale.

For many years afterwards, he made repeated visits to the silent cities of the Western Front, each time recording his experiences .

Involved in sport for over forty years he realised just how many talented sportsmen, both at international and local level, had made the supreme sacrifice.

An enthusiastic member of the Masonic fraternity for many years, he recognised too that many brethren had contributed to the war effort.

As well as visiting France and Belgium he has paid his respects to the war dead at Islandbridge Dublin, Gibraltar and in far off Gallipoli.

He was privileged to have served as an Ulster Unionist councillor for ten years on the former Craigavon Borough Council and represented the people of the area at many events commemorating the Great War.

Bibliography

Somme 1916 - A battlefield companion - Gerald Gliddon 2006 Sutton

The Somme Battlefields - Martin and Mary Middlebrook 1991 Viking

Before Endeavours Fade - Rose E B Coombs MBE 2006 After the Battle

Walter Tull 1888-1918 - Officer and footballer - Phil Vasili 2010 - Raw Press

McCrae's Battalion - Story of 16th Royal Scots - Jack Alexander 2005 - Mainstream Pub.

Fields of Glory - Gavin Mortimer - 2001 - Andre Deutsch

The Greater Game - Clive Harris and Julian Whippy - 2008 - Pen and Sword

When the Whistle Blows - Andrew Riddoch and John Kemp - 2008 - Haynes Pub.

British Battalions on the Somme - Ray Westlake - 1994 - Leo Cooper

The 16th (Irish) and 36th (Ulster) at the Battle of Wijtschaete - Tom Burke MBE - 2007 - RDF Assoc.

Forgotten Soldiers - The Irishmen Shot at Dawn - Stephen Walker 2007 - Gill and Macmillan Ltd

Battlefield Guide to the Somme - Tonie and Valmai Holt - 1996 - Leo Cooper

Battlefield Guide to the Western Front – North - Tonie and Valmai Holt - 2007 - Pen and Sword

Battlefield Guide to Ypres Salient - Tonie and Valmai Holt 1997 - Leo Cooper

Portadown Heroes - James S Kane - 2007 - Dargan Print

Pilgrimage - A guide to the Royal Newfoundland Regiment in WW1 - W. D. Parsons - 2009 - DRC

Greater Love - Rev David T Youngson - 2008 - Atkinson Print

G.L. of A.F. & A.M. of Ireland - Roll of Honour 1914 - 1919 - N and M Press

On Fame's Eternal Camping Ground - Trefor Jones .2007 - Cromwell Press Ltd

A Coward if I Return, a Hero if I Fall - Neil Richardson 2010 - The O'Brien Press

The Irish on the Somme - Steven Moore - 2005 - Local Press

The Road to the Somme - Philip Orr 1987 - Blackstaff Press

Cemeteries and Memorials in Belgium and Northern France - 2004 – CWGC

Symbol of Courage - Max Arthur - Sidgwick and Jackson - 2004

Courage Remembered - Major E Gibson & G Kingsley Ward - HMSO - 1995

Orange, Green and Khaki - Tom Johnstone - Gill and Macmillan Ltd - 1992

The Ypres Salient - Michael Scott - Naval and Military Press - 2002

Menin Gate - The Last Post - Dominiek Dendooven - de Klaproos - 2001

Victoria Cross Heroes - Michael Ashcroft - Headline Book Publishing - 2006

Blacker's Boys - Nick Metcalfe - Writersworld - 2012

A Wheen of Medals - W J Canning - 2006

A Call to Arms - Richard Edgar - 2014

Angels and Heroes - A Moreno & D Truesdale - RIF Museum - 2004

The Hounds of Ulster - Gavin Hughes - Peter Lang - 2012

Armagh and the Great War - Colin Cousins - The History Press Ireland - 2011

Walking with the Ulster Division - Jonnie Armstrong - Ancre Books Ltd - 2012

Battlefields of Northern France and Low Countries - Michael Glover - Guild Publishing - 1987

The First Battalion The Faugh-A-Ballaghs - Brig Gen A R Burrows - Gale and Polden Ltd

The Great War Explained - Philip Stevens - Pen and Sword - 2012

For Valour - Ulster VC's of the Great War - Ulster-Scots Community Network - 2014

Index of Cemeteries

D

E

F

G

H